FOOD SECURITY AND CHILD LABOUR
The Case of a Hazardous Occupation

FOOD SECURITY AND CHILD LABOUR

The Case of a Hazardous Occupation

SUDIP CHAKRABORTY
Reader in Economics
Ananda Chandra College
(North Bengal University)
Jalpaiguri (W.B.)

DEEP & DEEP PUBLICATIONS PVT. LTD.
F-159, Rajouri Garden, New Delhi - 110 027

FOOD SECURITY AND CHILD LABOUR
The Case of a Hazardous Occupation

ISBN 978-81-8450-308-1

Typeset by RAHUL COMPOSERS
358, Pocket-B, Phase-2, Sector-16B, Dwarka, New Delhi - 110 075

Printed in India at MAYUR ENTERPRISES
WZ Plot No. 3, Gujjar Market, Tihar Village, New Delhi - 110 018

Published by DEEP & DEEP PUBLICATIONS PVT. LTD.
F-159, Rajouri Garden, New Delhi - 110 027 • Phone : 25435369, 25440916
E-mail : ddpubs@gmail.com • ddpbooks@yahoo.co.in
Showroom :
2/13, Ansari Road, Daryaganj, New Delhi - 110 002 • Telefax : 23245122

Dedicated to

My Aunt, Anjali Chakraborty

Contents

Preface

We need to eliminate child labour for the sake of our own future. This is slur on humanity and stigma on our civilization. The children of today are citizens of future. They are future architect of our destiny. But they need to be made the same through nurturing, care, protection and education. They do not grow to be the same without state intervention. The nation needs skilled human resources for advancement. Skill does not automatically accrue to any one; it has to be acquired through education. This is a process involving a long gestation period. Children must receive quality primary education during the appropriate age and move further ahead to the successive levels of learning. Massive public investment is needed to provide education with an aim of skill formation of citizens. Public investment in education for children is not only compulsive but also rewarding for a nation. This is compulsive because the nation is bound by the United Nations Conventions of the Rights of the Child to provide universal quality primary education to all her children free of cost. India had ratified the Convention in 1992; therefore, she is also bound by the international legal obligation. We have also our national commitment for our children. Our Constitution's 93rd amendment compels the governments, both the union as well as state, to provide education to them. The pragmatic part of the action needs a little elaboration. National economic growth, as an outcome of expanded productive capacity, is impossible without contribution of human capital. The base and quality of the latter build the productive capacity, which in turn results in economic growth.

Therefore, education of children can ensure positive economic outcome for the nation in future. Denial of educational opportunity to a substantial segment of children is tantamount to lessening the likelihood of future economic prosperity of the whole nation. Thus, the first casualty of persistence of child labour is educational deprivation of these disadvantaged children. Evidently, this goes against the spirit of the UN Convention as well as the objective of our national legislation. There are other ills that go with child labour. The most crucial one is the risk of physical, psychological and sexual abuse of these vulnerable children. The neglect of their health is other worrying side. They have to toil for very long hours without rest in unhygienic and unsafe work places. This is unacceptable. We can not wait for an indefinite period. We need action plan to be followed immediately by public action.

But the problem needs to be diagnosed before crafting any action plan. There is variation in the intensity of economic exploitation of children. Therefore, child labourers do not form a purely homogenous category. The International Labour Organization now classifies them in three groups. The worst form of child labour needs to be eliminated in the first go. The present research study brings into focus the circumstances of one of the most hazardous occupation of children in one region in India. This form of child labour is most eligible candidate for inclusion in the 'worst' form as defined by the global body. But the upsetting revelation of our study is that the urgency of elimination of this hazardous form of child labour was not observed in course of our intensive field studies in those distraught locations. We have focussed on six villages in the district of Murshidabad in West Bengal to look for causes and circumstances of this hazardous variety of child labour. The study uncovers the dimension, determinants and degrees of child labour in tobacco processing in the region. The revelation of this in the successive chapters is enriching for all.

SUDIP CHAKRABORTY

Acknowledgements

I must acknowledge, in the beginning, the University Grants Commission for providing research grant to carry out the study on child labour. My first exposure to the enchanting world of childhood studies dates back to 1998 at the Indian Institute of Advanced Study, located in the picturesque hill city of Shimla. I must acknowledge, at the beginning, the contribution of this great national institute in shaping my mind. The University Grants Commission deserves credit for sponsoring my research on children. Above all stands, the University of Ghent in Belgium in motivating and enriching me in my work on children's issues from rights perspectives. I am indebted to them for providing me with generous scholarship to attend the International Interdisciplinary Course in Child Rights during 2004. I am obliged to Prof. Kathy Vlieghe and Prof. Arabella Weyts of the centre for motivating me for future work on children's rights. Child Line India Foundation needs no introduction. I must express my heartfelt gratitude to the foundation for selecting me as an honorary nodal director for the district of Jalpaiguri in West Bengal. This assignment has brought me very close to the underprivileged children in this part of West Bengal. I must thank the state government for inducting me as honourable member of the Child Welfare Committee (CWC) constituted as per Juvenile Justice Act. The committee works as a bench of magistrates in the district of Jalpaiguri to look after the children in need of care and protection. This involvement has further enriched my understanding of the intricacies of protection for distressed children. I must mention the name of Jalpaiguri Welfare Organisation (JWO), working steadfastly for protection of the rights of the disabled children. My association with this remarkable organisation has contributed to my practical knowledge on the rights and adversities of the disabled children.

I am indebted to the Fulbright Commission of the United States of America for nominating me as Fulbright Visiting Lecturer during 2008. The coveted fellowship has given me the opportunity of lecturing on children's rights issues at the Human Rights Centre of the University of Minnesota in the U.S.A. during fall semester. This book contains some of the lecture topics I had presented in the U.S.A. I must acknowledge the Jamia Milia University in New Delhi and Joyprokash Institute for Social Change in Kolkata for providing me opportunity for interaction and deliberation on child rights. I must thank my beloved colleagues at the Ananda Chandra College, Jalpaiguri for unvarying support and encouragement. My research assistant Dr. Abdul Hadi did wonderful work. His involvement all through out this work is commendable. Mr. Pallab Sarkar helped me in tabulation of data. Last but not the least, I am grateful to my wife Soma and to my daughter Saroni for propping me during the long course of writing the manuscript.

SUDIP CHAKRABORTY

1

Introduction

Child labour, as a problem of the global society, hardly needs any mention anew. We had faced this evil in our past. We bear with it in our present and it may remain with us in our future as a sticky virus. We did not pay much attention to this problem; even we did not mind it as a problem at all in the past. We all took it as a part of life and therefore condoned it. It had existed in all societies, in all continents, in North as well as in South. It still exists in all continents but in varied degrees, pervasive somewhere and very little in many locations of the globe including in the advanced western world. Many countries had succeeded in eliminating it altogether years ago. Elimination over time is certainly a function of economic development process in respective countries. It can hardly be contested that economic prosperity in the western world that followed the industrial revolution had impacted child labour adversely. Economic well-being and rise in the standard of living had brought about a change in the mindset and world view in the west. Child labour began to be regarded as social wrong. The idea gained ground that the right place for children is school, not work place. They are to be nourished, raised, cared and to be protected from all odds.

They should be allowed to grow in a healthy manner. Children can turn into productive adults if raised properly. It took many years even in the western world to accept that use of child labour is a damaging proposition. The persistence of child labour is dehumanizing, agonizing and economically disastrous for the country that fosters it. Rise in economic well-being coupled with state provision of education for children considerably brought down the incidence of child labour in the western society. Unfortunately this was not replicated in the southern hemisphere of the globe, a vast region of which is popularly known now as third world. Put in other words, the western action against child labour had no spread effects beyond their territories until at least the birth of the League of Nations in the aftermath of First World War. Concern was raised for the suffering children by this global body. Member-nations were persuaded to adopt a Declaration of the Rights of the Child in 1927. It was obviously a difficult job for the League to convince many member-states for accepting the Universal Declaration. It was arduous because children were and even still are not regarded as individuals in many societies. Children are reckoned as possessions of parents like many objects a family owns or commands. Children should not have the personal autonomy or the freedom to choose. Society confers the parent's right over children. Children are assets to be put to use like many other productive assets a family can own, livestock, for example. Children's labour power is utilized as a survival strategy for the family. More children implies more helping hands. Families living on the margins can engage them in various productive activities that can ensure family survival where state support is drastically insufficient or altogether absent. Children can tend cattle, collect fodder, fetch water, help parent in family agriculture, can do housework to release adults to join outside paid work, and can look after siblings and aged family members. They can join wage work outside home in busy agricultural season, as happens in many predominantly agricultural economies in the third world. There are varieties of activities waiting to take in them in virtually all societies.

High fertility and persistence of child labour are positively correlated. The affluent societies of the industrialized nations of the present time had to undergo that 'nexus' phase in the past. Many countries in the sub-Saharan Africa, in South Asia and in Latin America are going through that phase. Still many families aspires for more children as an insurance against economic adversity which may take the shape of starvation in worst situation. Child malnutrition and child mortality obviously enter into the high fertility and child labour nexus. Child labour, as an issue of social concern, however received scant attention from social thinkers. Adam Smith, venerated as the founding fathers of Economics, had tried to shed a light on the issue from the perspectives of political economy in the late eighteenth century. He had tried to look for the cause and found which is still valid for the subsistence economy even now, that high fertility is caused by higher value for children as they can be placed in labour force. Friedrich Engel had depicted a painful picture of the working children in the early phase of industrial revolution. Karl Marx straightway had blamed industrial revolution as cause for child labour. He had assumed that parent and capitalist did work hand in hand to employ children in factories. Thomas Malthus, the proponent of population explosion theory, was slightly off the genre, and he did not put all the blame on parents and employers. He argues that prevalence of child labour in the late 18th century is the reflection of the inabilities of families to meet the basic needs.

However, the modern theoretical construction on child labour was set in motion by T.W. Schultz way back in 1960. Gary Beckers and many others had later enriched that school of thought. Child labour is explained through the lens of human capital formation theory. Education forms a significant part of human capital formation process. Therefore, investment in children, both for the government and for the parents, is aimed at creating human resources, essential to contribute to growth and prosperity of the nation. The fundamental logic is that children cannot grow as productive adults if proper education is not imparted. Physical capital can not, on its own, take a country way forward. Human capital is as necessary as physical capital. Parents are confronted with two choices open to them relating to children's education. Parents will decide in favour of sending children to school if the perceived return to education is higher than the present cost of schooling. Cost of schooling for children, for the poor families particularly, comprises of two components; direct cost as well as indirect cost. Direct cost consists of costs on tuition, uniform, stationeries and various types of fees, indirect cost is the opportunity cost of time. The parents have to forgo child labour income if the children spend this time in school. Adults have to undertake many household works and unpaid works in family enterprises when children are in school.

This also amounts to cost in an indirect way. Thus child labour can persist and even swell if the present costs exceed the perceived benefit in future. Rosenzweig and Evenson's (1977) study on child labour in developing countries had applied this analytical framework. Research on child labour has recently gained momentum world-wide. World Bank has been sponsoring Living Standard Measurement Survey for last many years in many low income countries. The survey captures the conditions of children that also reveals the intensity and extent of child labour in respective countries. International Labour Organization (ILO) has launched International Program for the Elimination of Child Labour (IPEC) during nineties. It is still a puzzling social ills unyielding to preventive actions at the national level as well as at the global level. It is still amazing that many prosperous nations in the western world still have pockets of concentration of child labour. Enormous opulence in many western societies could not succeed in eliminating child labour altogether. The fruits of development are not shared equally and the prosperity seems to bypass a significant section of population even in the affluent world. Child labour still exist among communities who were left behind in the process of capitalist development. Income inequality and unequal opportunities for a section of population, even in the U.S.A., have helped to perpetuate child labour in agricultural sector over there.

CHILD LABOUR AS A GLOBAL PROBLEM

The International Labour Organization (ILO) in its 'Facts on Child Labour' released in June 2005, says that one out of six children in the world today is involved in child labour, doing work that is damaging to his or her mental, physical and emotional development. These children work in varieties of occupations. The teeming majority of them work in agricultural sector where they are exposed to dangerous chemicals, scorching sunlight, inclement weather, harmful pesticides. They run the risk of serious injury and wounds from using sharp agricultural tools and implements. Non-agricultural work for children comprises of far more dangerous and damaging occupations. Street children, visible in the cities and small towns in the developing countries are one such category. Millions of street children thus perish in the streets, running errands, peddling drugs, and they do whatever job they find for survival. The jobs obviously include petty thefts, snatching; pick-pocketing which render them vulnerable to torture and physical abuse. Children toil in factories, even in countries where factory work of children is legally prohibited. Girl children work as prostitutes. Sex tourism, which is flourishing recently, mainly in the aftermath of the removal of trade restrictions on goods and services across the globe, has been pulling in young girls from impoverished families. The list seems to be endless. Child domestics, in the third world, are another exploitative form of child labour mostly for girls. Hazardous occupation in mining, quarrying, gem polishing, glass bangle manufacturing, carpet weaving, construction, brick kiln, tobacco processing by the children are not only exploitative but also dangerous, monotonous, damaging and life threatening. They work without any gear or safety apparatus. These children, entrapped in such dire situations miss all the opportunities of life far away from what is called as 'decent childhood', and they are forced to lead humiliating and sub-human life.

Total elimination of child labour from the surface of the earth is virtually impossible in the short-run. It can be and must be abolished through removing the factors that generate child labour. Those factors can not be eliminated over night or even over next couples of years. But the removal must be prioritized in the long-term socio-economic goals a country must set to accomplish. While all forms of child labour can not be eliminated in the short-run but worst forms of child labour can be. Nearly three quarters of working children are engaged in what the world recognizes as the worst forms of child labour, including trafficking, armed conflict, child slavery, sexual exploitation, street children and child labour in most hazardous occupation and processes.

ILO that counts the child labour all over the world presents a very painful picture in its report entitled 'Facts on Child Labour' released in 2005. It says that—

(1) 246 million children are labourers.
(2) 73 million children are less than 10 years old.
(3) There are 2.5 million working children in the developed countries and another 2.5 million in the transition economies.
(4) Every year 22,000 children die in work-related accidents.
(5) Around 127 million children, under the age of 14 years, are working in Asia Pacific region.
(6) Sub-Saharan African tops the list in fostering highest proportion of child labour; nearly one-third of their children work. The magnitude over there is around 48 million.

The ILO finding also present that around 70% of these children work in agricultural sector, 8% in manufacturing, 8% in wholesale and retail trade and 7% in service sector. The most painful revelation in the report is that 8.4 million children are trapped in slavery, trafficking, debt bondage, prostitution, pornography and in many other degrading and illegal activities.

WHAT DO THE CHILD LABOURERS DO ACROSS THE GLOBE?

The last section sheds light on the classification of works in which children are engaged without going into the details of those works. We now turn on this, how and in which sectors the children work in respective countries where child labour is persistent. One commonality in the midst of variation in employment of children across all countries is the predominance of informal economy as employer of children. Formal economy as a site of child labour is hardly to come by in any country. However, removal of child labour from the formal economic activities has nothing to do with generation and perpetuation of child labour. There are many more takers. Formal economy can make use of children in circuitous way through outsourcing many labour-intensive manufacturing activities to informal and household sectors. This trend is in place for last couple of years, notably after the integration of national economies with global economy as a result of economic globalization. Multinational Corporations (MNC) are omnipresent and omnipotent. Entire globe is now their geography of activities. A substantial proportion of products are procured from tiny manufacturing units in informal sectors. In agriculture, highly organized commercial plantations may now contract out same production to small scale family farms.

CHILD LABOUR IN AGRICULTURE

Majority of child labourers can be traced in agricultural work, particularly in the developing world. But controversy is widespread in the nature of work of children in the agricultural activities. Child work in agriculture is not accepted as child labour by many scholars. The argument offered is that children in poor agricultural families learn skill during childhood. This is a kind of socialization process, much beneficial than damaging associated with child labour. Children work in family farms under the parental supervision that rules out any possibility of exploitation by outsiders. Children can attend school, can play and take part in leisurely and pleasurable activities. Over and above, agricultural activities are seasonal in which children can easily take part during school vacation. Opponents, however, raise the issue of numbers. They cast doubt that children engaged in this type of light work forms a very little fraction of child labour in agriculture. This attempt to condone and pass off as socialization process hides harsh realities of toil, many children undergo in the third world agriculture. Studies have shown that the combination of poor nutrition and agriculture work in childhood results in stunting, which impair earning ability in later life. Family-based agricultural occupation can sometimes be hazardous. It has been found in Philippines that family-based vegetable farming is dangerous for children as a consequence of exposure to infection from soil and water, the use of heavy watering cans and the lack of protective clothing. Agricultural processing like peeling, culling, grading cashew nuts can be hazardous for children. Fatal injury, cut, back pain and many other types of ailments are associated with these types of job for children.

GENDERED DELIMITATION IN CHILD LABOUR IN AGRICULTURE

Boys and girls do not perform the same nature of task in agriculture. Some of the tasks are meant exclusively for boys while some for girls. There is hardly any interchanging. In India, for example, on-field job like ploughing and levelling is male work while on-house job such as thrashing, peeling and many other post-harvesting jobs, undertaken in the courtyard of farmers are female dominated. In rural Bangladesh girls work longer hours than boys. Among the rural Tonga of Zimbabwe, both boys and girls help women with household task. Debt bondage or bonded child labour is found in the agricultural sector. This inhuman practice is still prevalent in parts of the third world where social safety net is very thin or altogether absent, institutional rural credit system is not in place, labour laws are virtually non-existent and government fail to protect the poor. A poor farmer without any assets, which might be a plot of land or any other variety, takes loan from private money lenders for an immediate and inescapable need. Money lenders and landlords are often the same persons. Thus borrowing by the farmer is tantamount to digging her own grave. The borrowers have to pledge the labour service of their sons and daughters in the agricultural activities of the lenders in the eventuality of default. The poor farmer invariably fails to repay the sum along with the exorbitant interest. Children have to work for the lenders as long as lenders wish without any wage payment. Terms of payment are fixed by the lenders and therefore children are at the mercy of the bond master. They have no escape route. Bonded child labour in agriculture is now regarded as one of the worst forms of child labour that needs immediate elimination. The world community has coalesced on this.

While the child labour in the family agriculture in the subsistence economy is certainly an issue to confront but child labour in commercial agriculture is much more serious. The production of commercial crop like cocoa, coffee, tea, rubber uses child labour in a bigger proportion. Studies in Brazil, Kenya, and Mexico have shown that children under 15 years make up between 25 and 30 per cent of total labour force in production of various commodities. Child labour in cocoa production in West Africa has drawn international attention. It is really puzzling and shocking to note that the United States, the land of immense prosperity and a symbol of democracy and human right still shelters child labour. It sounds unbelievable but unfortunately this is true. The site of her child labour is agriculture. Child labour in family farms is exempted from laws in the US provided parents employ them. It has been estimated that 7 per cent of all farm workers in the US are between the ages of 14 and 17. In the United States, this sector has the highest number of occupational fatalities for youths less than 18 years of age, accounting for 42.7 per cent of all fatalities reported for that age group.

CHILD LABOUR IN FISHING

Fishing is the source of sustenance for millions of people, predominantly in the coastal regions. It has become a major source of export income as global demand for sea food is on the rise. Small enterprises comprising more than half of the fish catch worldwide poses a real threat to health and safety of the workers. Small enterprises flourish on low cost fishing craft and use of child labour. Profit of these enterprises obviously swells on the back of child labour. In El Salvador, for example, children work in small scale, family-based or private enterprises in which boys and girls harvest shellfish. Children begin this work well before the age of ten. Child labour in fishing is found in the Philippines, not in small craft enterprises but in large vessels owned and operated by large monopoly houses. The technique of catching is known as *muro-ami* fishing. Children are engaged as swimmers and divers for catching reef fish. The dangers of such task for children need no explication. In Thailand, children work as fish sorters, factory workers and members of crew on fishing boats. They remain away from home and on sea for several months at a stretch. The work in the fishing, like agriculture, is marked by gender division. Boys work at night on the sea in small boats or in large vessels, while girls remain at home to undertake fish processing an even marketing. Strenuous work over night by the boys hampers their school achievement. Drop-out rate is very high among these 'fish catching' boys.

STREET CHILDREN

Street children are visible in the cities of Asia and Latin America. They are child labourers in every sense but they form a distinct category among them. One feature that differentiates them from others is their homelessness. Urban streets, slums, market places, railway yards and bus stands are their makeshift shelters. They are either trafficked or runaway and many of them are compelled to leave their familiar homes and neighbourhoods in search of livelihood in the cities. Sometimes, marital break up that culminates into the disappearance of parental care and protection pushes them to the city street for living. The causes are not far to seek. Poverty, family disintegration, lack of protection and care, lack of alternative community care, governmental apathy are collectively responsible for the generation and proliferation of street children. The pull factor works as well and the pull sometimes can be irresistible. Children can be lured by consumer culture and for better opportunities in the cities. Exposure to television among children in rural areas is associated with one particular adverse impact and that is weaning away their minds to consumerist lifestyle in cities. Children are thus entrapped in the fantasies of make-believe world. They flee their homes and ultimately land themselves in streets having no one to take care of them. The extreme adversities ensue from day one.

The nature of work, the street children are engaged, is diverse. It ranges from unlawful activities to most socially degrading jobs. They are engaged in shoe shining, vending fruits and vegetables, washing wind screens of the waiting cabs, repairing tires, scavenging, rag picking, begging, loading and unloading of merchandises and many others types of work. In many cities, street children go behind the bar for committing pick pocketing and petty theft. Boys outnumber girls in the crowd of street children. Girls are mostly engaged in low paid prostitution in the city streets. Work for street children is always associated with hazards. They are exposed to environmental pollution in the overcrowded cities, violence, torture, physical abuse and sexual abuse. They work in unhealthy environmental conditions and live in far more unhygienic conditions without any access to education and health care. Proper diet and safe drinking water seems to be miles away from their reach. They have to cope with vagaries of nature. Water logging as a result of continuous rainfall can wipe out their makeshift shelters. Floods are recurrent calamities that befall on Indian cities. Rehabilitation measures for slum-dwellers are not always sure to come by. Even if half-hearted measures are adopted in piecemeal fashion they are quite insufficient to take care of them in full. Hunger and dearth of gainful work in inundated streets make the street children vulnerable to various afflictions. Waterborne diseases are most common among them. Children living with parents on streets are somewhat better off than their peers without parents. Children without parents in the cities have to fend for themselves in this extreme adversity. Their presence is not felt, their livings remain unnoticed and no one is left to lament for their death. No body can listen to their cry in the din and bustle of the overcrowded cities. The cities move on, the business goes as usual; the high rise buildings stand still, no one grieves over the death of the children of the streets.

CHILDREN AT THE END OF SUPPLY CHAIN : CHILD LABOUR IN MANUFACTURING

Manufacturing activities cannot be labelled as the highest recruiter of child labour anywhere in the world, as agriculture holds that position. But the product variety and the shifting of sites for works of children are aspects to be explored to gauge the harsh reality of child labour. Manufacturing of certain products are now increasingly outsourced to family units in countries characterized by surplus labour force and lax labour laws. Women and children in the families can easily be engaged in various unskilled jobs at a certain phase of manufacturing. For example, tanning of leather is outsourced to families, stitching of soccer ball, rolling of tobacco cigars, processing in incense sticks and fire crackers and many other products are visible examples of such outsourcing to households.

Outsourcing in the manufacturing is widespread in the fast growing economies of both India and China. Private enterprises with an eye to high margin of profit make every effort to reduce the labour cost. They can earn enormous profit if bulk of production process is carried out by women and child in the family courtyard. Factories are subject to labour inspections and therefore bound to pay stipulated wage rate and must conform to the stipulated working hours and many other facilities that go with this factory work. The profit-seekers escape this route and smell very high profit in home-based units where factory act does not apply. Children work for very long hours at very little pay. The jobs are strenuous and expose them to cut, injury, infection, respiratory tract problem, and many types of hazards besides impeding schooling and leisure.

Outsourcing or sub-contracting has gained momentum in the aftermath of economic globalization and trade liberalization. Export sectors are rapidly flourishing in many countries as a result of removal of many trade restrictions. Manufacturing of exports goods has picked up in unprecedented scale in many countries. Translational Corporation have stepped in export sector of many countries that enjoy comparative advantage by way of production cost. Child labour manifestly comes within the list of comparative advantage for the producers as they have to pay very little for the labour. Shifting of sites from factory to homes is not a new development. But trade liberalization in the past decade has bolstered this process.

CHILD LABOUR IN TOURISM

Tourism sector in each country is undergoing unprecedented expansion in recent years. The ongoing economic globalization process deserves the credit. The flow of cross border tourism is rapidly on the rise as the restrictions that used to inhibit on tourists flow in the past is virtually removed now. Civil Aviation sector is now open in the global village. Entry of large number of airlines has resulted in massive reduction of airfare, flight frequency and many other advantages that have collectively work as impetus. Information Technology revolution in recent years has also contributed to the expansion of tourism sector. Booking for flight and hotels seems to be just one click away from any where in the world. Domestic tourism is also on the rise in parity with international tourism. Unprecedented rise in income of a certain sector in the middle class of the countries in the globalization era has created a massive demand for tourism in and outside their own lands. Hotels and restaurants have to come up in large numbers in the sites of tourist attraction everywhere. The scope of child labour use in the expanding hotels and restaurants has further widened.

Hotel industries often offer varieties of jobs for the children. They work as bell boys, maids, beach attendants, hawkers, golf caddies, porters. It has been estimated that around 10 to 15 per cent of workers between 13 to 19 million are under 18 years of age. In Acapulco, Mexico, children aged 7-12 employed by beach restaurants to bring in customers and they are paid exclusively by commission on the customer's drinks. Road side *dhaba* (a variety of rural motels in India) are the prominent sites of children working from dawn to dusk. They are ill paid, maltreated and are vulnerable to sexual abuse often by long distance truckers. A good number of hotel boys have been trafficked and therefore totally cut-off from their families rendering them more vulnerable to exploitation and abuse. One of the negative offshoots of the growing tourism sector is the emergence of sex tourism. Young girls are lured away to take up this degrading task of sexual gratification of the tourists for a little pay. The victims are either trafficked from different places, sometimes they are brought to this business with parental consent. Parents, unable to afford two square meals a day, do not always dither to say yes to the proposal. Parents are promised of better life prospects and jobs in the cities. The girls ultimately find them in the sex tourism to begin a new life of indignity, slavery and torture.

CHILD DOMESTICS

The most intractable category in the genre of child labour is child domestics. Children take up domestic service in their employer's home from very young age sometimes at a very low pay. Employer's home might be very close to the residences of the children, within a walking distance or within commutable distances. Children of the slum areas in the urban cities of the developing world do take up the job in the middle class families of the cities. However, this category of child labour is characterized by gendered division. Girls rather than boys are preferred in South Asian countries, because of inherent skills of the girls in housework. In the South Asian cultural context, girls grow up in the shadow of their mothers and look on to them as their role models. Daughters, from the very young age, help their mothers in the kitchen work as well as in household maintenance. Employers look for skilled helping hands to keep their households on track. Girls, thus perfectly fit in their requirements. In addition to that, girls are docile and are used to remain within four walls of homes for long hours unlike the boys. Girls outnumber boys in this category for the aforesaid reasons, particularly in South Asian context.

Children who commute daily to undertake the domestic service at master's houses seem to be a bit fortunate compared to other who has to stay with their master's family in far away places. Children in the latter situation are obviously more vulnerable to exploitation and abuse. Many girls in this category are brought to the master's house by traffickers. There are number of agencies in the cities of South Asian countries who deal in the deployment of young girls in the domestic service. These agencies have a liaison with the organized trafficking gangs for sourcing; very few of them might be runaway children. Girls who stay in their master's house have to undergo unspeakable misery. They are cut-off from their families and parents and as a result sever all contact with them. They are sometimes are not paid in cash. They are kept confined within the four walls and therefore totally secluded from the outside world. They do not find any one to interact. No one does listen to their agonies. They remain hidden from the public glare and are not counted in the child labour survey. There are innumerable instances of sexual assault in the master's house but a very few of them are reported to the police. The convictions of the offenders are rarely heard of.

The magnitude of child labour in the domestic service is quite high and it prevails in most of the regions of world. The Government of Haiti reports that around 2,50,000 children of disadvantaged parents are in domestic service. In Brazil, Columbia and Ecuador, 20 percent of all girls between the age of 10 and 14 are engaged in domestic service. Children working in other homes for wage with a view to support their struggling families are certainly deprived of the opportunities for growth and development. But many girls who undertake such tasks at home to release their mothers so that they can undertake paid work outside remain outside the statistics on child domestics. They work for long hours performing all odd jobs what adults are supposed to do. They forgo schooling as a consequence of their preoccupation with the domestic work. They earn indirectly through releasing adults. They ensure family survival by this involvement. They are hardly counted as child labourers in the child labour survey. Unfortunately domestic labour is not included in the labour laws in many countries. There is also a ray of hope in the darkness. In India, for example, child domestics, has been included in the prohibitive category of child labour act since 2006.

CHILD LABOUR IN MINING, CONSTRUCTION AND QUARRYING

City horizons are expanding in a massive way in the developing world. Surge in demand for housing in the cities is leading to boom in the construction activities. Construction of housing estates, roads, bridges, plants and parks in cities creates enormous demand for labour. The available labour force in the locality is insufficient in response to massive demand. The construction workers thus have to be sourced from urban outskirts or from the county sides. In view of the lack of alternative opportunities in the rural areas, adult labourers throng the cities in search of income opportunities. They bring with them their families including their children. They put up makeshift shelters around construction sites. The first casualty of this shifting of rural families is the loss of schooling of the children. They have to manage the kitchen when both the parents join the construction work. Children are exposed to health hazards as a consequence of living very close to construction site. Interestingly, child labour in construction is not only the phenomenon specific to developing world. There are developed countries as well who have yet to eliminate child labour from construction activities. One study in New Zealand reveals that injuries from construction work of the adolescents is quite high. A study by labour federation known as CGIL estimated that of the 400,000 child workers in Italy, about 10 percent was in construction.

In different countries of Africa, Latin America and Asia, children work alongside their parents or independently in underground mines, open cast mines and quarries. They also carry out support functions such as collecting, sorting and transporting collections or cooking and cleaning in remote mining enclaves. The hazards of such activities are immense and varied depending on the substances that are mined. Children are exposed to dusts or chemicals and have to suffer long-term bodily damage for carrying heavy loads. The ILO (IPEC) survey in Madagascar found that 53 per cent of the children in small scale mines and quarries were aged 12 or younger. In Guatemala as well as in Tanzania, children work along side their parents crushing rock to make gravel for the construction industry. Mining sometimes involves debt bondage. Child labour in brick kiln is prevalent in South Asian countries. Children are exposed to hazardous dust in these industries where labour laws in the respective countries are very loose to escape by the employers. Medical care hardly comes by in the event of accidents and injuries. Children have to survive with the ailments uncared and untreated. Almost all hazardous occupations that engage children are marked by same bad symptom: no medical care, no protection of workers, no rights, no social security. The magnitude of child labour in the hazardous occupation is certainly on lower side but the ill-effects and hazards are enormous.

WORST FORMS OF CHILD LABOUR

There are worst forms of child labour in the business of economic exploitation. Child labour is bad and needs to be eliminated through appropriate public action. But all forms within the genre of child labour are not equally or uniformly bad. Some are worst that needs instantaneous action. While abolition of child labour within a country is linked with the positive outcome of socio-economic transformation over time. We have to wait for many years to see the effect of socio-economic measures to make a dent on child labour. This is linked with socio-economic structure of the country that shelters child labour. So long as push and pull factors work in tandem to sustain and generate child labour, elimination of exploitation of children would remains a distant dream.

International Labour Organization that strives to eliminate child labour through global co-operation now understands the futility of calling for elimination of child labour as an immediate action for the member-states. It calls for long-term strategy for that aim to achieve. But it now segregates between worst forms and other generic child labour. The former is inhuman practice and amounts to slavery while others, although unacceptable, are not worst to be taken up on war footing for abolition right now.

Bonded child labour is one of such worst form. Children have to work for their bond masters as long as the debt burden remains. Children have to toil at agricultural fields from dawn to dusk without any cash payment in exchange of their labour. Poor parents pledge the labour of themselves as well as of their children in the eventuality of default of repayment. They invariably fail to repay for two reasons: one is the exorbitant rate of interest on borrowed funds. Secondly, the loan is contracted by the poor families to meet unforeseen financial needs which may comprises of medical treatment, wedding and many other types of contingencies which families, living from hand to mouth, cannot manage from their meagre means. The village money lenders appear at this moment of crisis posing as saviours. The trap is thus laid for the poor borrowers. Village money lenders are also land-owners. They need labour powers in a big way for farming. The terms of contract including repayment schedule for the borrowed funds remain shrouded in mystery. The terms are dictated by lenders putting the borrowers at the receiving ends. The poor in the villages have no access to formal credit institutions. The micro-finance institutions are yet to cover these vulnerable families. The system of debt bondage in many parts of the world places children in extremely inhuman situations.

Debt bandage sometimes leads to child trafficking. The trafficked children are employed in exploitative work in far off places. Children are taken away by the traffickers mostly in the garb of placement agencies, in exchange of meagre amount of loan to the families. Parents are falsely promised of better job and education in the cities for their children. Parents are sometimes persuaded and convinced craftily to elicit their consent. The traffickers sometimes take recourse to coercion and intimidation when persuasion does not work. Children are mute spectators to the deal where they do not participate in the decision concerning them. They have to pay-off the debts which their parents had incurred. The trafficked children end up in sweatshops, in hotels and restraints and in brothels in the cities. They miss their familiar homes and neighbourhoods and are deprived of family environments. They work in most hazardous condition exposing them to burns, injuries, physical abuse and sexual abuse. They cannot attend school and are thus deprived of life time opportunity of development. They are low paid and even not paid at all excepting one or two square meals a day just to keep them physically fit to continue the work. Children are unaware of the loan their parents took and they do not know how long they have to suffer to pay the debt.

SEXUAL EXPLOITATION OF CHILD

Another obverse of child labour in worst condition can be traced in sexual exploitation of children, mostly of girls. This is a billion-dollar trade now prevalent in major parts of the world involving young girls. Young girls are procured and placed in booming sex trade. Many agents and intermediaries are involved including parents and relatives of the victims. Income from the sale of those young girls is distributed as different points of agencies. The *modus operandi* of procuring the young girls is not always same for all places and for all times. The tricksters use different means depending on the ground situation. Fake marriage is one of many means to procure young girls. Traffickers sometimes pose as prospective grooms with financial offer to poor parents. The poor parents sometimes can easily be bought over. They can not resist the offer as it appears to be lucrative to them. They do not need to spend on their daughter's wedding. That amount, whatever may be, is a great saving. They would not spend for her food and clothing anymore as she departs for ever. Over and above, the offer of cash works wonder to win over their minds. The girls have no say in this deal about them. They accompany the 'fake' husband for journey to an unknown place. Finally, they end up in brothels of any city and begin a life of unspeakable adversities and deprivation.

Thus the procedures for procurement of young girls as an object of sexual pleasure for sale are varied depending on the demand for a particular situation. Abduction has also been reported in some places. Vulnerability of young girls to adult's misdeeds is omnipresent. Parents, who are primary care givers for their children, forget their responsibilities. States that are committed to protect children from exploitation and abuse, miserably fail to discharge their duties to their future adults. Millions of young girls all over the world thus perish in brothels as a result of neglect from all corners. Sexual abuse differs from commercial sexual exploitation as the latter is characterized by involvement of many actors. Sex trade has now been profit-making venture, a billion dollar industry that thrives on poverty and vulnerability of the victims. Two actors are involved in the sexual abuse; the abused and the abusers or the predator and the prey. Surprisingly both of them may belong to the same family and therefore connected by kinship relation. Government's report on sexual abuse of children reveals that relatives are sometimes abusers. Sexual abuse of children within four walls of their familiar homes is the severest violation of child rights. Such misdeeds by relatives whom they trust as protectors are the grimmest situation where the misdeeds never come to light. Children are sometimes not safe within their homes.

Commercial sexual exploitation, in comparison to abuse is a trade where a third party gains financially. The victims are either ill-paid or sometime, paid nothing in exchange for their service. There is another distinction between these two forms of this sexual maltreatment to young girls while sexual abuse may occur to any child irrespective of economic well-being. Children in the rich families are equally vulnerable where relatives may be abusers. Children of poor families are more vulnerable as a result of the lack of protection. One can not just rule out the possibility of such adult misdeeds in rich homes and in prosperous neighbourhoods.

Commercial sexual exploitation, on the other hand is largely associated with poverty and household vulnerability. Girl children often join this trade to support their families. Culture among many communities in South Asia encourages this sex trade of young girls. But one cannot invoke cultural sanction to condone the dastardly crime against children. The adverse impacts of sexual abuse and exploitation are manifold: physical, psychological, social and moral. Girl children are most likely to be infected by HIV and many other sexually transmitted diseases. Unwanted pregnancies, frequent abortion cause permanent damage to their reproductive system. Improper and inadequate health care provision to fight away those debilitating diseases reduces their survival chances. Those who survive somehow, lead a life of severe destitution, devastation and servitude.

Psychological impact is more damaging than physical or bodily damage. Young girls, uprooted from their families and familiar neighbourhoods, are engaged in sex trade for the financial benefit of their procurers. They are forced to lead an isolated and secluded life in the dark confines of the brothels.

They are not allowed to interact with others. They are not even allowed to keep contact with their families; they are deprived from educational opportunities. Children victims of sexual abuse also undergo trauma that often leads to physic disorder. Their learning process is hampered as a result of the lack of concentration in studies. Traumatized mind cannot pick up classroom transaction. These learning impediments adversely affect their competency that sometime result in school discontinuation. Thus sexual exploitation and abuse of children are blatant violation of human rights of children. Their helplessness is exploited by adults for sexual pleasure and exploitation. There are laws in almost all ratifying nations to prevent this inhuman trade in children. Ironically, laws and enforcing mechanism have miserably failed to stop these adult misdeeds perpetrated on children in counties where state initiatives on protection of children are altogether absent. Millions of children, mostly girls among them, in developing world, are thus lost in the darkness of destitution.

2

Perfect Childhood

The issue of child labour has to be construed and contextualized in the perspectives of what is known as 'decent childhood'. The UNCRC aims to bestow the decent childhood for all children on this planet by obliging all member-nations to implement the articles of the Convention. The Convention lays down a uniform structure for all children across geography and culture. This was certainly the biggest triumph at the floor of the United Nations to reach at a global consensus, winning over the hearts of defiant members. The discordant tones from the leaders of many third world nations in the beginning of the process put a big hurdle on the road to adoption. The debate centred on the conception of decent childhood to be provided uniformly. The third world leaders debated that childhood is a sociological construction pertaining to culture specific contexts. Thus adoption and ratification of the CRC amounts to acceptance of the western norm in the third world societies. This was a ploy to intrude upon cultural autonomy of the third world societies.

The decent childhood was constructed in the western industrial societies in the aftermath of the industrial revolution that in turn led to the birth of affluent middle class over there.

The age of enlightenment had an impact on the attitude, world view and ethical orientation of the western societies. The construction of decent childhood was thus influenced by many historical developments preceding the adoption in 1989 at the U.N. The anti-slavery movement, civil rights movement, the establishment of the League of Nations, the first Declaration of the Rights of the Child in 1921, birth of the United Nations in the aftermath of the Second World War and the adoption of the Universal Declaration of Human Rights. All these supportive developments spanning for hundred of years, had definitely created a favourable condition for the acceptance of the Convention for the world children.

The debate persists on the construction of childhood as a distinct phase in the life of mankind. During medieval period children were young adults. They did everything what an adult used to perform for survival. There are evidences to support medieval attitude towards children. Children were regarded as family pets by adults, born and raised in the families to be used for labour service. Compassion, affection and emotional attachment were altogether missing. High fertility, high child mortality and use of children as labour power were interconnected in this phase of social evolution. Thus childhood as a formative phase in the earliest part of human life, which should demand attention from the adults, was virtually non-existent until the advent of industrial revolution. The latter was followed by the emergence of affluent middle class in Western Europe. Underage people are no longer regarded as miniature adults in the new era of enlightenment and prosperity. Society began to differentiate between children and adults. The former category of human beings needs care and protection, upbringing, emotional support because of the physical and psychological immaturities. Childhood is thus a period of adult support for their defencelessness. They are very vulnerable seedling to be protected and nourished for growth and development. There was, however, other reason for this change in outlook towards these young numbers of the new industrial society that emerged in the new era. The need for labour power of the children for livelihood activities, the dominant feature of the agrarian society, gradually disappeared in the urban-based industrial societies. Production technology displaced the nimble fingers from the factory sites. Mechanisation of production process decimated the need for child labour in the western world. The demand for skill and education for young members of the families in the cities led to establishment of schools and learning centres in the upcoming industrial cities. Parents began to send their children to school to acquire skills and literacy. Thus childhood was accepted as a period of learning, caring and protection. Education began to be perceived as investment on children for a better future.

CHILDREN AS 'INDIVIDUALS'

It took hundreds of years for human society to accept that their young members are individual human beings not the objects to own. The advancement of humanity from the medieval and pre-modern phase to modernity, the ushering of industrial revolution, the emergence of cities, the rise of middle class, enormous opulence, the spread of science and technology and the dawn of enlightenment in Europe, collectively changed the attitude towards their young members. The period from the first Declaration of the Rights of the Children under the auspices of the League of Nations down to the adoption of the United Nations Conventions of the Rights of the children was a remarkable phase in the recent history in the advancement of human rights for children. The world now accepts children as rights-holders as they are individuals. The world community now recognizes and accepts that the children are active participants, not passive recipients. They have rights to protection, right to provision, right to survival and physical well-being, right to participation and to development. Their voices cannot be muted by parental rights over them. They must be heard and must be allowed to take part in any decision concerning them. Thus conferring them the right to participation by the world community is the reflection of society's acceptance of children as individuals.

But despite the universal acceptance and commitment by way of the global treaty on the rights on the children that confers them rights to be treated as individuals, children in many societies are still treated as objects of exploitation even today. The prevalence of child labour in many regions of the world is the testimony to this remnant of medieval social attitude to children in the world of twenty-first century. States are unwilling to eliminate child labour, parents utilizes their labour services for family survival. Employers exploit them for economic gain keeping their wages at a very low level and stretching their work schedules for very long hours. The states are unable to protect their children from exploitation in the market place. They are just productive assets in many struggling families living on the margin of bare subsistence. The states fail to protect those families from severe economic adversities and prevent the economic exploitation of children. Children, thus, in this dire circumstance have no voice. They have no part to play in the decision concerning them. Thus the persistence of child labour is thus the reflection of society's reluctance to accept their children as individual human beings in the first go. The second one is the lack of political will and sincerity of the state to protect them from exploitation and abuse. The states tend to invoke poverty and under-development as excuse for the perpetuation of child labour. This is certainly and indisputable reason for many countries in sub-Saharan Africa, in Latin America as well as in South Asia. But child labour still persists in massive scale in many countries where economic growth in recent times has substantially reduced poverty but child labour still persists.

CHILD RIGHTS AND CHILD LABOUR

The United Nations Convention of the Right of the Child is a great leap forward in the advancement of the global movement for the protection of children on this planet. The tangible positive outcome of the adoption of CRC is the recognition of childhood as a vulnerable phase in the lives of mankind. This phase of life is to be protected from all odds that damage this childhood. All children of this world are entitled to a decent childhood. The states, the communities and the families are legally bound to ensure the decent childhood to the children. The UNCRC is unique in the sense that it is an enforceable international treaty which obliges all state parties to legislate as part of domestic legal structure. The state parties will evolve policies in conformity with the basic spirits of the Convention. The Convention provides for elaborate check and balances. State parties must report to the UN about progress on the implementation of the Convention from time to time. Non-governmental Organizations, working within the national boundaries are also encouraged to send alternate report about the progress of realization of rights in the respective country.

States are also encouraged to seek all sorts of assistance from the UN and from other international organizations for the effective implementation of the Convention. The rights for the children as articulated in the Convention are comprehensive and inseparable. One piece of rights cannot be realized excluding others. The comprehensive rights for the children cover all aspects of protection to ensure a decent childhood to the young members of the humanity. All rights must be realized simultaneously.

The UNCRC provides for rights of the child to protection against economic exploitation. The Article 32 of the Convention articulates that "State parties recognize the right of the child to be protected from economic exploitation and from performing any work that is likely to be hazardous or to interfere with the child's education or to be harmful to the child's health or physical, mental, spiritual, moral or social development". The article further lays down that all state parties must stipulate minimum age for admission to employment. This article thus exclusively deals with the issue of child labour in all cultures and in all geographies. Employment of children that jeopardizes their health and well-being, derails their education and development and hampers their moral, spiritual and social development is unacceptable. The state must ensure that this harmful employment of children must be stopped with appropriate legal, political, social policies and implementation in conformity with the CRC. Abolition of child labour must be the priority agenda of all states ratifying the UNCRC.

The perpetuation of child labour is not only the violation of Article 32 of the UNCRC but other rights, the realization of which can only guarantee a decent childhood are simultaneously violated. Take the case of a child labour, working in a factory for very long hours in a day. The apparent fallout of this sort of engagement of the child is missing of school. The child is obviously out of school; she might have enrolled before but have dropped out or had never enrolled. The child in question is thus deprived of his or her right to education as a result of his employment as child labourer. Another sort of her right, very crucial for her survival and physical growth is her right to health. A child labourer, working for long hours in a cramped, unhealthy and fusty factory shed, is vulnerable to serious illness that can jeopardize her physical and mental health. Her spiritual and moral development is equally derailed. The child labourer is vulnerable to sexual abuse, physical and psychological abuse in the work place. Thus her right to protection against all sorts of abuses is violated. Thus all rights are inalienable and composite.

INTERNATIONAL LABOUR ORGANIZATION AND CHILD LABOUR IN INDIA

International Labour Organization, known to the world by her abbreviated name, i.e. ILO needs to be mentioned and her role must be perused in the discourse on child labour world-wide. It would be interesting to assess her role in eliminating child labour in India as a largest reservoir of child labourers in the contemporary world. ILO was created in the aftermath of the First World War to protect and promote the interest of the industrial workers. The plight of the workers in the upcoming factories in the wake of industrial revolution in the Western Europe is chronicled in the human history as severest form of exploitation. There is immense prosperity but that was at the cost of unspeakable human misery. Workers, both adult male and female as well as children had to perish in the factories, toiling from dawn to dusk with very little pay. There was no law to stipulate fixed working hours for the workers. In fact, there was no protective shield for these vulnerable workers. It took many years and after a prolonged struggle, the minimum wage act and stipulation of working hours where legislated and came into effect in industrial countries. Thanks to ILO for creating a climate in favour of workers, for motivating employers and respective government to protect the right of the workers.

ILO was created in 1919 to give effect to certain missions to accomplish through global consensus. Abolition of child labour and forced labour including slavery are among the principal objective of her global initiatives. ILO Conventions and Recommendations are instruments to apply to achieve the objectives. These Conventions and Recommendations are drafted, adopted and ratified with a view to put in place international labour standard for protection of workers' rights in all works places. These rights include rights to adequate living wages, right to stipulated working hours, rights to protection against discriminatory treatment and rights to adequate health provisioning and most fundamental, among the rights, is freedom of association and freedom to form trade union. The International Labour Conference, the most effective organ of the ILO is a collective body of representatives from governments of each member-states representatives from workers' organization as well as from employers' organizations. Thus any decision on the issues of protection of rights for the workers and adoption of any convention are outcome of thorough discussion and consensus of all stake-holders. Any Convention, once adopted by all members, binds them to implement in the respective states. Child labour was a major concern in the beginning and is still now in the thought and actions of the ILO.

The widely well-known instrument in the armoury of ILO is the Convention no. 138 adopted way back in 1973. The convention stipulates that the minimum age of entry in employment must be 15 years of age, by the time of which children complete their primary education. It was reduced by one year to 14 years in case of developing countries. Hazardous work for children was altogether prohibited up to 18 years of age. India's major legal provision: Child Labour (Regulation and Prohibition) Act to fight child labour sets the minimum age of 14 years for entry in employment in certain industries and in processing. Another ILO instrument, convention no. 29 calls for abolition of forced and compulsory labour. India's bonded child labour problem, the perpetuation of which has been brought to light in many studies comes within the purview of that Convention. ILO was alarmed, by the end of the last century, at the massive magnitude of child labour, particularly in the developing world. It begins to understand that abolition of child labour in the immediate future was an impossible task. The issue of poverty and underdevelopment are linked to the issue of child labour. The latter can not be addressed without addressing the former. Economic growth and development that will reduce poverty and child labour is a long-run process.

ILO began to segregate between less harmful child labour and worst form of child labour. It calls for immediate elimination of the latter. The Convention no. 182 was adopted at the ILO during 1999 and was ratified by 157 countries as of January 1, 2006. This Convention obliges all ratifying nations to take steps on priority basis, for elimination of child labour that jeopardizes health, safety, education, liberty, integrity of the children. The worst forms of child labour including child trafficking, child prostitution, child pornography, children in armed conflict, children in drug trafficking, child slavery including bonded child labour and many other forms of child labour in various countries that entail inhuman exploitation of children. ILO has its own list of worst forms but allows respective countries to locate and define worst forms in their own territories. ILO thus admits that abolition of child labour of all forms and natures is dependent on the overall socio-economic development of a country. But abolition of worst form of child labour must be immediate task of all state parties. The humanity can not wait for an indefinite period to witness that their children are engaged in most degradable, dehumanizing and extremely hazardous forms of child labour. It must be eradicated through concrete action right now. The decent childhood, the bestowal of which is the ultimate goal of the Convention, may be a little far but can be achieved through dogged determination and firm political will of all nations.

3

What is Child Labour?

Debate as to what constitutes child labour persists imposingly, thwarting sometimes, the examination of this inhuman abuse of children in the world today. The immediate outcome of the definitional disagreement is the conflicting estimate of child labour at any point of time. For example, child labour estimate in India has varied from 12 million to 100, even 110 million during nineties. Government of India brings out the figure, which is obviously lowest in the aforesaid spectrum of magnitude. NGOs, who are working for children in India, do not accept the government statistics. They assert that child labour is shockingly alarming in India and the figure is more than 100 million. Government of India, like any government in the world, obviously would be, quite obviously, hesitant to bring to light its own failure of its governance. The latter is not confined to maintaining law and order within the country or to ensure external security. The functioning of a police state is limited to these. The modern welfare state is expected to strive for peace, prosperity and highest possible well-being of its people. Persistence of child labour in a country is an indication of failure as welfare state. No government on this earth would drumbeat its own glitch.

Therefore, the stand taken by one group is quite far from the one taken by the other. Those who subscribe to higher figure of incidence belong to 'broader definition' school. Government prefers to go by 'narrow' or restrictive definition and contradicts broader definition. Professor Myron Wiener, the U.S. political scientist and a great commentator on child labour issues in India argues that children out of school are child labourers in some way or other. Those are children who are currently not in the labour force but are sure to join it very soon. They are potential child labourers. He rules out the possibility of any other category like 'idle children' in India. NGOs in India working for elimination of child labour firmly believe in this interpretation of what constitutes child labour. One N.G.O., based in Andhra Pradesh, is pioneer in propagating the concept and in application of the same in rural districts of Andhra Pradesh. M.V. Foundation is a widely admired organization working for universalization of primary education through formal schooling. The organization believes that providing enrolment and retention of all children in formal school can ensure total elimination of child labour. They emphasise that poverty is not always inhibiting factor, poor parents can be persuaded to send their children to schools. Government must ensure school accessibility to all children through opening up new school and through improvement of existing ones.

Broader definition of child labour is challenged by restrictive school on the ground that the former definition includes child work which is acceptable to many extent by a society as a socialization process. The work engagement does not hamper child's development process. It does not derail proper schooling, health care, nutrition and recreation. Child labour is rather harmful, exploitative and deters the process of development. It brings about schooling deprivation, illness, hazards and much other maltreatment in the workplaces. Broader school tends to put together these two categories into one broad group. Magnitude of child labour thus turns out to be too overwhelming to tackle by the governments of less developed countries. This definition is more likely to upset the child labour elimination programme. It is very easy to associate child labour problem with overpopulated low income countries of the third world. The image of India, for example, in the 'western' eye as a vast reservoir of child labour is embedded. Thus a very high figure or estimate of child labour in India is unquestionably accepted in the western world. This high figure never begs the question on methodological accuracy of data collection. Citing and shouting such high figure of incidence of child labour in India weakens rather than strengthens our child labour elimination efforts.

They argue, therefore, that child labour should be defined as economic exploitation of children that derails the process of development. The economic engagement of the child prevents his or her access to proper schooling. It can jeopardise his or her health by way of exposure to unhealthy work environment. Children are denied appropriate medical care for any ailment, caused by overwork, strain and drudgery. Child labourers are prone to physical as well as psychological abuse. Child labour thus hampers the psychological development of the children. On the whole, child labour is demoralizing, degrading, hazardous, exploitative and detrimental to well-being of the children. Article 32 of the UNCRC says "State parties recognise the right of the child to be protected from economic exploitation and from performing any work that is likely to be hazarders or to interfere with child education or to be harmful to the child's health, physical as well as mental.

SPIRITUAL, MORAL OR SOCIAL DEVELOPMENT

Children's economic engagement or any non-economic engagement must accompany the odds, stated above to be qualified for describing as child labour. Not all economic or non-economic engagements are child labour. Bundling all kinds of engagement in one category of child labour does not stand to practical reasoning. One successful attempt to get at a realistic figure of child labour is through segregation of children occupation between child work and child labour. The former may be used to signify a general engagement of children in any work that does not hamper the process of development. Many call it as socialization process and therefore beneficial for a child's growth and development. Child work is acceptable while child labour is intolerable and unacceptable. Child work is enabling while child labour is disabling. ILO, in the beginning, was swayed and it accepted the high figure of global incidence of child labour which did not segregate between child work and child labour. ILO now, categorises children economic activities in terms of severity and calls for immediate action for certain category and long-term action for others. The first category comprises of working children. ILO defines work as participation in any economic activity that does not derail the process of growth and development of the child. ILO had estimated that there were 190 million working children in the work during 2004. Child labour is now defined by ILO in more restrictive sense. It excludes all children legally working in accordance with ILO convention 138 and 182. ILO now says that there were 165 million child labourers in 2004.

ILO now carves out a section of children within the category of child labourers and specifies that section as worst form of child labour. This category includes extremely exploitative, harmful, degrading and dangerous child labour. The worst forms include child slavery, children in armed conflict, street children, child beggars, children sex workers, trafficking of children for unlawful economic use, child pornography and children in sex tourism. ILO calls for immediate action to stop these worst forms of child labour. It is also pleasing to notice that this inhuman form of child labour is on the wane. ILO reports that the magnitude of worst form has come down to 126 million in 2004 from 171 million in 2000. The immediate next category in descending order is child labour, less dangerous than the former but needs to be eradicated. Child labour is economic engagement of underage children that impede this growth and development, deprives them of education and leisure and adversity affect their health and well-being. Article 32 of the Convention of the Rights of the Child (UNCRC) stipulates that the perpetuation child labour is violation of child rights.

The Constitution of India prohibits child labour. Elementary education is now fundamental rights of all children in India. Right to education has recently been included in the right to life under Article 21 of our constitution. Child labour has to be eradicated through short-term and long-term action, poverty alleviation programmers, punitive measures for employers of child labour and most effective investment in the armoury is the provision of free and quality education to all children. Many scholars tend to cite poverty as a dominant cause of child labour. The invocation of poverty as a dominant reason does not explain the demand side factors. There should be market for child labour in all locations where child labour persists. Poverty works on push side but availability of market work has to present in all places. Market based intervention like prohibition and regulation act has to be coupled with anti-poverty programmers. Thus child labour even if it falls short of worst category is detrimental to health and education of children. It needs to be eliminated through short-run and long-run action, through prohibitive and punitive action, through developmental and rehabilitative strategy and the effective implementation of recent constitutional amendment to bind the state with legal obligation of education to all children.

Child work is rather a benign category that has not invited infuriating wrath from all corners. It has not attracted that much world attention and spearheaded worry. Child work is unobjectionable while child labour is not. Child work is socializing, educative and beneficial for many societies. It does not collide with schooling attendance as well as educational achievement and does not impinge on physical and mental well-being. The global magnitude on child labour until very recently, aroused scepticism among many scholars of the third world. The figure appeared to be too overwhelming as it put child workers and child labourers in the same bowl of child labourers. Third world countries that shelter this burgeoning number of child labourers fit well with their images as overpopulated and poor countries. ILO later realized the folly of mixing two different groups and presenting as a single category of child labour. It now differentiates between them and now the fog around the definitional disagreement and controversy is now clear. This is never logically acceptable to ask for abolition by the third world countries such an overwhelming number of child labour. The challenge is now less intense with separating out exploitative and disabling child labourers.

GLOBALIZATION PROCESS AND CHILD LABOUR

Globalization, in its latest variant, is currently under way. This is an economic action by the countries and for the countries for mutual benefits. However, this is one of the most controversial global actions. Critics, activists and protesters quickly blame globalization for causing or creating global economic crisis and unprecedented economic divide among nations as well as within nations. Proponents, on the other hand, praise this process as harbinger of prosperity, driver of economic growth and provider of new knowledge and technology through exchange and interconnection. The economic globalization is accomplished through integration of national economies with global economy through removal of all barriers to trade and exchange. The economies which were insulated for many years through high tariff wall are now opening up for trade and investment. Privatization is thus a necessity to make room for investment. Industrial licensing that traditionally earmarks certain sectors of production and distribution to be exclusive domain of the government is no longer in place in the wake of trade openness. Liberalization, Privatization and Globalization (LPG) is now widely recognised as well as extensively challenged as panacea for many poor countries to come out of the shackles of poverty and low income. Public sector industries during prolonged years of license raj in India did not deliver positive results. Inefficiency and escalating cost of the public sector enterprises turned them into unviable units only to be kept alive by budgetary subsidy.

Private investment began to flow in after the opening. Multinational Corporations are now free to establish factories and can sell their products anywhere in the globalized world. Private investment is now solicited for the loss-making public sector companies to make them more competitive to survive and flourish in the competitive world. The shrinkage of public sector and expansion of private sector economic activities evidently swell child labour. Economic activities seem to move from formal sector to informal sector.

One outcome of the privatization initiative is the growth of informal sector of production activities. Formal sector or organized sector cannot evade or bypass statutory law that stipulates works, pay and working conditions of workers. Organized sectors are to protect workers' rights as articulated in the ILO charter and in national labour policies. Formal sectors are getting downsized and informal sectors are flourishing for two reasons. Firstly, government's withdrawal from production activities and delicensing, secondly, informal sector of production activities can generate more profits as a result of reduced cost of production. Labour cost forms a major portion of production cost. The bill can be drastically brought down in the informal sector. Workers in the informal sectors are subject to hire and fire with no obligation to pay compensation. The informal sectors are far off the factory inspection system, minimum wage act and statutory working hours. Profit, the driving force behind massive expansion of informal sector in the third world countries, is generated out of inhuman exploitation of workers who are paid low wage and are employed for very long hours in a day. India for example, has acts to deal with both these issues but unfortunately, these legal instruments are ineffective the informal sector.

DOES GLOBALIZATION INTENSIFY CHILD LABOUR?

Flourishing of informal sector can intensify child labour in developing countries in the neo-liberal global order. Employment of female and child labour in such unmonitored enterprises can increase the profit manifold. These two vulnerable groups are subject to exploitation by their employers. Informalization of many production activities in the wake of privatization is also associated with outsourcing of job to home-based working units employing family labour. Children of the families are therefore prone to be engaged in such work. Child labour prohibition act does not apply to this home-based work for children. Many of the processing jobs can now be shifted to family-based units. This outsourcing can substantially reduce production cost and increase profits of the enterprises. These enterprises use child labour for production and processing of their products where they can easily absolve themselves as employers of child labourers. Privatization has made it possible.

There is opposite line of argument that not only defends but also praises economic globalization. They argue that main economic ills those were afflicting and are doing still now are negative fallout of economic isolation. Economic insulation through erecting high tariff wall to pre-empt entry of goods, capital and technology in developing countries has been breeding poverty. Thus opening up of domestic economies to other economies especially the economies of the affluent north could reduce poverty and its associated other ills, most prominent among them is of course, child labour. Poverty would come down through economic growth and prosperity for those countries that could not make a mark as a result of inaccessibility to capital and technology. Globalization, would thus, open the flood gate of technology, information, new knowledge and resources. Economic prosperity, transformation and industrialization of those economies would need skilled manpower. Demand for education will rise as a result of ushering in new opportunities. Poor parents will then tend to send to their children to school instead of sending them to work places. Thus globalization will reduce child labour through creating demand for education and skill.

There is however an attempt to reconcile the extremely polarized views. This strand of argument points out that the impact of globalization process on child labour in developing countries depends on quality of governance and its commitment towards vulnerable population. Public action can significantly protect the vulnerable families from ill-effects of privatization, liberalization and globalization. Child labour can intensify even in the absence of globalization. Globalization cannot be singled out as a villain and as creator or perpetuator of child labour. Thus the effect of globalization on generation and perpetuation of child labour may be adverse or may be beneficial. It depends on how the respective states handle the globalization process. The government must make room for private investment to let in latest technology that would result in rise in export. Public sector must be made more efficient by way of cost efficiency. The rise in GDP will eventually raise income and standard of living. Government must protect the poor through provision of social security measures.

CAUSAL FACTORS DEBATE

Professor Weiner draws a painful picture of India's working children. His seminal book on child labour in India has ignited many minds to delve deep into this pervasive menace. Subsequent studies have either reaffirmed his position or have cast doubt on his reasoning. He does not find much credibility in official estimate *"since official figures generally omit children engaged in non-wage domestic work"* (Weiner, 1996). He raised question on the status of 90 million children as per government estimate during 90s who were not attending school. A high drop out rate of 47 per cent in the primary stage of education and a higher rate of 62 per cent in the elementary stage that includes primary and upper primary level would be swelling the rank of out of school children. Government estimate counts those children among them as worker only if they are engaged in economically productive activities that result in production of tangible output or intangible services. Children's labour inputs have to be used for commodities or services to be sold in the market. However, this restrictive definition excludes many works of children, the output of which may not find its way to market. Exponents of broader definition vehemently contest this underestimation. Weiner (1996) observes:

> "Most of the 90 million children not in school are working children. Some are paid by employers, others contribute to family income by caring for cattle, working in the fields or engaging in household industries and still others work at home collecting water and fuel and taking care of young siblings".

He further claims that one may be puzzled to detect no child labour in organized industries. *"There are some parts of India's economy where you will not see children at work. Children do not work in the large textile mills, or in any of the large industrial plants. The factory acts ban the employment of children in large factories"* (Weiner, 1996). The Child Labour (Prohibitions and Regulation Act of 1986) is the comprehensive legal instrument to deal with child labour in organized industries. The act, in its spirits, lays emphasis on regulation rather than on prohibition. The act bans employment of children in hazardous industries but does not restrict children's employment in non-hazardous occupations. Children are not legally permitted to work in large factories but are allowed, as per the provision, in small scale units, in cottage industries, in home-based units, in home-based sub-contracting.

Working conditions in large factories are rather better by way of ventilation, lighting, sanitation, wage payment, incentives. Small units are rather fusty, unhygienic and characterized by low payment and long hours of work. Paradoxically abuse of working children is intense where the child labour act permits children to work and rather less where the act bans child labour. Weiner (1996) mentions many such areas: much of the carpet weaving in India is done in household workshops where children and their parents perform piecework. Though children are prohibited from working in the large match factories in Sivakasi they are free to work in the numerous small workshops scattered outside the town. Large number of children works in tens of thousands of tea stalls and restaurants. And of course most children work in the agricultural sector often as agricultural labour. Many middle class households also employ children as sweepers and household servants. The main point is that there are hundred of thousands of employers of children in India (Weiner, 96). The existing child labour Act fails to bring into its purview the millions of employers engaging children in far more abusive manner than the large industries.

Child rights activist and researcher Shanta Sinha also upholds Weiner's observation on the state of child labour in India. She asserts *'any child not in school is immediately drawn into supplementing family labour on a full time basis assisting in family occupation, managing family assets, or simply engaging in a wide variety of domestic "adult releasing activities"*. Strictly speaking, therefore, no child is ever kept idle and one cannot invoke the concept of idle children to explain the large number of missing children in the binary categories of students and child labourers. She suggests, as a method to resolve the issue of missing children to consider all of them as child labourers. She argues that segregation work done by a child into exploitative 'labour' and non-exploitative 'work' suffers from basic flaws, as there is no simple method by which some activities engaging a child could be classified as 'work' and some as 'labour'. There is wide variation in the work situation of children. Therefore, such a categorization is extremely difficult to accomplish. The distinction should be rather based on working conditions rather than on the work itself. She argues:

> To judge and distinguish between child work and child labour is highly subjective and artificial process. This task is rendered even more arbitrary by the fact that there is nothing to prevent the child from transiting from one category to another. In the ultimate analysis, any working child is in reality a child labourer, the degree of exploitation in the current employment not withstanding. Since any child out of school is ultimately put to work and the concept of an 'idle child' is not really appropriate in the Indian context, any child out of school has to be treated as child labourer *(Sinha, 1996)*.

Many scholars oppose this 'advocacy' stand marking all out of school children as child labourers. Richard Anker (1999) argues that exaggerated figure that emerges from this all encompassing definition will have unexpected negative impact on the government commitment to eliminate child labour. He points out:

> But this is often misleading since different types of child labour are combined into one number resulting in the proverbial mixing of 'apples' and oranges'. The basic problem is that one all inclusive child labour estimate includes conceptually different types of child labour, and therefore cannot be very useful for policy purpose (Anker, 2000)

Thus, we are landed in queer situation on the precise definition of child labour. The pendulum swings between broader definition and narrow definition. Opponents of broader definition are certainly concerned with extent of deprivation meted out to all children out of school by the educational delivery system of the state. A child's fundamental right to education is denied. This is violation of child rights. A child remains outside the school because of two types of factors: supply side and demand side. Supply side factors include school quality, school curriculum and easy accessibility. School quality encompasses a host of factors broadly divided in to two: physical infrastructure and learning conveniences. The classrooms may be stuffed, seating space may be inadequate, and classrooms may be fusty with little or no ventilation. Schools may not have proper sanitation, no provision of drinking water and toilets. Lack of infrastructure is also compounded by difficulties in learning and attainments. Teachers may be in short supply far below the minimum number for effective teaching. Teaching aids and other kits those attract students may not find their ways in many schools.

School curriculum may be out of date that hardly catches the fancy of the young minds. Single teacher schools, plenty in rural areas, are serious impediments to attendance and learning attainments. Absence for a day of the lone teacher is undeclared closure of the school. Medium of teaching and learning at school often proves to be formidable barrier to children of tribal communities and children of linguistic minority. Children are uncomfortable with the language at school they do not speak at home. Difference of language at home and at school impairs learning ability. Dropout rate in tribal habitations is on the rise partly due to this language barrier.

PUSH FACTORS

Demand side factors are equally at work to influence children's schooling and retention. Decision to enrol a child to a school and continue thereafter is exclusively parental. Poverty plays a crucial role in this decision. Poor families beget more children as they consider them as economic asset. Many studies have established the relationship among household poverty, family size, child labour and schooling. Cost benefit approach is offered to analyse the parental decision about children schooling. The familiar quality and quantity trade-off is apparent even in children's schooling decision. Poor parents compare between costs and benefit, of children schooling. If benefits exceed cost only then parents send these children to school. Survival is the only concern that haunts poor parents. Education may be a costly option, which they cannot afford. A child remains in school indicates that he or she foregoes a day's wage or unpaid economic work at home. The cost is two-fold: indirect and direct. Indirect cost is opportunity cost of child's time and the direct cost is private cost on education that includes textbooks, uniforms and stationeries. Poor parents do not have access to educational credit system that may smooth out their hardships during the entire period of schooling. Parents should have positive perception towards education. A positive return to education also encourages schooling. In absence of such a return for poor parents, work is the best option. Schooling takes back seat. Work in family enterprise, in family profession is a kind of apprenticeship for the children. It is a smooth passage to productive adulthood. Work under the caring supervision of parents, and within the contour of home is often beneficial for the children. There is strong argument favouring such work even at the cost of schooling. A farmer's son should know how to handle a plough with precision that pay dividend in future. If it is learnt during childhood, it will be better for the child. Affluent parents can afford schooling of their children. They do not depend on children's income for survival as they opt for quality children that right kind of education can ensure. Thus poverty and low income deters schooling of children.

Parental illiteracy is also a prominent factor in demand side. Parents having had exposure to schooling are supposed to realize the value of education. Children's schooling is determined by these supply side and demand side factors. A child remains out of school not necessarily because of compulsion of labour. Thus all children out of school are child labourer as claimed is exaggeration and far away from reality. Listen (2000) has tried to clear the fog. He distinguishes between child work (*Kaj* or *Kam*) and child labour (*Bal Majduri*). He reminds us of the misconception about child labour that pervades discourse on the issue. He opines that children undertake a wide variety of work like weeding the fields, looking after cattle, household chores or collecting firewood. These engagement of children should be termed as work not as labour. Child work should be used as generic term and would refer to any type of work in any mode of employment relationship. The concept of work should be based on the physical or mental involvement in a job. Lieten emphasizes that the notion of labour should be restricted to the production of goods and services that interfere with the normative development of children as defined in the UN convention. The nature of the labour relation (paid-unpaid, hired or self-employed full time or part time) is immaterial to the definition. He vehemently opposes the conceptual framework that considers any work engagement of the children out of school is labour. Stein and Davies (1940) have delineated as "any work by children that interferes within their full physical development, the opportunities for a desirable minimum of education and their needed recreation." This definition is in tune with the UN Declaration and with ILO strategy of targeting the intolerable. The Convention of the Rights of the Child (CRC) in 1989 did not blatantly condemn all work engagement of children but rather stipulates: *The right of the child to be protected from economic exploitation and from performing any work that is likely to be hazardous or to interfere with the child's education or to be harmful to the child's health or physical, mental, spiritual moral or social development.*

The argument of cultural exclusiveness is offered to condone the high magnitude of child labour in India in particular and for third world in general. Universal concept of childhood on which universal rights of the children is structured, do not fit in to the specific perspectives of third world countries. The exponents of socialization theory of child labour argue that the use of child labour is socialized as an integral part of family-oriented social and institutional order. Weiner (1991) supports this cultural exclusivity argument and he is very specific that the acceptance of child labour is not because of feudal or capitalist economies.

He is hesitant to accept poverty or low per capita income as much relevant factor in explaining perpetuation of child labour in India. Rather the belief system of the state bureaucracy is responsible to sustain this menace, the set of beliefs that are widely shared by educators, social activists, trade unionists, academic researchers and by members of the Indian middle class. He opines that at the centre of the belief system lies the hierarchical caste system that determines the respective roles of upper and lower strata. In this analysis, Hinduism is depicted as exclusive religion and exclusively ideology of India. Indian policies and practice are different from other countries because Indian people and leaders, leftists and rightists alike are closely tied to religious notions and premises of the hierarchical caste system. Thus traditional Hindu notion of social rank and hierarchy are subtly incorporated into the ways, Indians distinguish between people who are destined to undertake manual labour and those who should be educated to escape such a life. This view that positions Indians as collapsed in to Hindu orthodoxy reinforce a conventional discourse underwriting the distinction between the developed child labour free *West* and the orthodox child labour prone *East*. But this view that distinguishes developed world and developing world by cultural traits also deflects the debate of poverty and child labour away from other prominent factors: the impact of past colonialism and the impact of the structure of global economy. This slanderous image stigmatising third world countries helps to sustain the magnitude of child labour in excess of official estimate.

DEBATE AND DISCOURSE ON EXPLANATORY FACTORS

The definitional precision is needed not only for policy guidelines but also for investigating casual factors. The formulation of child labour programme must precede the identification of its beneficiaries, i.e., a realistic definition of child labour. If child labour refers to all children not attending school then the explanatory factors will differ from the explanation, which will come up, when category of child labour is confined to children actually selling their labour power or others appropriate their labour power. It has often been argued that child work is essential to the survival of the children and their families. It is thus obvious that poverty is an important reason why children work. If they were not to work, survival of the entire family could be in jeopardy. However, it would be wrong to assume that poverty is the one and only cause of child labour. A typical instance of a poor region, measured by per capita state domestic product, with a low level of child labour is Kerala. A state in Indian union with a remarkable record in human development index despite considerable poverty can reduce child labour contrary to Andhra Pradesh whose per capita income is higher that of Kerala. The enormous difference between Kerala and Andhra Pradesh cannot be explained with reference to the poverty factor. These exceptions indicate that it is possible to reduce child labour without having to wait for the breakthrough in economic development.

Focus has been so far and so widespread on push factor. It is a common view that poverty is pushing poor children into the labour market. But for poverty to lead to child labour there should be a pull factor as well. ILO (1996) notes this one-sided analysis and observes: *research on the cause of child labour tends to concentrate on the supply factors both because of justifiable pre-occupation with the victims, and because of the commonly shared view that poverty is the driving force. But the demand for child labour plays a critical role in determining the involvement of children in hazardous work.*

One casual factor in the pull side is profit motive of employers. The nimble finger argument drives certain employers to engage children for docility and dexterity. But studies conducted by ILO did not confirm this argument, as a strong motivation for employing children is specific industries.

> 'In the industries where the argument is being used, for example in carpet weaving, diamond polishing and sports good stitching, adults and children work side-by-side. When some of the task performed exclusively by children, the skills required are so minimal that child labour is clearly replaceable by adult labour. Profit margin would drop marginally if child labour were to be replaced by adult labour. In the carpet and bangle industry the difference in production costs between adult labour and

cheaper child labour has been calculated to be lower than 5 per cent' (Chndrashekhar, 1997, Sharma, 2001).

The other prominent factor in the pull side is structure of labour market characterized by substantive segmentation. The segmentation of job market usually occurs in an environment in which there is a reasonably high demand for labour and lower extent of labour empowerment. Under such circumstances employers create selective market for child labour in addition to labour market for adults.

TABLE 3.1
Child Labour, Literacy, Income and Work Participation

Major States in India	*Child labour (%)*	*Per capita domestic product (In Rs.)*	*Female literacy (%)*	*Work Participation*	
				All (%)	*Female (%)*
Andhra Pradesh	17.8	7006	24.8	81.0	72.4
Karnataka	13.9	7242	34.6	74.9	61.3
Himachal Pradesh	13.6	6896	51.5	79.9	72.9
Rajasthan	12.2	5315	15.0	77.6	67.2
Tamil Nadu	10.4	8051	42.8	74.8	64.7
Madhya Pradesh	8.7	5516	22.1	76.5	63.0
Orissa	7.4	4662	30.5	65.3	45.7
Maharashtra	6.5	12010	39.7	77.7	70.5
West Bengal	5.1	6247	40.7	58.9	28.5
Uttar Pradesh	5.0	4794	22.9	61.9	34.7
Gujarat	4.1	9054	36.1	73.2	57.9
Bihar	3.7	3417	19.7	56.6	26.9
Punjab	2.7	12934	43.9	58.7	32.4
Assam	2.6	5520	52.1	54.5	23.9
Haryana	2.6	12934	43.9	58.7	32.4
Kerala	0.8	6524	81.7	53.4	32.5

Source : Mahendra Dev and Ravi (2002).

Child labour exists along with high level of employment as is evident in the table. Andhra Pradesh with highest level of employment is also characterized by highest rate of child labour. Pull factor is evidently working in this correlation. The logic is that after adult male and adult female labour power, child labour power will also be pulled into employment. The segmentation of the labour market leaves the most vulnerable and marginalized families to fend for survival at the lower end of the income scale. Indebtedness, illness, failed marriage and social exclusion help to push the most impoverished families in to labour condition where wages are far below the family reproduction level.

The attempt to establish poverty as an explanation is also beset with problem as at is difficult to define poverty precisely. Poverty that can explain the prevalence of child labour is some thing beyond economic poverty. There are certain thresholds below which people will find it difficult to survive. These thresholds are defined by nutrition, sanitation, health and shelter. At the level of deprivation below this level, there is no option or alternative between work and no work. Deprivation often causes as a shock effect: the death or severe illness of the adult breadwinner has been found to be a direct cause of child labour. Thus poverty that entails human deprivation, not only measured in term of per capita income, goes to the root of the child labour problem.

WHY ELIMINATION OF CHILD LABOUR IS NECESSARY

Child labour must be eliminated in India for two reasons. Firstly, the elementary logic in development economics says that child labour thwarts the human capital formation process. Child of today is human capital of tomorrow. All human beings are not poised to turn in to human capital automatically. They are to be made. Education and heath care comprise of this making process. The resultant of this making process is perfect human capital. No country can prosper with endowment of physical capital only. Human capital and physical capital must work hand in hand to ensure economic growth. History of economic development of the first world countries and most prominently of our south-east Asian neighbours buttresses the role of massive public investment on education 'particularly, on elementary education and provision of quality health care'.

Japan and Korea had accomplished universal literacy and compulsion education well before they had emerged from shackles of poverty. Their public investment on education and heath care was relatively higher when their per capita incomes were relatively lower. Provision of quality primary education and quality heath care build the pillar of human capital formation. Perpetuation of child labour in any country is the reflection of educational failure. Child labourers are those children in a county who have no access to education, or put in other words, education delivery system has eluded numerous children. Child labourers along with many other hapless categories of deprived children fall within the category of educationally deprived children. Children who stay outside the portal of school remain unlettered, unskilled and untrained. They do not acquire the ability of numeracy, literacy and cognitive skills. They are sure to miss many opportunities that would come on their way. They are not only deprived of the benefits of educational development but also they themselves deprive the nation from their productive participation in national economic transformation. A country may suffer from supply side constraints in relation to availability of skilled manpower. Persistence of child labour is sure to cause supply side constraints through denying access to education of many children. Thus countries will miserably fail to accomplish a desired level of economic growth and development if child labour is allowed to grow and flourish.

The second reason for immediate elimination is prompted by the issue of human rights for children. The United Nations Convention of Rights of the Children (UNCRC) was adopted at the General Assembly in 1989. India had ratified the Convention in 1992. These were Declarations on Child Rights preceding this Convention. But those Declarations were in the nature of appeal to the state parties which were devoid of any legal obligations and bindings. In contrast, the Convention was an international treaty that comes into force in the national legislation through ratification. This exercise is not only a positive gesture to any UN resolution but a legally binding action. All state parties, on ratification of the Convention, has to conform by enacting legislation framing policies and implementing programme accommodating the spirits and core values of the Convention.

The Convention stipulates in Article 32 that economic exploitation of children amounts to violation of child rights. The state must stop child labour through enacting appropriate legislation and through provisioning of development opportunity for those children. Child rights are inalienable. One type of right cannot be advanced at the exclusion of others. Child labourers are not only denied their right to protection against economic exploitation but also are denied their right to education and right to protection against many other forms of abuse and maltreatment and they also denied their right to health. Child labour prohibition act can stop economic exploitation of children but that is only a step forward. There are other steps, to be undertaken, to reach the destination of decent childhood. All other rights should be simultaneously realized to give back those children their rights to childhood.

4

Child Labour Estimates in India : The Provider of Statistics

India can be an example to emulate by many developing nations by her exemplarily mechanism, well-oiled and well-managed, to collect and disseminate data on child labour. We have more than one organizations engaged in this task. There is hardly any scope of verification when there is only one organization providing the data for the entire country. This is next to impossible for a huge country with more than one billion population. The statistics provided for the whole nation by the sole organization can hardly be disputed and sought for cross-verification to check the authenticity. India is a class apart in this exercise. It has three national organizations and agencies, taking up the task of periodic publication of child labour data. The reference period may not exactly coincide but the data are verifiable. The accuracy of data is assured by the government. There are three major sources and two minor sources in India. Population census, NSSO employment unemployment survey and Rural labour enquires arė principal sources for child labour data. National Council of Applied Economic Research (NCAER) and National Family Health

Survey are also sources but receive scant reference. It will be a bit interesting to dwell on the methodology, tools and concepts used by the two major sources—Census and NSS. Census reports workers or persons engaged in gainful economic activity according to age and sex every ten years. We can estimate child labour by considering workers between 5 to 14 years of age. Likewise NSS conducts Employment and Unemployment survey every five years. The definition of worker is same as followed in the census.

CHILD LABOUR ESTIMATES IN INDIA : INTER CENSUS PERIOD, 1991-2001

However, the data on child labour in India, released by government agencies, explained in the last section, are not accepted indisputably by NGOs and human rights organizations. NGOs, social activists and many scholars are in favour of broader definition. They allege that government always presents and accepts very restrictive definition. Governments tend to offer census estimate based on economic participation of children. The Census of India recorded 11.20 million working children during 1991 while the latest census of 2001 has recorded 12.66 million working children in the ages of 5 to 14 years. Ninety percent of the child labourers were from rural areas. It is evident that the magnitude of child-labour has gone up in India, even by this restrictive definition during last 10 years. However, there is very marginal decline in child labour ratio, work participation rate, rather, from 5.4 percent to 5 percent. The increase in the magnitude of the child labour during 1991-2001 is unacceptable and uncomfortable. The reference decade had witnessed tremendous efforts by government the United Nations and other international agencies and NGOs, for universalizing primary and elementary education and removing children from work through education and other rehabilitative intervention. The results depict that only education interventions without integrating poverty alleviation programme in the policy may not yield desired result of reducing child labour.

TABLE 4.1

Child Workers in Two Census Period and Out of School Children

State	*Child Workers 1991*	*Child Workers 2001*	*% Workers 1991*	*% Workers 2001*	*Change 1991-2001*	*Out of School Children**
(1)	*(2)*	*(3)*	*(4)*	*(5)*	*(6)*	*(7)*
Andhra Pradesh	1661940	1363339	9.98	7.7	-2.28	2477695
Arunachal Pradesh	12,395	18482	5.65	6.06	0.41	3239
Assam	327598	351416	5.46	5.07	-0.39	78882
Bihar	942,245	1117500	3.99	4.68	0.69	8453648
Chhattisgarh	N.A	364572	N.A	6.96	6.96	N.A
Delhi	27351	41899	1.27	1.35	0.08	1122443
Goa	4656	4138	1.95	1.82	-0.13	98178
Gujarat	523585	485530	5.26	4.28	-0.98	0
Haryana	109,691	253491	2.55	4.78	2.23	1136131
Himachal Pradesh	56438	107774	4.55	8.14	3.59	123290
Jammu & Kashmir	N.A	175630	N.A	6.62	6.62	331417
Jharkhand	N.A	407200	N.A	5.47	5.47	N.A
Karnataka	976247	822665	8.81	6.91	-1.90	93505
Kerala	34800	26156	0.58	0.47	-0.11	375103
Madhya Pradesh	1352563	1065259	8.08	6.71	-1.37	1489236

Maharashtra	1068418	764075	5.73	3.54	-2.19	0
Orissa	452394	377594	5.87	4.37	-1.50	642000
Punjab	142,868	177268	3.04	3.23	0.19	1123234
Rajasthan	774199	1262570	6.46	8.25	1.79	212715
Sikkim	5598	16457	5.18	12.04	6.86	00
Tamil Nadu	578,889	418801	4.83	3.61	-1.22	347065
Tripura	16478	21756	2.29	2.79	0.50	71365
Uttar Pradesh	1410086	1927997	3.81	4.04	0.23	15940996
Uttranchal	N.A	70183	N.A	3.24	3.24	N.A
West Bengal	711691	857087	4.16	4.5	0.34	2134655
India	11285349	12666377	5.37	5	-0.37	35360017

Census 1991 and 2001.

**Source* : Rajya Sabha Unstarred Question No. 1908, dated 10.3.2003.

REGIONAL DISTRIBUTION : CHANGES BETWEEN TWO CENSUS PERIODS

Kerala, a tiny state in India's southern peninsula is just a few notches off being garlanded is India's first child labour free state. It is a remarkable feat by a state where poverty and low income are still persisting. The story is altogether different in another southern state, Andhra Pradesh; very close to Kerala geographically; child labour rate of 10 per cent during 1991 in that state has come down to 7.7 per cent in 2001. The most interesting part of this is that Andhra Pradesh is richer than Kerala measured by per capita state domestic product. Child labour is alarming at 8.14 percent in Himachal Pradesh, followed by around 7 per cent in Chhattisgarh, 6.91 per cent in Karnataka in the latest census of 2001. Sikkim is catapulted to the top most position in sheltering 12.04 percent child labour as per latest census.

Child labour has gone up between 1991 and 2001, in Bihar, Haryana, Himachal Pradesh, Punjab, Rajasthan, Sikkim, Uttar Pradesh and West Bengal. It has come down in Andhra Pradesh, Assam, Karnataka, Kerala, Madhya Pradesh, and Tamil Nadu. There is no perceptible regional pattern in the incidence and growth of child labour in India. Child labour-prone and almost child labour-free states in India, Andhra Pradesh and Kerala, are within southern region. Karnataka, another state in the same region and referred as IT hub in India also shelters around 7 per child labour. The prosperous states in Northern India, Punjab, Haryana and Delhi have witnessed rise in the incidence of child labour. The picture is rather mixed in Hindi heartland characterized by poverty and illiteracy. Child labour has gone down in Madhya Pradesh but it has gone up in Bihar, Uttar Pradesh and Rajasthan.

SECTOR-WISE DISTRIBUTION IN THE CENSUS ESTIMATE

We now attempt to present distribution of child workers according to occupational categories. Children are engaged in almost all categories of employment. Most of the working children are found to be working in agricultural activities as wage labourers or cultivators. As per census report around 84 percent are employed in primary sector of activities. The primary sector comprises of wage labouring as well as cultivation. The plight of child labourer in agriculture in India is well known. They have to toil in agricultural fields for long hours without any protection from scorching sun rays or any head gear. They have to handle pesticides and chemicals that increase the risk of life threatening illness or permanent disability. They have to work with sharp tools and implements that run the risk of serious injury.

Work in family agriculture, is rather less tormenting and less exploitative compared to work as wage labourer. Agricultural work does not come under the purview of Child Labour (Prohibition and Regulation Act), the only legal instrument of intervention. Thus the work remains unmonitored and unverified. Child labourers are thus placed in a vulnerable situation and are subject to inhuman exploitation. There is hardly any possibility of learning any skill from this job. The cycle of poverty and agricultural wage work remains undisturbed and will remain so in foreseeable future unless serious measures are not taken up. They are engaged in agricultural wage work not for the reason that adult workers are not available for employment. They are employed when adult workers remain idle. They hunt for children not for any special love, but for pure economic reason. They can be managed with lower wage rate. They are docile and never protest against injustice. They enter the job as unskilled labour and end up as unskilled. This child labour in agriculture, particularly the wage work is characterized by a vicious cycle of low wage, low skill, poverty and illiteracy.

Gender-wise segregation of child labourers in agricultural work is revealing enough to take note. Girl children are more in agriculture wage work than the boys indicating a phenomenon of gender-based exploitation. Girls are more in low paid and unskilled jobs than the boys. Non-agricultural works which comprise of factory work, household manufacturing and service sector engage the remaining i.e., 16 percent of child labourers in India. Male children are increasingly drawn towards non-agricultural activities in the urban informal sector. The latest census report of 2001 confirms that child labour is on the rise in prosperous states in India. Those states are industrially developed; Delhi, Haryana, Punjab and part of Uttar Pradesh are among them. Manufacturing units in these states are coming up and flourish in the favourable environment of neo-liberal regime. Industrial climate, already in place in these states, supplemented by tax concessions, delicensing and export incentives have worked collectively in favour of flourishing unorganized sector of manufacturing and processing. Girls have restricted mobility and therefore are confined to primary and household occupation.

CHILD LABOUR : THE GLOBAL MAGNITUDE

Work force in India constitutes a very large group of population from 15 years old to 59 years old. The minimum age of entry into labour force however differ from country to country. Generally, developed nations would not allow children below 18 years to enter any income earning vocation. The upper age limit for remaining within labour force is also dependent on general longevity and work capacity of people. This also substantially varies among nations of the world. The poor countries are characterised by shorter life span, weak health and inadequate quality health care. Old age and infirmities besiege their people earlier than their counterparts in relatively advanced nations where working age is far more stretched. On the other hand, a poor country's entry age for labour force is lower. The United Nations Conventions on the Rights of the Children stipulates that children below 18 years should not be allowed to join labour force that would jeopardise their health and development. In India, child labour is prohibited for certain occupations and processes for children below 14 years of age. Therefore, there is no legal binding for employing children aged 14 years in any occupation. India is a home to the largest number of child labourers in the contemporary world.

However, the scale of the problem of child labour is hard to obtain. Data on the extent of child labour is not very precise for several reasons. Firstly, the child workers are spread widely in unorganized sectors as family or hired workers. With the globalization of the economy and increasing informalization of the labour markets this problem has intensified manifold. Secondly, some countries do not include 0-14 years age group in their labour force. Hence it is problematic to gauge the extent of working children, as they work beyond school hours. Thirdly, employers do not always supply correct data on child labour in order to evade legal restrictions. Lastly, data on child labour is extremely scant also because of the absence of an suitable survey methodology for studying the work of children, which for most part is a secreted happening. Problem is far more shocking in the third world countries but on the whole, child labour participation rates over time are on the wane extensively in almost all the countries, particularly from 1950 to 2000. The table below reveals the secular decline over a period of half a century.

TABLE 4.2
Trend in Labour Participation Rates for Children

	1950	*2000*
World	27.57	11.32
Africa	38.42	24.92
Latin America and Caribbean	19.36	8.21
Asia	36.06	10.18
Europe	6.49	0.04
India	34.52	12.07
China	47.85	7.86

Source : Basu (1999), Kambhampati & Rajan (2005).
Quoted from Niti Mehta at http://ssrn.com/abstract= 996574.

The reduction during 1950 to 2000 has been remarkable in all the regions, bringing the average down from 27.6 to 11.3 percent. Even in India the child labour participation rates have come down to a great extent. Majority of the child labour is employed in the unorganized and informal sectors, as the organized and factory sectors are subject to national laws, banning such work. In the unorganized sector the child labour remains highly susceptible to exploitation. Moreover, a large number of the child labourers belong to the 10-14 years age category, still children below 10 years also work in a significant number.

The majority of child labourers are traced in developing and in least developed countries. According to ILO (International Labour Organisation), 250 million children between 5-14 years in the developing countries who are child labourers. Nearly half of them (120 million) perform work on a full time basis while the remaining combines it with schooling or non-economic activities. This estimate of 250 million is, according to ILO, exclusive of children engaged in regular non-economic activities, including those providing domestic services on a full time basis at parental homes (Ashagrie, 1998). They constitute about 15-20 percent of the child population of the same age group.

Child labour is widespread in developing regions. Asia, the biggest continent, has the most child workers (61 percent of world's total), as compared to 32 percent in Africa, 7 percent in Latin America. However in relative terms, Africa leads in economic activity participation rates of child labour. The corresponding proportion in Asia is less than half of the level of Africa. Participation rates in economic activity in all the regions are more for boys than girls, and much higher in rural areas than in urban centres. The probability for children to engage in economic activity is twice as high in rural areas. The persistence of child labour is clearly an indicator of poverty, unemployment and illiteracy along with the annoying presence of segmented labour markets, demand for low wage labour or specialized labour.

MAGNITUDE OF CHILD LABOUR IN INDIA

India, by way of magnitude, tops the list of countries of the world sheltering child labourers. According to the census report of 1981, 13.59 million child labourers were working in the country. In 1991, it slightly came down to 11.28 million again rose to 12.67 million in 2001. Census estimates of child labour traditionally seem to be underestimates. As per the NSS (National Sample Survey Organization) data, there were 16.33

million child workers in 1972-73, 16.25 million in 1977-78, 17.36 million in 1983. The decline in the numbers of labouring children is reflected even in the NSS estimates. If we look at the age wise distribution of persons by principal activity to get a rough estimate of child workers, we find that by 1993-94, NSS reported the extent of child labourers to be 9.27 million and further down to 5.94 million in 2004-05 (as per the latest Employment-Unemployment Survey of 61st Round). These estimates, however, keep out the subsidiary workers. If the number of subsidiary workers amongst the age group of 5-14 years is added, it may further augment the magnitude of child labour in India during 2004-05. The ratio of marginal workers to main workers amongst child labour in 2001 census can be used in the estimate of 2004-05. Children in the age group of 5-14 years constituted 0.53 percent of male marginal workers and 0.62 percent of the female marginal workers in 2001. Thus there were nearly 1.29 million child workers as subsidiary workers and hence about 7.23 million total child workers in the country in 2004-05. Match up to of data strictly cannot be maintained over time, but the statistics point out that the magnitude of child labour has fallen off from early 1980s to a large extent. Still the problem persists in India overwhelmingly. India is now on high economic growth path that does not match with her present image as a faster growing economy flourishing within democratic set-up.

School participation of children, particularly school attendance, is always a deterrent to child labour exploitation. The efficacy of compulsory education of children in eliminating child labour is now widely acknowledged. Not all forms of child labour can be eliminated through this measure but the whole time labour engagement of children is stoppable. Universal school enrolment is just the beginning of the initiatives in this direction but the state must not be smug in taking this action. Regularity of attendance in school must be ensured. Children must enjoy schooling for a major period of the day. That only can keep them away from labour employment for long hours. The education should be free of all cost involved. Parents sometimes allege that they have to cough up various fees demanded by the school authority. These meagre fees can turn out to be huge burden for poor

TABLE 4.3

Estimates of Child Labour in India, 1972-73 to 2004-05

(million)

	Age Group	Rural male	Rural female	Rural	Urban male	Urban female	Urban	Total
(1)	(2)	(3)	(4)	(5)	(6)	(7)	(8)	(9)
NSS (1972-73)	5 to 9	0.88	0.63	1.51	0.05	0.03	0.08	1.56
27th Round	10 to 14	7.78	5.75	13.53	0.8	0.41	1.21	14.74
	5 to 14	8.66	6.38	15.04	0.85	0.44	1.29	16.33
NSS (1977-78)	5 to 9	0.88	0.63	1.51	0.05	0.05	0.1	1.61
32nd Round	10 to 14	7.96	5.21	13.77	0.94	0.53	1.47	15.24
	5 to 14	8.84	5.84	14.68	0.99	0.58	1.57	16.25
Census 1981	0-14	7.34	5.21	12.55	0.76	0.29	1.05	13.59
1983	5 to 9	0.9	0.64	1.54	0.06	0.06	0.12	1.66
	10 to 14	8.44	5.59	14.03	1.07	0.6	1.67	15.7
	5 to 14	9.34	6.23	15.57	1.13	0.66	1.79	17.36
NSS (1993-94)	5 to 9	0.35	0.42	0.83	0.02	0.02	0.02	0.85
50th Round	10 to 14	4.19	3.15	7.34	0.72	0.38	1.08	8.42
(principal usual activity)	5 to 14	4.54	3.57	8.17	0.74	0.4	1.1	9.27
Census 2001	5 to 9	0.18	0.16	0.34	0.13	0.07	0.2	0.54

(main+ marginal)	10 to 14	1.17	0.94	2.11	0.65	0.29	0.94	3.05
	5 to 14	1.35	1.1	2.45	0.78	0.36	1.14	3.59
NSS (2004-05)	5 to 9	0.09	0.09	0.18	0.02	0.01	0.05	0.23
61st Round	10 to 14	2.67	2.05	4.72	0.65	0.33	0.99	5.71
(principal usual activity)	5 to 14	2.76	2.14	4.9	0.67	0.34	1.04	5.94

Note : During 1994 and 2005, involvement in activities status-wise from 91 to 99 is excluded, that also includes attending to domestic duties and free collection of goods.

Source : For NSS 27th round, 32nd round, Census 1981 and 1983, Mehta (1991). For NSS 50th round, estimates derived from table 1A, Report No. 406. For NSS 61st round, estimates derived from Table 17, Report No. 515, part 1.

Quoted from Niti Mehta at http://ssrn.com/ abstract= 996574.

parents. Therefore, free education should be free in letter and spirit. The enrolment and continuation in school, therefore, largely depend on the ability to afford the private cost. The Government must ensure that the parents are kept out of varieties of hidden cost that inhibits enrolment and school continuation. The growth of enrolment and retention of children in school can thus reduce child labour. In India, part time work of children does not come in the way of education, therefore a large number of children combine schooling with work in family farms, in family business and in many other paid job where work schedule is flexible. Sometimes these works, even if for shorter period, may be detrimental to child development. Children may join family occupation after and before school hours to help her family. Unfortunately, this part time work is not captured by the Census or the NSS. In India, primary education for children below the age of 14 years is free; hence the child population between the ages 5-14 years should be normally in school. Despite this, of the estimated population of 87.12 million in the age group of 6-14 years in 2001 were out of school. An estimated 12.66 million (as per Census 2001) were workers. Thus, nearly 74.45 million children are "idlers" or "nowhere" children. The National Sample Survey (NSS) estimated in (2004-05) that out of 226 million children between 5-14 years, nearly 7.23 million are workers. 'Idle' children neither work nor are part of the education system, and precise understanding of their status is contentious. It may be that underreporting of domestic work, unemployment and unobserved health issues are responsible for a significant part of the "idleness" status. It has been conjectured that a child does not attend school when the marginal utility associated with the returns to education are less than the forgone utility caused by schooling costs (Edmonds, 2007).

There is a dominant belief, particularly in Indian context, that the presence of 'idle' children is notional construction unconnected with ground level actuality. This view is widely held by many social scientists and NGO activists. They argue that idle children are working in some way or other. Their work engagement is not captured in official statistics. They work on family farms as well as in family business. The other reason of their 'idleness' is the lack of schooling facility in their vicinity. Whatever is the reason this is an issue of considerable concern as these children shockingly suffer from deprivation and poverty (Mehta, 1991). It may be added here that the persistence of child labour is a denial of our basic principle of social justice articulated in our Constitution, which proclaims universal, free and compulsory education for children in the age group of 6-14 years. Articles 24 and 39 of our Constitution clearly prohibit labour engagement of children and spells out protection against any form of exploitation and abuse. In addition, there are much legislation enacted on child labour to keep children away from certain specific occupations and industries. The provisions of these acts prescribe the minimum age, minimum wages and working conditions of child labour in various employments such as factories, mines, transport, construction, etc. (Mehta, 1991; Hirway, 1991).

DISTRIBUTION OF CHILD LABOUR : AGE GROUPS AND ACTIVITIES

Sectoral distribution reveals that rural areas have 60.1% of child labour, while 39.8 % of it is in the urban areas (2001 Census). The NSS estimates of 61st round show that 82 percent of the child labour is in rural areas. Since we do not have the detailed industry-wise distribution of NSS 2004-05, we will discuss the 2001 census information. Nearly 14.7 percent of the child labour fall between ages 5-9 years and about 85.2 percent is between 10-15 years. The ratio is more or less the same for male and female child labour and also in rural and urban areas; although in case of urban female the proportion of younger child workers is greater. In 1983 nearly 90 percent of the child labour were between 10-15 years of age. This is still alarming that there is deterioration in the situation as larger proportion of younger children (5-9 years) is now working as child workers.

Tables 4.5 and 4.6 brings to light the activity, sex and location-wise distribution of main and marginal child workers between the ages 5-14 years in India. During 1981, nearly 92 percent of the child workers in rural areas were involved in primary sector, followed by 5.7 percent in secondary and 2.7

TABLE 4.4
Age-wise Distribution of Child Workers (Main), 2001

Total Rural-Urban

	Male	*Female*	*Male*	*Female*	*Male*	*Female*
(1)	*(2)*	*(3)*	*(4)*	*(5)*	*(6)*	*(7)*
5-9 years	199807 (14.1)	116779 (16.1)	101532 (13.0)	69576 (15.0)	98275 (16.0)	47203 (19.0)
10-15 years	1217349 (85.9)	610584 (83.9)	707231 (87.4)	410907 (85.5)	510118 (83.8)	199677 (80.8)
Total	1417156 (100.0)	727363 (100.0)	808763 (100.0)	480483 (100.0)	608393 (100.0)	246880 (100.0)

Source : Census of India, 2001.
Quoted from Niti Mehta at http://ssrn.com/ abstract= 996574.

percent in the service activities. In urban areas then, 53.7 percent were engaged in secondary activities, 26 percent in primary and 20 percent in the tertiary sector. As is the case with the workforce, the occupational distribution of child workers has changed significantly in the last few decades. In 2001, amongst the main workers, only 28.1 percent of the rural child labour was engaged in primary sector, 51 percent in the secondary and 21 percent in the tertiary sectors. In urban areas the percentages were 2.7, 56.3 and 41 respectively.

Overall during 2001, the share of child labour in manufacturing and repairs within the secondary sector is quite significant (46.6%) and also in trade, hotels and restaurants (14%), apart from the primary sectors. In the urban areas, services, trade, non monetary services, hotels and restaurants engage large sections of child labour. In this context educational deprivation and lack of skill training limit their opportunities for upward mobility. The provisional information from Labour Bureau (2001) indicates that on an average only 2782 children are employed in factories registered under the Factories Act. This is clearly indicative of the fact that employment of children is mainly in the unorganized and informal sectors of the economy, where they face greater risks of exploitation and discrimination. Organized sector is covered by national laws which prohibit child labour.

State-wise information from 2001 Census regarding age-wise distribution of workers is not readily available, so we can take a look at the latest NSS round (2004-05) for analysis. For the states, child population could be ascertained from the NSS for the combined group of 5-15 years. However, the work force participation rates are provided separately for the age groups 5-9 and 10-15 years. In order to arrive at the numbers of child workers (males, females, rural and urban areas separately) the work force participation rates of the age group between 10-15 years is applied to the child population of 5-15 years and hence the extent of workers may not be accurate. Actually these may be over estimated considering that participation ratios for 5-9 years are far lower. Keeping this caution in mind let us look at the state-wise distribution of child labour (as a share of the total workers in each state) as given in Table 4.5.

Table 4.5
Activity, Sex and Location-wise Distribution of Main Child Workers (5-14 years), 1981 and 2001

Main child Workers (%)

Sl. No.	*Activity*		*Male*		*Female*		*Total*	*% CL to main workers*
			Rural	*Urban*	*Rural*	*Urban*		
	(1)	*(2)*	*(3)*	*(4)*	*(5)*	*(6)*	*(7)*	*(8)*
1.	Primary	1981	91.53	38.63	91.76	9.68	82.46	6.16
		2001	29.71	2.87	25.39	2.30	17.97	3.28
2.	Secondary	1981	5.52	33.48	6.13	80.08	12.42	3.62
		2001	45.17	53.48	60.81	63.27	53.12	2.07
3.	Tertiary	1981	2.95	27.90	2.11	10.24	5.12	1.52
		2001	25.12	43.65	13.79	34.43	28.91	0.78
4.	All sectors	1981	6.68	0.93	3.46	0.71	100:00	5.01
	(million)	2001	0.81	0.61	0.48	0.25	100.00	1.47

TABLE 4.6

Activity, Sex and Location-wise Distribution of Marginal Child Workers

(5-14 years),
1981 and 2001
Marginal child workers (%)

Sl. No.	*Activity*		*Male*		*Female*			*% CL to marginal workers*	*% CL to total workers*
			Rural	*Urban*	*Rural*	*Urban*	*Total*		
	(1)	*(2)*	*(3)*	*(4)*	*(5)*	*(6)*	*(7)*	*(8)*	*(9)*
1.	Primary	1981	93.79	94.90	98.85	47.88	77.95	11.44	6.76
		2001	32.91	3.46	31.31	3.89	26.3	10.66	5.00
2.	Secondary	1981	3.90	2.83	4.13	37.68	3.61	7.50	3.83
		2001	47.59	61.36	56.20	74.40	55.14	6.66	2.89
3.	Tertiary	1981	2.30	2.27	1.02	14.44	18.44	5.00	1.59
		2001	19.88	35.18	12.50	21.71	18.69	4.07	1.04
4.	All sectors	1981	0.65	0.32	1.70	0.04	100.00	10.92	5.55
	(million)	2001	0.534	0.17	0.62	0.12	100.00	6.52	2.14

Source : Mehta (1991) for 1981; Census of India, 2001.
Quoted from Niti Mehta at http://ssrn.com/ abstract= 996574.

TABLE 4.7

State-wise Child Labour Distribution (5-15 Years), 2004-05

(per 000 of total workers)

States	Rural			Urban			Total
	Male	Female	Persons	Male	Female	Persons	
(1)	(2)	(3)	(4)	(5)	(6)	(7)	(8)
Andhra Pradesh	39.78	69.97	52.36	22.23	48.59	29.73	47.75
Assam	27.92	24.19	23.95	5.16	55.43	11.48	22.84
Jharkhand	21.42	50.88	30.20	19.52	52.57	25.14	29.51
Bihar	21.06	23.85	21.59	23.44	49.11	25.85	21.95
Gujarat	20.36	24.87	22.04	12.76	28.18	15.19	20.09
Haryana	11.50	3.97	10.56	8.69	5.07	8.23	9.95
Himachal Pradesh	6.43	14.19	9.72	0.00	3.78	0.82	8.92
Karnataka	31.38	47.91	38.06	6.55	14.87	8.25	30.68
Kerala	1.07	0.00	0.99	1.41	4.95	2.00	1.22
Chattisgarh	27.07	48.30	36.53	26.70	21.16	26.40	35.35
Madhya Pradesh	21.29	57.50	33.44	13.59	32.17	17.05	30.34
Maharashtra	24.19	35.44	29.13	7.34	6.97	7.11	21.79
Orissa	33.33	64.23	42.00	15.83	36.29	19.42	39.43

Punjab	17.58	35.00	18.54	8.45	0.00	7.18	14.60
Rajasthan	33.96	98.03	55.25	38.13	56.46	42.09	52.61
Tamil Nadu	7.48	14.74	10.39	6.93	20.52	10.68	10.49
Uttaranchal	28.58	7.02	20.55	3.85	4.23	4.02	17.19
Uttar Pradesh	33.29	50.43	37.50	39.78	132.69	49.88	39.96
West Bengal	25.76	69.04	32.18	21.40	76.52	29.23	31.41
All India	25.59	47.20	32.38	16.31	35.95	19.79	29.46

Note : Calculated from Estimated Population data and Usual Status (ps) WPRs.
Number of child workers are normalized by total workers.

Source : NSS Report No. 515 part 1.
Quoted from Niti Mehta, at http://ssrn.com/abstract=996574.

As per NSS (2004-05), on an average, rural areas support between 84 percent of the child labour in the country. Ranging between 62 to 99 percent of the child labour in all the states is in the rural areas. In 1981, in all the states 90 percent of the child workers were concentrated in the rural areas (Mehta, 1991). There has been a veritable shift since then. The growth of urban centres and expansion of informal sector economy in the urban areas have encouraged large scale migration from rural areas to upcoming urban areas. Children do join their parents in their uncertain journey for seeking livelihoods. Informal sector in the urban areas offers a wide variety of employment for children. This is reflected in the trends of fall in magnitude in the engagement of child labour in primary sectors (2004-05) as compared to that of 1981. More opportunities are created in the secondary/tertiary sectors to employ the children.

By way of magnitude of child labour, Andhra Pradesh, Rajasthan and Uttar Pradesh have more than a million child labourers each and these states together account for nearly 44 percent of the total child workers in the country. In Karnataka, Madhya Pradesh, Maharashtra, Orissa and West Bengal the occurrence of child labour is between 0.5 to 1 million each. Nearly 78 percent of the child workers are found in these eight states. However, the incidence of child workers in the total worker population defines the problem more accurately. In this respect, Table 4.8 reveals that for the entire country. Andhra Pradesh, Orissa, Rajasthan and Uttar Pradesh have the highest concentration of child labour (more than 40 child workers per thousand workers), followed by Jharkhand, Karnataka, Chhattisgarh, MP and West Bengal (between 25 to 40 child workers per thousand workers). Remaining states have a lower concentration of child workers (less than 25 per thousand workers).

The following template portrays the swing in the incidence of child labour across the states between 1981 and 2004-05. Over time, states that have done well in bringing down the magnitude of child labour significantly are Bihar, Gujarat, Haryana, Maharashtra, Punjab and Tamil Nadu. Uttar Pradesh and West Bengal have not done anything significant. In Andhra Pradesh and Rajasthan child labour problem

Table 4.8

Relative Concentration of Child Labour, 1981, 2004-05

Nature of Incidence (child workers per thousand workers)	*1981*	*2004-05*
(1)	*(2)*	*(3)*
Low (Less than 25/000)	Kerala.	Kerala, Bihar, Gujarat, Haryana, Maharashtra, Punjab, Tamil Nadu
Medium (26 to 45/000)	Bihar, Gujarat, Haryana, Punjab, Tamilnadu, Uttar Pradesh, West Bengal, India	Karnataka, Madhya Pradesh, Orissa, Uttar Pradesh, West Bengal, India
High (More than 45/000)	Andhra Pradesh, Orissa, Karnataka, Madhya Pradesh, Rajasthan	Andhra Pradesh, Rajasthan

Source : Table 5 and Census of India 1991, "Working Children in India : An Analysis of 1991 Census Data". Quoted from Niti Mehta at http://ssrn.com/abstract= 996574.

remains as acute as during 1981. The occurrence of child workers is an indicator of the negative outcome of development. Rural economy is characterized by higher levels of poverty, unemployment and illiteracy compared to the urban economy, as the per capita rural incomes and the head count of the population below the poverty line is lower in urban than in the rural areas. Adult literacy rates in rural areas were much lower at 54.5 percent as compared to 75.2 percent in the urban areas. At the disaggregated level (states), we have attempted to find the relationship between the magnitude of child labour with the incidence of poverty, level of unemployment and illiteracy among the general population for rural and urban areas separately. (See Table 4.9 for the proportion of child workers, headcount ratio of population below poverty line, unemployment rates on current daily status and literacy rates in rural and urban areas during 2004-05).

In the years following market reforms (particularly in the period between 1999-00 to 2004-05) the poverty level, as per Planning Commission estimate, has declined significantly. Urban-rural differentials in poverty levels too have narrowed down significantly at least at the aggregate level as revealed in the government estimate. Variations between states in the occurrence of poverty still overwhelmingly persist. The gap between rural and urban poverty is still quite visible in several states and poverty levels in rural areas are quite high in Bihar, MP, Maharashtra, and Orissa, UP, WB, Jharkhand, and Chhattisgarh. We find that there exists a positive relation between the number of child labour and the head count ratio of poverty though the relation is not very significant, especially in rural areas. Such an inference finds support in recent literature, where it is shown that higher incidence of poverty is not always correlated with child labour. Economic growth sometimes creates more opportunities for child labour. Structure of demand is an important factor in this process (Swaminathan, 1998).

The table offers interesting revelation. The head count ratio in Andhra Pradesh is 10.8 per cent but child workers' proportion is 52.4 per 1000 workers in rural area. Contrastingly Kerala has head count ratio of 13.2 per cent but child labour is

TABLE 4.9
Relation between Child Labour, Literacy Rates, Poverty Ratio and Unemployment by States (2004-05)

States	Rural				Urban			
	Child Workers (per 000* workers)	Head Count ratio** (%)	Unemployed Rate*** (per 000)	Literacy Rate (%)	Child Workers (per 000* workers)	Head Count ratio** (%)	Unemployed Rate*** (per 000)	Literacy Rate (%)
(1)	(2)	(3)	(4)	(5)	(6)	(7)	(8)	(9)
Andhra Pradesh	52.4	10.8	109.0	47.5	29.7	27.1	79.0	69.6
Assam	23.9	21.7	65.0	69.6	11.5	3.7	90.0	82.3
Jharkhand	30.2	42.9	66.0	47.3	25.1	20.7	88.0	76.5
Bihar	21.6	42.2	68.0	43.7	25.8	38.1	100.0	68.4
Gujarat	22.0	19.4	41.0	58.5	15.2	14.2	47.0	79.5
Haryana	10.6	13.6	62.0	58.1	8.2	15.6	69.0	73.8
Himachal Pradesh	9.7	10.9	57.0	71.5	0.8	5.0	49.0	79.7
Karnataka	38.1	20.0	67.0	54.5	8.3	33.3	60.0	75.9
Kerala	1.0	13.2	256.0	82.7	2.0	20.6	252.0	85.6
Chhattisgarh	36.5	42.0	82.0	53.9	26.4	40.7	71.0	75.9

(Contd.)

TABLE 4.9 (Contd.)

(1)	(2)	(3)	(4)	(5)	(6)	(7)	(8)	(9)
Madhya Pradesh	33.4	35.8	56.0	48.1	17.1	42.3	64.0	72.2
Maharashtra	29.1	30.0	93.0	63.6	7.1	32.8	88.0	79.8
Orissa	42.0	46.9	102.0	54.2	19.4	43.7	150.0	72.1
Punjab	18.5	10.0	97.0	63.3	7.2	5.0	75.0	77.1
Rajasthan	55.3	19.0	44.0	45.3	42.1	28.5	61.0	63.7
Tamil Nadu	10.4	22.7	151.0	63.4	10.7	24.1	86.0	80.6
Uttaranchal	20.6	14.9	41.0	60.3	4.0	17.0	68.0	76.3
Uttar Pradesh	37.5	33.9	37.0	47.3	49.9	30.7	63.0	65.5
West Bengal	32.2	28.5	112.0	61.0	29.2	15.4	105.0	80.5
All India	32.4	28.7	82.0	54.5	19.8	25.9	83.0	75.2

Source : * Table 5.
** Calculated from grouped data from NSSO Report 508. Our Source : Himanshu, 2007.
*** Current daily status unemployment rates, from NSS Report 515, part 1.
Quoted from Niti Mehta (at http://ssrn.com/abstract= 996574).

virtually nil at only one per thousand workers. In Assam, head count ratio of poverty is 21.7 per cent but child workers' proportion is 21.7 per 1000 workers in rural area. Thus the co-relation between child labour incidence and the head count ratio does not seem to be robust.

5

Contextualizing the Issue of Child Employment in Beedi Rolling

The present research study has been undertaken out of an inner urge to find an answer to question that has been relentlessly provoking me for last few years. The question that posed is "why beedi rolling as household enterprise is so predominant in the two districts of West Bengal: Murshidabad and Malda? I am convinced that I got the answer from my field study in Murshidabad. I choose the latter for study for two reasons: one for the convenience of my field study as I was stationed there with unhindered flow of co-operation from all sides. The same did not come by, in that way, from the other district. An additional reason, I must disclose, is the easy access to numerous household units located in contiguous region, comprising many block areas. The northern region of the district has the highest concentration of beedi units. Logistic convenience, thus, drove me to focus on these areas intensively to delve deep into working of beedi units and the nature of involvement of children in that occupation. The second reason for concentrating only Murshidabad, leaving the other adjoining district which is almost equally infamous for use of child labour in beedi, is the limitation of time and resources. But limiting the empirical study on Murshidabad will not render our findings less than the true revelation of what is happening to numerous children engaged in one of the most hazardous occupations in West Bengal.

These two districts are geographically separated by the river Ganges. Location of these districts on either side of the mighty Ganges has advantages as well as disadvantages. The river Ganges provides fish aplenty to the people, living on both sides. Fishing thus is a source of living for many. The river, in addition to creating livelihood opportunities, also enriches the dietary intake through eating fish that contain protein, iron and many other types of nutrients. The river, thus, contributes to physical well-being of people, residing very close it. But the blessing is not unmixed. People have to face the fury of the river every year. It wrecks havoc during rainy season and causes unspeakable misery to the people. It overflows submerging the low lying areas on both sides. It swallows every year one or two villages during this terrifying season of the year. Loss of life and property are recurrent phenomenon that speaks of government's inability to protect the vulnerable people from the wrath of the mighty river.

Both of these districts are victims of calamities created by the river and recipients of some of the meagre benefits for perilous living on both sides. One crucial advantage that really makes a difference, is reaped by the farmers. Flood sometime becomes blessings in disguise. A few can gain when a vast majority suffers. The landed farmers benefit from the flood if silts are deposited in their croplands. Deposition of silts can enhance fertility manifolds. Thus benefits accrue to very few landed farms whose farm lands are close to the sides and whose lands are not washed away by the flood. The two districts share the same benefits and suffer the same magnitude of losses for their geographical location, close to the mighty river. There is noticeable similarity between the two districts, as if one resembles the other. The semblance of the two areas strengthens the argument for taking up one instead of two. The findings of the study in Murshidabad will reveal the circumstances in which beedi manufacturing units are working in the courtyards of poor families. The study will bring to light the condition of children employed in beedi units as part of family labour. The survey will surely unfold the conditions, causes and consequence of child labour in beedi rolling. The study will probe into the issues of poverty and lack of employment opportunities of the areas where beedi processing is the mainstay of the survival strategy.

The question that evokes utmost inquisitiveness and concern is the predominant presence of the occupation for last many years. Diversification of employment over time does not seem to work here. The job of beedi rolling is being passed on from one generation to the next. The people and the place are identified with this particular work. Thus it seems that the cycle of poverty and intergenerational transfer of occupation are mutually interlocked.

There is dearth of study on child labour in tobacco processing. Exact statistics on the number of children in this hazardous form of child labour is hard to come by. Some studies on the nature of child labour in different hazardous occupation, in processing as well as in manufacturing are enriching sources of information. But those studies were undertaken at established industries in the manufacturing sector Industries that are infamous for employing child labour are brick kilns, slate, gem and jewelleries, bangle, carpet, incense making units. One study to probe into child labour in these industries was undertaken by a group of scholars led by Professor Deborah Levison of the University of Minnesota, U.S.A. This book is not only a treasure store of information on the nature and extent of child labours in hazardous occupation but also lay bare the failure of the state and inefficacy of the law to punish the offenders. The book shows the way and charts out the path for future possible action in a bid to get rid of these dangerous social ills. The present study covers the home-based beedi units not factory-based units to track child employment therein. This study is thus a new attempt in new area having very few or altogether missing material on the subject to get light from. The road is thorny but the journey is challenging and interesting to take on.

WHY IS THE STUDY UNDERTAKEN?

The latest census reports a rise in magnitude of child labour in West Bengal. Censes defines child labour in restrictive sense where work is defined as participation in economic activities that results in production of goods and services. Censure data in every likelihood, may not reveal true incidence. Children who attend school may not be counted as workers in the census enumeration. Many children may be merely enrolled but may not be attending school as they need to join family labour for beedi rolling. Children in large number combine beedi work and schooling. A significant segment of them might be fulltime worker. Census captures data of workers and puts them in two categories: workers and non-workers. Workers are then further divided into main workers and marginal workers. The latter division is carried out on the basis of duration of employment during the year preceding the day of remuneration. The main worker should be in productive employment for more than six months during last one year. Census categories evidently fail to capture various combinations relating to work and schooling, 'work and idleness', 'no work and no schooling' and full schooling and no work of children.

We need to bring into focus the varied occupations and engagement of children in a rural setting where work in tobacco is the principal source of living. Census data does not furnish the complete fact. We need to go into further details. The present study is thus planned and undertaken to plug the holes. It is interesting to understand why thousand of children partake in this dangerous job for a prolonged time that exposes them to tobacco dust and pong. Exposure to tobacco results in severe lung diseases, prolonged cough and cold, breathing difficulty and many other ills. We are all aware of the danger of passive smoking. The study aims to look into the circumstances that compel them to undertake this detrimental work. Inter-generational transfer of the same job is an issue to be probed. Diversification of job, a shift from low paid work to more rewarding work is associated with economic transformation process. The latter has, it seems, by passed the study area where people are seeking livelihood from beedi work for a last half a century or even more. It is intriguing to find why this low paying, monotonous, exploitative and highly hazardous job is still a dominant economic activity and mainstay of the local economy in a particular region within the state of West Bengal.

Is the pre-eminence of the work in beedi rolling poverty driven? Is any factor, other than poverty, can explain the predominance of this occupation in this are? Poverty and illiteracy nexus has to be looked into. Are culture and mindsets of their people someway connected to continuation with this degrading occupation? What are the alternatives and how is the motivation to shift to other alternatives? The state of West Bengal is applauded everywhere for initiating land reform programs during eighties with a view to raise the standard of living for the people living on the margins in the agrarian economy of Bengal. Small farmers, marginal farmers and landless agricultural labourers are those people who were expected to be exclusive beneficiaries of land reform programme. The three tier Panchayat system was revamped to ensure popular democracy at the grass root. Participation of people, across class and caste in the rural society in Bengal was the primary objective to accomplish by this grass root democratic institutions. The underdogs in the rural society can now take part in planning and in execution of rural development programme. Thus radical land reforms and rejuvenation of Panchayat system were two revolutionary steps of the left front government undertaken more than three decades ago. These steps were aimed at bringing a radical change in the agrarian economy steeped into unequal land relations and mass poverty. These measures were undertaken to alter the agrarian conditions by giving away land to the tillers. This was expected to bring about rise in agricultural productivity and rural income through intensive and efficient cultivation in small holdings. Increased income would raise the standard of living. Growth and expansion of rural market were natural outcome of the increase in rural income.

Rise in rural income demands expansion of rural market. The demands for non-agricultural goods and services would go up as a result. Non-agricultural activity will jump start in response to demand for non-agricultural goods. Agricultural and rural manufactures will flourish simultaneously. Rural institution will foster this growth process through facilitation, provision and protection. The question that naturally comes up is why this transformation had eluded certain areas in the state. Why the distribution of poverty so skewed. Can poverty alone explain this predominance of this dangerous and dehumanizing occupation? The connection between poverty and beedi processing can not be established as permanent and omnipresent. There are many regions in the state of West Bengal where poverty is more acute or even at par but this occupation in tobacco rolling is almost absent.

One may be interested to look into educational opportunities, children of the study area can access. Are there any supply side constraints of schooling? Is the number or schools adequate for all children? Number of school matters less than the facilities schools can provide. School quality and attractiveness of curriculum can enhance school attendance. Dysfunctional schooling can dissuade attendance. Children tend to bunk school if the class room transaction fails to arouse interest in them. The frequent bunking can turn into permanent drop-out. A child who stops going to school may join family work in beedi processing. Thus, in many cases undertaking work in beedi processing becomes a default activity that is not always caused by poverty or need for income support by the children. Push factor is generated from the school side. Parental education is also a factor that influences children schooling participation and academic achievement. We need to look at schooling backgrounds of parents. On the whole, the study is undertaken to uncover the circumstance of children engaged in labour processing. We need to think about the possible way out of this entrapment of numerous children in home-based tobacco processing.

SPECIFIC RESEARCH QUESTIONS

We try to find the factors responsible for continuation of child labour in the area chosen for household survey. We begin with searching household characteristics that may have some connection with situation of children. Religious affiliation of a household in question does not appear to have any relation with the generation and perpetuation of child labour or any other sorts of deprivation. We are a bit curious to know whether that connection exists at all in locales of study. Class and caste nexus is issue in Indian rural society that still triggers debates. There is a dominant conception that caste and class always move along side. This means that lowest caste families are invariably the poorest and *vice versa*. There is also a different kind of inference about the relationship which says that the relationship is not linear and consistent. There are instances of deviations which establishes that lowest category among the caste hierarchy may not be poorest in the economic class. Castes association may influence children's well-being and their participation in labour force via class affiliations. Cultural instincts or a particular world view of certain caste groups may have an effect on children's situation. This cultural effect may outweigh economic predicament.

Children are likely to suffer when they have lost their fathers as head of the family and as a sole bread winner. The crisis deepens and vulnerability engulfs when state support in the forms of social security is not forthcoming. Father may disappear once and for all. Children born and raised in joint family structure are better placed as they receive support from other relations. Children of the nuclear family are in worst predicament. Disappearance of father may be due to death, abandonment, divorce or for any other reason. Disappearance of father in a nuclear family amounts to taking away the protective shield from the defenceless members of the family. Mothers take up the bread winning task when there is no alternative. Suffering of the children goes up obviously as the mothers have to shuttle between house work and paid work. Mother may not earn that much which their father used to do. Thus family heading is a significant factor in determining children's plight. Children of a family headed by father are more likely to be better placed than children whose families are not. We will bring forth this connection, the relationship between family heading and children's relative situations.

Father's age is equally important factor influencing children's situations in the society. Children are obviously in distress if their fathers cannot move and work due to old age.

We are also interested to see whether such relations hold good in our survey. Children's participation in education, to a large extent, is determined by father's education experiences. Fathers who had exposure to schooling and had realized the benefits of education are likely to send their children to school. Economic well-being sometimes is related to educational level of the earners. This connection may prevail upon fathers to send children to school and encourage uninterrupted continuation in education. We are interested to look into this connection in our study.

Mothers' education and occupation also have influence on children's educational and work participation. Girls' participation is more influenced by mothers' characteristics. Mothers having schooling experience, tend to encourage children, particularly girls, for attending schools. Mothers' occupations can have an impact on the children particularly on girl children. Girls, take up kitchen work in the absence of mothers when the absence is caused by her paid work outside home. Girls' rather than boys are likely to suffer in case of mothers' outside work. Thus mothers' education may have positive influence on children but mothers' work outside may adversely affect children particularly girls. We will explore this connection also.

There is hardly any dispute over the well-known connection between poverty and child labour. It is now widely accepted, axiomatically, that the former causes the latter. We will verify this casual connection in our study covering thousand of households in the sample villages. We will, in the first go, be guided by 'tagging' of households by the local government. The grass root local governments all over the country are assigned with the task of identifying families who will be recorded as poor families. They prepare a list of Below Property Line (BPL) families for providing special benefits and subsidies to the distraught families. The Panchayat maintains the statistics on poverty in their respective jurisdiction. This database is most crucial for anti-poverty programs and actions. The quantum of government grant from the central or as well as from state government to be allotted to a particular Gram Panchayat depends on the poverty figure. Each family, identified as BPL, is allotted a card as a gate pass to the portals of benefits. We had recorded this government identification in our enquiry schedule as a rough measure of poverty as a determinant of child labour. One exercise that may evoke interest from all corners is the verification of the correctness of the selection. There are two types of error involved in identification of poor. Type I error entails inclusion of non-poor in the category of poor. Type II error relates to inclusion actual poor in the category of non-poor.

OUR OWN MEASURE OF POVERTY

Panchayat enumerators interact with households to elicit all information abut their coping mechanism for survival. There is almost uniforms structure and points of query in the schedule to be canvassed in each household. Housing type and quality, productive assets especially cultivable land and livestock, family members, consumption expenditure, income, employment and even clothing are included in the household survey schedule. The data, thus collected are rechecked and verified to ensure accuracy. Tabulation and analysis are carried out in the next phase. A cut-off score is designed by the government to conceive as poverty line. Households that fail to achieve that prefixed score are identified as below poverty line.

BPL listing from its very inception particularly in West Bengal has been an issue shrouded by controversy. The listing procedure, survey methods and the battery of questions, contained in the survey template are widely contradicted from many corners. The critics have pointed out that subjective, rather than objective judgment, has prevailed in such listing. Vote bank politics has come into the making of the BPL list. The result, quite evidently, is either overestimation or under estimation. Two kinds of error as explained above are likely to be committed. We have calculated Engel's ratio, per capita consumption expenditure, and standard of living index score for each family. We will now take these score with government identification of BPL to get at the true story of household poverty.

FOOD SECURITY : OUR QUESTION

Food Security is a tangible obverse of household poverty. Richer households are obviously food secure households while poorer households are not. Insufficiency of food for all members of the households are outcome of inability to buy enough food from the market or produce enough food crop in the farm, owned and operated by the household themselves. Food deficient households will search for all option in a bid to avert food crisis. One option may be engagement of children in income earning work. Demand for work is not enough to find a paid job for children. Jobs are to be available to them. Children can easily get into any job where there is no law to prohibit child employment. Employers would be very keen to employ children for two conveniences as they deem it economically profitable. One is the advantages of low wage for children that reduces wage bill for them. The second one is the benefits of docility. Children can be engaged for long hours without extra cost on labour. Possibility of non-compliance can be easily ruled out. The study is undertaken in an area where home-based manufacturing of beedi is dominant economic activity. Children of tender age can be pulled into this avocation by the head of family to augment family income. Thus the perception of food insecurity can increase child labour. We are interested to look into possible connection between food insecurity and child labour

EMPLOYMENT AND UNEMPLOYMENT OF ADULTS

A crucial question that comes up is the relation between adult employment and child labour use. Employment that is gainful results in accrual of income to the employed person. The outcome of employment is positive contribution to quantum of goods production or service generation. This characteristics of employment contrasts with disguised unemployment where a person is visibly employed but that does not yield any output nor generates income. Quality of employment does also matter. Employment that does not bring in reasonable payment fails short of what is known as quality employment. Employee should get wages according to her skill and efficiency. Underpayment is the symptom of the malfunctioning of the labour market as well as lack of check and balance by the state. Number of adult earners and accrual of reasonable payment are signs of relative affluence of the households. Child labour use is obviously related to the days and quality of adult employment. Families having more than one adult earner are less likely to engage their children for contributing to family income.

STRUCTURE OF THE FAMILY

Presence of both parents in a family is always beneficial of the children. Single parents evidently find it difficult to manage the family. Care for children, in the face of many adversities, is the first casualty. Families having protection from both parents are better placed, economically. They can absorb economic shocks that are characteristics of informal employment and economic activities in the unorganised sector. Both parents can overcome the crisis in a prudent way. Children may not feel the pinch. Children can benefit from quality parenting, a vital input in their growth process, mentally as well as physically, when they grow up in the warm presence of both parents. Single parenthood is associated with multiple adversities, economic, social and psychological. Children are prone to receive less care and attention when they miss either their father or mother, children's upbringing is sure to suffer in this situation. Single parent families, as a coping mechanism and survival strategy, can engage children in employment to make up the loss of income caused by death or disappearance of either parent. Thus children's well-being in a family is largely dependent or where both parents are living and staying with them. We will look into this connection in our study on the children.

CHARACTERISTICS OF CHILDREN

The focal point of the present study is children and childhood. The features and endowments of childhood vary from child to child depending on age, sex, and many other attributes of them. Age of a child is a factor in determining the nature of work in which a child can be engaged. Older children are more likely to be engaged in paid work outside home. Poor parents would like to send their relatively grown up child to other places of work, away from home. The workplace may be close to their homes or even in many cases far away from home requiring stay outside home for many weeks or even many months. The frequency of home visit, however, depends on the distance, transportation and on magnitude of child labour income. Poor parents, even if they are poor, generally do not like to send their younger children to work outside. Gender of the child is also a determining factor in the nature of job, they undertake. Girl children are always at the receiving end of educational opportunities. School completion rate is comparatively less than that of the boys. The reason for school withdrawal of daughters is their engagement with kitchen work, which is gender determined task in families. Girls are generally not sent for outside paid work, even in the worst situation of poverty. We will explore this connection in our study.

SCHOOLING CHARACTERISTICS

Schooling participation has all along been our point of query. We are not only interested to find the school participation rate of the children but also the gender aspect of this. School availability within the precincts of the village, where children need not take too much stride to attend school, is to be ensured. This is most crucial particularly for an area which is poverty-ridden in the one hand and presence of irresistible pull of work in tobacco processing on the other. Distance of the school from the house of the school does matter in areas where transportation is altogether absent and children have to take long hours to reach to and return from school. Continuation of schooling in this case is threatened by high cost of child time. Spending time for schooling is a costly option where remunerative work for children is available around the vicinity. We have calculated the distance of school from the homes. We have included formal school as well as informal school such as SSK and MSK. Truancy sometimes leads to dropout if the former recurs off and on. We are also interested to look into the school attendance of the children and its possible connection without child labour engagement.

ACADEMIC COMPETENCY OF STUDENTS

Quantity and quality debate in educational participation of children in India is an area of interest. The general perception is that and is logically grounded also, that quantity and quality do not move in the same direction with each other. It means, in the jargon of economics, that there is a trade off between quality and quantity. Quality of education has to be sacrificed when quantity is pursued vigorously and *vice versa*. There has been a spectacular expansion in elementary education in recent years. Enrolment and retention have gone up manifold. *Sarva Sikhsa Abhiyan* (SSA) as a centrally sponsored programme to implement Education for All (EEA) in India has taken up the daunting task to bring all children to school. Positive outcomes are surfacing up. There is, evidently, a quantum jump in school attendance. But what is missing in the crowd of numbers, is quality. Despite pedagogic innovation, infrastructure enhancement provision of many facilities, teachers training, learning competency is taking a back seat. Many studies in recent years, have pointed out this grey spot in the stride for educational expansion. Supplemental tuition is now making a difference. Poor parent cannot afford private tuition for their children. Poverty and poor quality of education seem to be linked to each other. We try to explore in our study, the linkage between household affluence, supplemental tuition and school competency.

CATEGORIES OF CHILDREN

Mutually Exclusive but Collectively Exhaustive

Our dependent variable is child status not child labour as such. We want to look at different combinations of situation in which children are placed. Children in a rural setting combine schooling with paid work. Not all children are engaged in full time work, many of them may be part-time workers. We want to reveal the entire situation. Therefore, we must consider many probable pairs. Each pair is mutually exclusive but collectively exhaustive. Its means no other combination can emerge where all the possible pairs are tried and exhausted. Multinational logistic regression technique will be used to find the impact of all explanatory variables considered for the present investigation. We are interested to see that factors primary responsible for situating children in a particular situation. One group of children may be full time student and they do not undertake any work. Other group may be doing part time job, in the morning or in the evening but attending school. The other group of children may be full time child labour and do not go to school. We will consider five pairs of different situations of combination. A child can belong to any one of this pairs.

INVESTIGATING

Localisation of Home-based Tobacco Work

Economists across the globe had engaged themselves in finding the causes of regional concentration of certain type of economic activity. The question that stirred many inquisitive minds is why a particular means of livelihood persists for last many years in a particular geographical area. The economic theories on industrial development say that industries come up and flourish in an area where they can find optimal backward and forward linkages. Industries produce output by using inputs of all kinds in a bid to sell in the market. Output must be sold at a price that must include a portion called profit as an incentive for the industrialist or the enterprisers to continue with the business. The location of industries and of any manufacturing units is determined by the consideration of profit in a market economy. In a controlled economy however the state enterprises come up in places chosen by the state. The mixed economy, as of ours, contains many elements of both these opposite economic system. Private industrialists do not have a free hand. They are reined in by licensing system adopted in the industrial policies which declares that purpose of industrialization, who ever accomplishes it, is for national development. Governments in mixed economic structure provide incentive in the form of tax exemption and subsidies to industrialist to set-up industries in areas where industries do not come up by market rules. A government strives for balanced regional development. Incentives sometimes attract investment. Costs significantly come down in the wake of showering of incentives.

Tobacco processing, in which a sizable work force comprises of children and women, is the means of livelihood in the area. This evokes a question, naturally, why this particular work is so widespread in that particular area? Are the people of that area especially deft in that work? Do the people acquire exclusive skills for that work through intergenerational transmission? Is the work is the exclusive domain of a certain caste or of a certain community in a caste-ridden society. One consideration that work, for coming up of any enterprise is the adequate availability of cheap raw-materials. Raw-materials may be produced in the same locality where enterprises are located. Sugar mills in India are located very close to sugarcane producing fields. The proximity of raw material source that prompts processing to come up in its vicinity does not apply in case of tobacco processing enterprises in our study area. Raw materials are sourced from far off places, mainly from North India states.

The other reason that makes a very strong ground for establishing manufacturing units is the proximity to market centres. Industries or so to say any business venture of manufacturing generally comes up near big railway stations or near ports for easy shipment at a lesser cost of their produce to different market centres. Transport and communication facilities that help in sourcing of raw materials as well as shipment of finished product are major consideration for establishments of manufacturing units. Our keen observations at the work places and survey over the villages did not find any big railway station, sea port or any other communication that can facilitate their transportation of input and output without any extra hassles or cost. A small railway station is not far from the villages. Goods train is visibly an important transportation of their produce. Villages are connected with motorable roads the health of which does not remain well through out the year. The rainy reason spells doom for the arterial roads connecting the villages. Adequate materials that should conform to the quality and standard requirement for strong, weather resistant and durable road, is never put to use. Lack of monitoring, absence of people's participation, neglect of the respective government departments and corruption from the beginning to the end is collectively responsible for the horrible plight or the road. Transportation and connectivity are there but not of any high mark to generate any cost efficiency.

Proximity to the source of raw materials and to the market centres do not seen to be a factor to reckon in explaining the prevalence of this work in the region under study. Poverty and illiteracy are factors to explain the immobility. People are not moving from one level of livelihood to better ones that goes with economic development over time. One tangible outcome of development is of course, the scaling of higher ladders of income receipts and employment prospects. People are stuck to the same occupation which is neither rewarding nor acceptable as a reasonable means of living. People in the study area are found to be seeking their livelihood in this enterprise for last many generations. How one can explain this 'sticking syndrome'. One can contentedly explain this phenomenon by invoking the argument of inherent skill for the particular processing, acquired from the childhood. A child grows in this work environment where she can observe the work of other member in the family from dawn to dusk. She picks it up easily. She catches hold of small implements before she catches pencil and slate. She learns different stages involved in tobacco processing before she learns alphabets. A child begins to join the work at very young age to help her parents. Particular dexterity in the work of vast magnitude of population inhabiting a particular area may work as a major cause of pervasiveness of a certain type of livelihood.

A grandfather might be a farmer in his working life. He might be tilling his land with obsolete implements, bullock driven plough, local variety of seed and a local market for produce dominated by middlemen. He would have found it difficult to feed all the mouths in the family. This is the picture of agrarian society characterized by subsistence living. State sponsored development was in its nascent stage. Public investment in building rural infrastructure was meagre or private investment in rural economy was hard to dream. The grand father's grand son is not supposed to lead the same life of subsistence. In the eventuality of constant or stagnant life and livelihood for a period of half a century, one can comfortable conclude that development process has not been initiated or there is no trickle down of the process for certain segment of population inhabiting certain area. Shifting of occupations, from low paid one to remunerative one is the positive symptom of development process over a considerable period of time. The history of economic development of advanced countries of the contemporary world teaches us this growth trajectory. Gradual shifting of occupations of people in their societies in the earlier phase of underdevelopment, a vast majority of people was dependent on agriculture. Poverty, malnutrition, death and diseases made lives miserable. With the passage of time people began to leave, in various stages, agriculture and joined industries in large number.

Urbanization and industrialization went side by side in the aftermath of industrial revolution. Industrialization brought about immense prosperity. People began to demand something else than food and manufactured goods. Service sector began to flourish. Service sector was more paying than the other two. Now, service sector absorbs more people than other two sectors in the affluent countries of the world. This is the natural process of economic development that results in such occupational shifting of work force. However, the stickiness of tobacco or processing work for last many generations speaks volume of occupational immobility of the area. The work is exploitative, informal, home-based, hazardous, low paying and detrimental to health. People still find the job as means of living that provides two square meals a day. They do not change this work nor are they able to do so. One reason for this immobility is the lack of any other skill that could place them some where else, in other less harmful but more remunerative job. The present job is highly acceptable as the work is home-based so the women and children need not move out of home. Women, particularly adjust this work with other household work which no other paid employment can offer. The work schedule is flexible that does not bind the family workers with fixed time during the day.

The field survey has enlightened us with a new aspect of connection of girls with home-based tobacco work. Skills in this particular work are obtained through inter-generational transmission and are learnt through hands-on training pays dividend for the girls. A girl is likely to be married off comfortably if she can demonstrate her skill in *beedi* rolling work. The prospective bride groom and his family are always in search of bride who excels in the work. The reason of this preference is the guaranteed hand of income. The girl who is going to join other family as daughter-in-law is expected to join the same work in her husband's family. Her entry as earning hand will augment family income of her new home. Matrimonial benefit out of the daughter's involvement in the work derails the girl's schooling attendance and academic achievement. There is thus a possibility that girls who attend school, concentrate on studies and achieve in schools are less likely to be married off. Parents out of fear not to miss the bus in right time discourage schooling of daughters and encourage work of girls in tobacco processing. Thus girl's involvement in home-based tobacco that we come across in course of our field survey in these villages is driven by the consideration of prospects of marriage. The boys join on part time basis to help families and to contribute to family income. Thus poverty, illiteracy, lack of alternative employment opportunities, easy access to this home-based job, specialised skill for the job, acquired through direct observation are some of the factors responsible for the perpetuation of this hazardous and exploitative work in these particular areas.

THE WORKING OF THE HOME-BASED UNITS : THE SUPPLY CHAIN

The finished products of these units are *beedis* known as poor men's cigars. Filtered or unfiltered cigarettes are beyond the reach of the poor. They take to *beedi* as cheaper alternative. Thus rural areas in India consume *beedi* more than the city areas reflecting a rural urban divide in the pattern of smoking of these tiny items excepting of course the *beedi* habits of large number of smokers in slum areas of cities. The production of these tiny objects, in the same way is undertaken in informal sector. Addiction to *beedi* for Indians and even for the South Asians in general goes back to a very long past. Tobacco or an intoxicating produce was brought to India from outside like many other crops including fruits and vegetables. Trading among the neighbouring countries and with distant lands, during the *Harappan* era helped this transfer of agricultural variety from one land to other. The cultivation of tobacco in India received a boost for its intoxicating ingredients. Tobacco, as a cash crop in India, began to be source of livelihood for many. The demand for *beedi* or an item of pleasurable consumption among the poor sections went on unhindered. Cigarettes, filtered as well as unfiltered, look quite differently from *beedi* although they satisfy their smokers in the same way. They differ in length, in shape as well as in colour. *Beedi* is smaller compared to cigarettes. The exterior of beedi is brownish as tobaccos dust is stuffed and rolled in dried *tendu* leaves. The cigarettes are white in appearance as it is rolled in paper. The former is hand made and is therefore labour intensive while the latter is machine-made and therefore capital intensive. Cigarette is manufactured in organized sector of industries while *beedi* is done mostly in unorganised home-based sector. The smell out of smoke from them also differs. The smoke from cigarette smells less obnoxious than that of *beedi*. The smoking of cigarette marks the sophistication and relative affluence, while that of *beedi* speaks of lower social positioning and weak economic standing. Workers of *beedi* are exposed to severe health hazards while the cigarette manufacturing is subject to protections, health benefits and insurance. Mechanized system of manufacturing that needs few human hands are obviously less hazardous. The most dangerous consequence of prolonged exposure to tobacco dust is lung infection that may lead to tuberculosis and breathing disorders. Cough and cold concomitant with intermittent fever are common among *beedi* workers. They do not have any protective gear, musk and any other means of protection from ill effects of tobacco.

THE PRDUCTION SYSTEM

Tendu leaves and tobacco dusts are raw materials for making *beedi*. Three items are supplied by the *Munshis* (agents of the company). There are various companies of different sizes and business turnover located in the *Aurangabad,* a small town in the *Jangipur* Sub-division of Murshidabad district. *Beedi* companies also abound in *Dhuliyan* and in *Raghunathganj* of the same sub-division. A few among them, namely, *Pataka beedi, Mrinalini beedi, Mother India beedi* are known brands. They have significant market presence in northern India as well as in the state of West Bengal. Companies buy those raw materials from outside state in bulk and bring it through railway transport to their go down or storages. *Munshis* work as commission agents of the companies. They might also work as regular paid employee of the company. They procure the raw materials from the company stock to deliver at the door steps or the households. *Munshis* keep record of the households within their catchment areas. Families may not know the company for which they are working. They only know the *Munshis* with whom they make deal. *Munshis* work as conduit between the company and the workers. This remote linkage and indirect employment in the form of outsourcing of job help the companies to get rid of all liabilities to the workers.

Households own the capital equipments which are simple, inexpensive and few. They need scissors, tiny knives, boxes and wire nets. Scissors is used to cut the tendu leaves to give it proper size and shape. It will take a perpendicular shape. Tobacco dust of fixed amount is stuffed in to the cut leaves and it is rolled. The workers bind the rolled stick at a point half an inch away from one end with a thread. The stick may be two inches or one and half inches long. One end from which the smoker takes a puff must be sleek so that it can comfortably be placed between tow lips. A single *beedi* is thus made through these stages. A packet contains twenty to twenty five *beedis*. These packets are then bound by a cotton thread to prepare for roasting. The latter stages of work including roasting and labelling are undertaken by the companies. They get the work done by casual employees of the company. This finishing phase also can be carried out by home workers on payment of additional wage.

One can come across during a tour through the village this group work. Male worker of adjacent families congregate at an open space in the neighbourhood to begin their work for the day. They sit in a circle to finish last phase of work where they put the dust and roll. The cutting of leaves is done by women folk. There is thus a division of labour in the work pattern.

Each stage of the production process is taken care of by each member of the family. Members take it up as a family task. Responsibilities are shared. Each member even the younger one is concerned about the commitment to deliver the produce to the *Munshi* on a prefixed date. Members work according to their ability and strength. Women perform kitchen work; take care of young siblings and of elders and frail members. They obviously work in between these household tasks, taking up and adjusting the work schedule.

Production Chain

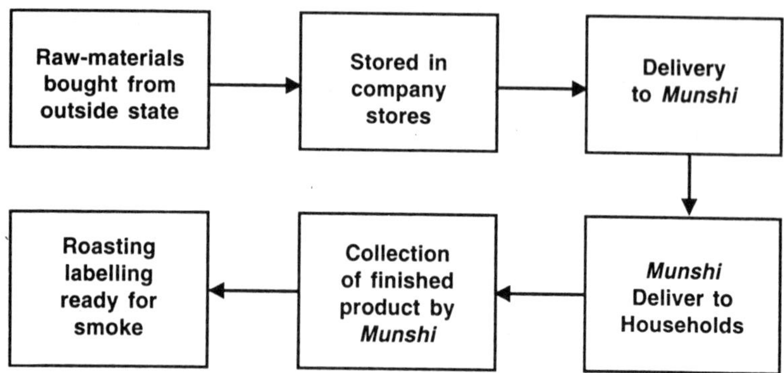

Source : Author's Field Observation.

Children take part in large numbers in the home-based production. They combine schooling with work and many of them are engaged in full time basis after dropping out from school. School continuation depends on circumstances, particularly the need for full time work.

The work with *beedi* is year-round unlike others which have a seasonal character. One can take a glimpse of the work site on a trip to these areas. Radio is placed in the centre around which all workers sit in the courtyard or in and open space in a rounded way. They work, as it appears, with the tune of Bengali music, emitting from a wrecked radio set. This inexpensive entertainment is supposed to tone down their drudgery. The music acts as energizer. The wage which contractor or *Munshi* pays to each household or to the adults of the household is paid as per rate decided and accepted mutually. The rate was low a few years ago. It has gone up after protest and movement by the workers. The wage is paid at the rate of Rs. 41 per one thousand of *beedis*. The adult members are enlisted as workers for what ever benefits the companies are compelled to provide for them. One noticeable achievement in recent years is of course the extension of provident fund to the enlisted adult workers. An amount of Rs. 4 is deducted from the piece rate for credit in P.F. account of the adult workers. The working age is fixed between 18 years at the minimum and 60 years at the maximum. Obviously, the official list of workers does not contain the names of children below eighteen and older members above sixty. The company needs not worry about below or above the stipulated age. Children and elderly people work actually in the enterprise but do not work officially.

Adult male members look for other jobs outside home. Children and women take charge of the *beedi* work at home. Adult males join the family work only when other jobs are not forthcoming. Family income depends along with other irregular and under remunerative sources, on the quantity of *beedi* produced. They, therefore, tend to take as much raw materials from the contractors sometimes beyond the capacity and availability of family labours. The acceptance of bulk order from the *Munshi* is driven by higher prospects of income. In this predicament of tight commitment, the adults would obviously engage all members including the young children. Children would not only be employed, they would be forced to work long hours to ensure completion of work. The plight of the women is even worse as they have to take care of kitchen and urgent household work. Income volatility and food insecurity may be reasons for such over work imposed on all members. But there are such households that may toe the same line to catch up with better life and consumerist consideration. Easy availability of the work, an irresistible urge to acquire, for the family, better gadgets, consumer durables and luxuries sometimes jointly causes the overwork.

6

Economy, People and Society : Exploring Linkages with Tobacco Work

The circumstances of the households trapped in this degradable but unavoidable source of living need detailed probing. We have seen in the last section, how this particular economic activity that provides bread and butter to thousand of vulnerable families in our study area is pervasive. We also need to know whether the areas which we have surveyed in course of our household visits are backward regions in the district which exhibits better human development results and satisfying social indicators. It may appear that the study areas are exceptions not the general picture which the district presents. We need to look at the place of the district of Murshidabad in the list of rankings of the districts in the state of West Bengal. The relative position of the district in economic and social performance will shed light on the state of poverty and general economic well-being of the district. However, at the end we see that our chosen villages are not exceptions but actually reflect the true picture of the vast rural landscape of the district. Rapid urbanization in a developing country is always associated with one vice that keeps on breeding and alters the demography in urban areas. Migration has become unstoppable every where particularly in third world countries where economic opportunities are sprouting in urban area and getting dried up in rural area. Migration does not seem to be a bothering issue in the district of Murshidabad.

Urban population comprises only 12 per cent of a total population size of 5.8 million. Urban population inhabits seven municipal towns and the rest of the people reside in 1925 villages in the district. The pace of urbanization here is far below the state average which stands at 28.03 per cent. The rural area is overpopulated even by the standard ratio estimated for the state of West Bengal. Population density measured by number of persons per square kilometre is 1102 in Murshidabad. The state average is 904. West Bengal stands at the top of all states and union territories in India for populating every inch of her land. Per capita land availability, measured by land man ratio is alarmingly low. Migration from neighbouring poor states and illegal migration from neighbouring country are invoked as a contributing factor in swelling the population size. The recent desire by the state governments to woo investors in establishing industries in West Bengal is dampened by the acute supply constraint of suitable land. The peasant's resistance to big industrial projects in recent time also points to the land crisis. Peasants are unwilling to part away with their cultivable land even rejecting handsome compensation offer in cash.

The apparent explosion of rural population in the district located in an already overpopulated state of India is a sign of distress. Overpopulation is likely to cause poverty which, in turn, is also the result of overpopulation. The National Sample Survey Organization, Government of India, had conducted Consumer Expenditure Survey in 2004-05 to estimate the level of living as a measure of poverty in India. They had computed Monthly Consumption Expenditure per head (MPCE) in rural as well as in urban India. The Average MPCE in the district of Murshidabad is Rs. 428 which is far below the state average of Rs. 562 and rural Indian average of Rs. 559. Among the districts in West Bengal, the district of Murshidabad tops the list in sheltering poor people. The NSS survey in this 61st round, finds that almost 56 per cent of rural people are poor. Population has gone up, between inter-census period, 1991-2001 by 23.70 per cent. This is decadal growth rate of population in the district. The average annual growth rate thus stands at 2.37 per cent which is far above the national annual growth rate of 1.80 per cent. Many people, in course of our informal conversation with them, aired their anxiety over uncontrolled influx of people from across the border. Crossing of border, they allege, is easy now. Inter-state migration is also a big issue that is also causing the abnormal growth of population. This will continue to go on unchecked in a situation where disparities of development persist. Poverty is acute somewhere and less severe elsewhere. Migration in search of livelihood from one poverty region to other is a common occurrence. This appears to hold good in our study area.

EDUCATION

The positive contribution of education is immense. Education is the driver of development. Education does not only mean attainment of literacy and enrolment. It implies something more than the enrolment figure, school infrastructure and the literacy rate. Education is a process that results in effective learning, understanding and assimilation. Education enhances skill. Education is therefore regarded as most crucial public investment for human capital formation. An educated person can contribute to national economic development through his productive participation. Delivery mechanism of public education is therefore a crucial task. The outcome of education delivery is reflected in adult literacy rate. Female literacy is widely accepted as the best indicator of social development. Education of mothers is always associated with lower facility, child nutrition, child care and girls education. Many positive outcome and positive externality are associated with female education. We will look into literacy attainment, particularly of female literacy of the district of Murshidabad. We then compare this attainment with the same of the state of West Bengal.

The rate of adult literacy in the state of West Bengal is 68.6 per cent. The same is 54.3 per cent in the district of Murshidabad. We get these figures from the 2001 census. Thus the district lags behind the state average by 14.30 percentage points in literacy attainment. Educational backwardness is therefore a serious issue of concern. Murshidabad, Maldah and Uttar Dinajpur collectively make the dark zone in the education in West Bengal's landscape. Fight against illiteracy is still in its nascent stage. We have many miles to go to raise this rate at least to the state average. The performance of this state in literacy achievement as revealed by census of 2001 is far below satisfactory and just close to national average. West Bengal's position in the middle of the list of states arranged in ascending order of literacy does not go with her image as a historical site for education and culture. The performance of this district within this 'mediocre' state is visibly dismal. Let us now look at female literacy and compare it with the state of West Bengal. Female literacy is 47.60 per cent here in Murshidabad. The same, for the state of West Bengal, is 59.60. Thus, the district here also lags behind by 12 percentage points from the state average.

Deficiency of infrastructure in the delivery of education can adversely affect the educational outcome. Literacy for general as well as for female is the visible result of educational process. Physical infrastructure, particularly the school building forms the initial edifice of this infrastructural build up. Lack of such infrastructure speaks volume of government neglect of this crucial area of human development. Number of schools should be adequate to serve the children. We take the subject of primary education of the district to gauge the adequacy of schools compared with the state as a whole. The statistical abstract released by the Department of Statistics and Applied Economics, Government of West Bengal, released in 2004 furnishes the data on number of primary schools and the number of primary students currently enrolled. We find that there is one primary school for 259 primary students in Murshidabad district. For the state of West Bengal, there is one primary school for 180 primary students. This is one indicator of infrastructural shortfall: inadequacy of primary schools. The district is lagging behind the state in providing enough primary schools for their primary school going children.

ECONOMY AND EMPLOYMENT

Predominance of rural population in the demographic pattern of the district is an indication of persistence of informal and rural economy. Big industrial projects did not come up here. Manufacturing enterprises in the organized sector are few and far between. One exception is the Farakka Thermal Power Project that came into being at one end of the district. It does not have spread effect so to speak in promoting industrialization of the adjacent areas. Thermal project is manned by skilled and highly trained technical persons. Most of them are from outside the district and from other states also. Thus the employment effect of this big project is conspicuously unobservable. The project has failed to create ancillary and down stream enterprises in and around the district. The agrarian economy is facing constraint of different kind. Public investment in irrigation as well as rural road is not adequate: Paddy, Jute, Potato and vegetables are principal agricultural crops. Only 28 per cent of the total cultivable area is under irrigation. Thus initiative to raise productivity in agriculture by investment in irrigation is of urgent necessity.

Small holding is a formidable impediment to growth in agricultural productivity. Rising input prices especially the escalating cost of diesel to run pump set for irrigation turn the agricultural operation into an unviable economic activity. Mechanized tools such as tractor or thrasher can not be put to use in tiny land. Small plots can be irrigated through the system of paying user's fees. In the absence of such pay and use water projects in the vicinity, the farmers have two options. They can install pump set on their own. The second one is to allow their tiny plots to go dry until monsoon rain waters their lands. The first option can easily be ruled out as the small peasants can not afford the capital cost as well as operation cost.

Many small peasants were benefited by state government land distribution from the land pool created through surplus land grabbed from big farmers by implementing rural land ceiling act. A large section of landless agricultural families were endowed with new bounty of land under the auspices of the state. The rank of small holding agricultural families swelled shortly thereafter. This was hailed by many as silent revolution poised for radical change in rural power structure as well as impending economic well-being of the majority of rural people. This radical measure was expected to bring about reduction of poverty and inequality. The bestowal of land rights to a large number of rural masses thirty years ago is failing now to bestow the benefits as was expected. Many such land assignee holdings are on the verge of extinction now and many of them had already left the farming. They had parted with their land out of distress. Land reforms measure by the state government was hailed as a radical step towards socialist practice. 'Land to the tillers' became a catchphrase when government distributed surplus land to the landless families in West Bengal. The main objective was to raise the standard of living of the poorest of the poor in the agrarian society. They become landed farmer decades ago only to slip into depth of landlessness after a couple of decades.

A little less than one half of the working population of Murshidabad (46%) is engaged in agriculture as principal as well as subsidiary activity. Out of a total working population of 2 million, 18 per cent are cultivators. Cultivators, according to census definition, own and cultivate lands to raise agricultural produce. Agricultural labourers, who constitute the lowest rung in the order of destitution, comprise 28 per cent of the total working population in the district. The class of agricultural labourers have already been swelled manifold during last many years. The figure, refereed for them relates to census 2001 which has already become a little outdated. We have no other alternatives, right now at the moment, to replace the census date. The magnitude of agricultural labourers has gone up, by quite a high proportion from 1991 to 2001 in West Bengal. Farmers are increasingly joining the horde of agricultural labourers after parting with their land; they were gifted with during the glorified land reform programme. The average holding size is 0.73 hectors in Murshidabad. Marginal and small farmers still comprise the largest category in the operational holdings category in the district. The predominance of small holdings, rare access to irrigation, rising input cost and marketing bottlenecks thus characterize the agricultural economy. The surplus labour in agriculture can hardly find alternative employment in non-agricultural enterprises which did not come by adequately to take them in.

INDUSTRY

Agricultural is the primary and dominant occupation of people at an early stage of economic development. The shifting of occupation from agriculture to industry and from there to service sector is a gradual process in the trajectory of economic development process. Rich countries of contemporary world were primarily agrarian, a couple of centuries age. Development process is thus transformation of agrarian economy to industrial economy. One of the indicators of development is the share of employment in and share of income from agriculture in national income. The less is the share of agriculture and more of the share of industry and service is indicator of economic prosperity. The district of Murshidabad, by that account, is yet to be placed in growth path. Organized industries have no significant presence to employ a sizeable portion of surplus labour force in agriculture. However, household industries, mainly in unorganised sector, employ around 20 per cent of the working population. Work in *beedi* in which a massive number of workers are employed in home-based contract system of manufacturing is in informal sector. Their work is not regulated by act or inspection system to monitor work hours and wage of the home-based family workers.

Murshidabad which now cries for industries has a glorious industrial past. Her silk industry alone attracted East India Company to establish trading in the district. Good quality silk of Murshidabad had huge demand in England. Ivory and craft work by gifted artisans of this area drew applauses from different parts of India. Handicrafts and art work, that could be upgraded to meet the rising demand, had seen their gradual demise over a period of time that followed the onset of colonialism in India. The industrial revolution in England had adversely affected the growth of handicrafts and sericulture. The possibility of a vibrant indigenous industry that could herald the onset of industrial take-off from this part of Bengal was nipped in the bud. Government apathy and invasion of cheaper textiles from England brought about a devastation of the local economy. The horrible state of industrial expansion owes to much extent to the tragic past of imperial de-industrialisation design. Bell metal and Brass utensils are manufactured now at Khagra, Berhampore, Kandi as well as in Jangipur. But the impediments to their growth and expansion are quite formidable. Sourcing of raw materials for these struggling industries is problematic. Government does not, as it appears, come forward to facilitate easy and timely sourcing of raw-material.

Silk Sari, the object of pride and a treasure possession, is still produced despite various odds, by skilled entrepreneurs. It seems that a few artisans are still fighting their last battle. The skill which they have learnt from their earlier generations is put to use in making the immaculate sari for the relatively affluent sections and finds its limited market in Bengal. Their struggle for survival through seeking livelihood from this occupation is becoming very hard in the present circumstances of competition from cheap import. Synthetic silk sari now hits the local market. These inexpensive saris are being imported from neighbouring China. The opening of trade in the aftermath of liberalization has almost decimated the indigenous silk enterprise of the region. Availability of raw silk is seriously constrained by factors such as crop loss, ineffective pest control and overall government neglect in the production of the basic raw material. Silk industry is languishing, bell metal and brass industry is struggling for survival, iron chest industry is starved of raw material, modern electronic industry is yet to step in. Falling agriculture fails to sustain the growing population. Tobacco processing enterprise involving family labour has thus filled the vacuum. Tobacco companies are mushrooming to exploit the availability of cheap labour, particularly of children and women coupled with abysmal adult unemployment.

MURSHIDABAD AND HER HUMAN DEVELOPMENT PERFORMANCE

West Bengal Human Development Report, published in 2004, in line with National Human Development for the entire country, is an eye opener. This is a welcome initiative by the state government to assess its own performance in all areas of human well-being. Income as a singular measure of wellbeing is out of currency now. Income is one aspect, not the entirety, to measure development. Development must result in enhancement of human capability, functioning and freedom of choice. Physical well-being and education should go hand in hand with rise in per capita income which means higher purchasing power that would enable people to command more goods and service for better life. Human development thus incorporates health, income and education. Health outcome is measured by life expectancy at birth, the average life span. Health index is the score the value of which lies between 0 to 1. The scores on education and income are obtained by same mechanism. The state report not only contains the performance of the state on each of these fields but also ranks the districts in order of performance. The report presents scores of seventeen states as the district of Dinajpur was not divided during the preparation of the report. Human Development Index (HDI) is the composite or aggregate of Health, Income and Education Index. Murshidabad stands at 15 in the set of 17 districts in West Bengal HDI outcome.

The HDI score for the state of West Bengal is 0.61 and that of Murshidabad is 0.46. The horrible performance of the district puts it in the company of worst performers in human development outcomes. Let us look at its performance in each field separately. The score in health index for the state of West Bengal is 0.70 and for the district the same is 0.57. The health score speaks a lot about precarious health delivery system prevailing in the district. The score in income index for the district is 0.29 as against 0.43 for the entire state. Income index is same measure of poverty. The low score thus indicates general economic adversity in the district under study. West Bengal is a middle order state in the national ranking in order of per capita income. The state score of 0.43 in income index place her at 18th position in the ranking of 35 states. The performance of the state in the field of income generation is far below the satisfactory level compared to many other affluent states like Punjab, Haryana, Gujarat and Maharashtra. The state of West Bengal used to be in the top rank in income, in literary as well as in industrialization during fifties and sixties. The down sliding of the state in the areas of human development seems to be unstoppable. The situation of poverty in the district of Murshidabad needs no separate emphasis. The ranking in the lowest order in a state where poverty is pervasive speaks volume of its utter economic distress.

Education is the most crucial obverse of human development process. Illiteracy and poverty go hand in hand. Low income countries are characterized by widespread illiteracy. This linkage is present everywhere. Many regions within a developing country are lagging behind in certain aspects compared to what the country herself fares on national scale. The grey areas of the landscape are those laggard regions where illiteracy and poverty are persisting for quite some times. The inefficacy of anti-poverty programme is quite evident over there. These areas may be inhabited by indigenous people or ethnic people who are far off the mainstream. There are the dark areas where rays of development have failed to penetrate. The regional growth imbalance and lopsided growth are features of many developing countries. These economic ills also affect India. Incidence of poverty and illiteracy varies from state to state as well as varies from one area to other area within the same state. For example, the district of Darjeeling in North Bengal obtains a score of 0.72 in education index, the state of West Bengal obtains 0.69 and Murshidabad district receives a score of 0.52. The score of the district is far below the state average. Taking the three areas of human development, income, health, education, the HDI score of Murshidabad is 0.46, the state score is 0.61. The backwardness of the district has been brought forward by human development report.

FALL BACK ON BEEDI

Beedi the brownish local cigar, are made for the relatively poor, that goes into their essential consumption basket. The item of addiction, a cheaper alternative to branded cigarettes, and an object for pleasure for the poor is also offered to a visitor as a sign of welcome in many rural communities. The unique feature of *beedi*, which differentiate it from many other items of mass consumption, is that it is made for as well as made by underdogs in the society. This item is consumed as well as made by the lower rung of economic categories. Thus involvement of people in making the item depends on economic predicament. Beedi is the overwhelming economic activity, dominant sources of livelihood, in the district under study. As per the district statistical handbook of the district for 2006, three lakh (0.3 million) workers are employed in home-based *beedi* processing. Only 2846 people work in *beedi* companies. There are 55 *beedi* companies in the district who are, to much extent, subject to government regulation regarding safety and wage payment. Individual employers, the number of which is as many as 510 as per the district statistical hand book enjoys more freedom to exploit the workers as they are immune from any act legislated for the workers of the formal company.

THE LOCALE SELECTED

The district of Murshidabad in which our survey area is located is divided in to five sub-divisions. A cluster of community development Blocks makes a sub-division, the second tier in the administrative hierarchy of a district. Development blocks are now synonymous with *Panchayat Samiti* in the aftermath of the introduction of three tier Panchayat system in West Bengal during late seventies. We have focused our study on Jangipur, the sub-division located in north western part of the district and the hub of *beedi* industry. All most all *beedi* companies have set-up their operations in the sub-division. The pervasiveness of tobacco processing is more intense here in the sub-division than any other sub-divisions of the district. We have selected six blocks

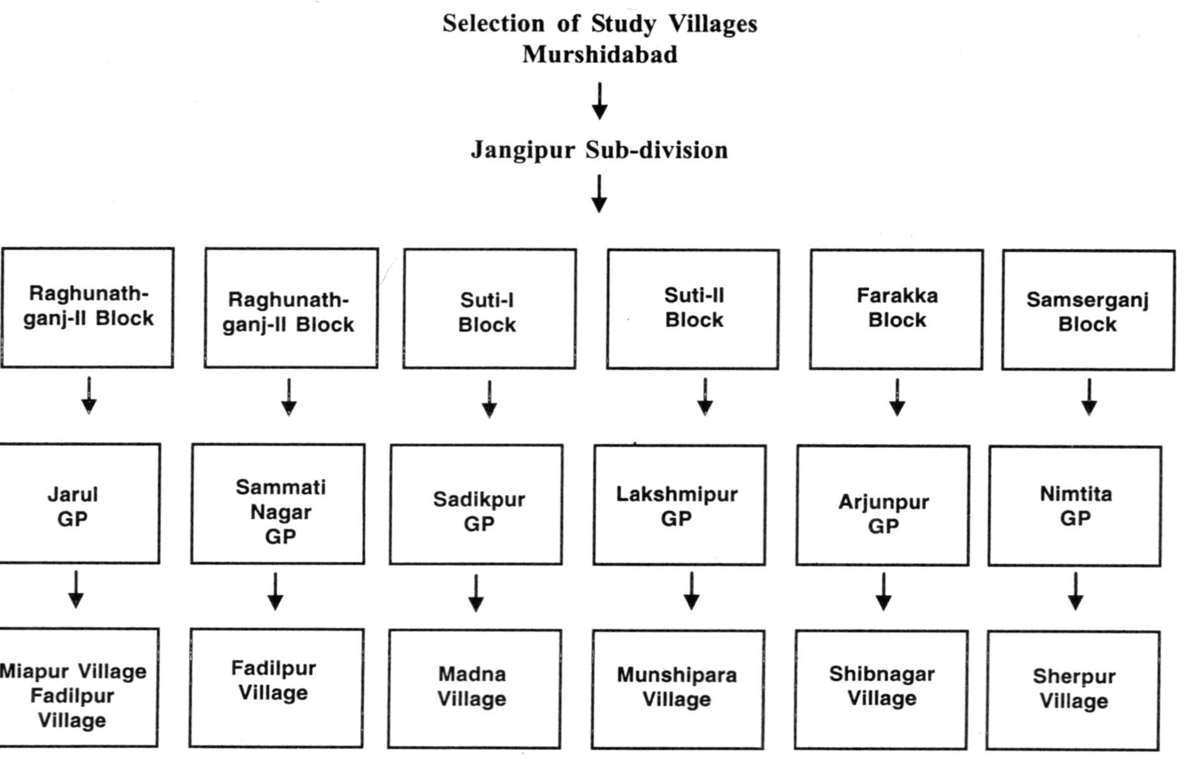

Selection of Study Villages
Murshidabad
Jangipur Sub-division
Raghunath-ganj-II Block
Raghunath-ganj-II Block
Suti-I Block
Suti-II Block
Farakka Block
Samserganj Block
Jarul GP
Sammati Nagar GP
Sadikpur GP
Lakshmipur GP
Arjunpur GP
Nimtita GP
Miapur Village Fadilpur Village
Fadilpur Village
Madna Village
Munshipara Village
Shibnagar Village
Sherpur Village

in the sub division, namely, *Raghunathganj-I Raghunathganj-II, Suti-I, Suti-II, Farakka* and *Samserganj*. A block or Panchayat Samiti is constituted of a number of Gram Panchayats (G.P.). The third-tier in the Panchayat system is Gram Panchayat which is, in turn, is formed by elected representative from gram sangsad, the grass root constituency of rural voters. We have selected a gram Panchayat from each of the blocks of the sub division of Jangipur. The foregoing chart describes the selection of study village.

The selection of the study villages were thus done on multistage sampling on random basis. The sub division, Jangipur, was selected for the highest concentration of home-based manufacturing of *beedi* as a first stage. One G.P. from each block was selected at random in the second stage. In third stage, one village was similarly selected at random from each of the G.Ps. Thus the selected villages are taken up for our intensive household survey.

SELECTION OF HOUSEHOLDS

Household is the ultimate unit of our study. Children are raised in household settings and they join family enterprises at different level of their childhood growth. A child may undertake *beedi* processing at very young age or other may join at relatively grown up stage. Joining and intensity of involvement in the work obviously depend on family circumstances which may differ at micro-level. Poverty persists in the area under our study. Many economic ills would come to sight to any visitor paying a casual visit to those places. One need not take recourse to quantitative poverty measurement to verify one's reading about the locality and economic unwellness. Still economic adversities are not same for all households. A few are better-off relatively speaking than others who are relatively worse-off. A few families might have many mouths to feed and a few may not. Two households in the same neighbourhood may have received same income. Still poverty might well differ between these two hypothetical families. Family size causes the variation in the intensity of poverty. Per capita income pertaining to a household does matter than gross family income. Studies on child labour, therefore, focus on family size and fertility along with family income as proximate determinant of child labour. Thus how many and when the children of a particular age join beedi work depend on household economic circumstances.

TABLE 6.1
Household Selection

Villages	*No. of Households*	*No. of Children 6-14 years*	*Average Children per Household*
Miapur	163	317	1.94
Fadilpur	187	376	2.01
Madna	259	588	2.27
Munshipara	265	585	2.20
Shibnagar	194	409	2.10
Sherpur	156	385	2.47
Total	1224	2660	2.17

Source : Household Survey in Murshidabad in 2008.

We did not include, firstly, the households without any children. We had excluded households with all children more than 14 years old as well as households without any children aged six years, we have considered only children's households whose magnitude would obviously falls short of total households living in each village. Thus a children household means any household having at least one child from 6 to 14 years old. We have excluded children below six years as they do take part neither in work nor in school in the villages.

We did not include children above 14 years old because our objective of the present research is to investigate the situation of child labour in tobacco processing. The most prominent anti-child labour in India is Child Labour (Prohibition and Regulation Act) of 1986. The act spells out that child labourers are children who have not completed their fourteenth birth day. Put in other words, the Act prohibits and regulates of certain kind of works for children who are below

14 years of age. The upper age of 14 years is also the age by the time of which a child is supposed to complete elementary education. Our enquiry relates to child labour and therefore we have set the age in conformity with child labour act as well as the age of completion of elementary education. In the beginning, on completion of selection of villages, we made a list of households for each village. The listing was done through household visit. During listing stage, the name of the head of the household and age of each child of the household were recorded to prepare a final list for household survey. We prepared the list of all children households of the six study villagers. Every second household from the list was taken up for household survey.

SURVEY TOOLS

The questionnaire for recording the data from the household head was developed after consulting similar research studies, seeking opinion and comments from scholars who had a longstanding research experiences on child labour, woman's labour, home-based economic activities and informal sector employment. The comprehensiveness of our questionnaire leaves very little room for leaving out vital information about the household that are related to child labour exploitation. The questionnaire has three segments: children characteristics, parental characteristics and family characteristics. All attributes of children, related to children's possible involvement of family-based work in *beedi* are included for canvassing. Ages, religion, caste, sex, schooling, attendance rate, score in the examination, supplementary tuitions, are attributes that can influence children's participation in school as well as in work. We have included in the questionnaire the influencing attributes of parents. Single parenting, parental educational background, particularly of mothers. Parental occupations, ages of father and mothers, literacy level are recorded in the questionnaire. Family characteristics which include, per capita consumption expenditure, regularity of job, food security, membership of BPL category, family size, family structure, standard of living are incorporated in our survey questions. The draft questionnaire was canvassed on experimental basis for few households to locate any inconsistency in the question setting.

After scrutiny the final questionnaire was ready by April 2007. The household survey was conducted during 2007-08. We devoted much time for each household to elicit information from them. We did welcome their inquisition about the purpose of the survey. Many of them were reluctant to share with us any information about their families. A few aired their suspension and disgust about our project of the study on child labour. All inhibition in the beginning disappeared very quickly after the candid disclosure of our purpose. We made a frank admission to the villagers that our purpose is research. We were not working on behalf of government agency or organization working for any NGO. We let them know that we are from university and amazingly they were convinced. The co-operation from them unexpectedly came by spontaneously. We could befriend them easily. We preferred that the head of the household must be joined by other family members while responding our question. We tried to make sure that the answers received from the household head can be verified or cross-checked by other members. This joint sitting reduced the possibility of feeding us with wrong information. At the end of the day we used to scrutinize each filled in schedule to look for any inconsistent information. We would revisit the same household to verify any information.

TOOLS FOR ANALYSIS

Data collected from the survey were inserted into SPSS data editor after giving variable name, missing value and coding. SHAZAM Econometric Software is used to run logistic regression. Frequency distribution table is constructed for the variables. Correlation tool is used to find the strength of relationship between variables. Cross-tabulation with the variables is conducted to see the relationship among them. We need to know, an important objective of the present research, what are the factors that causes child labour in the study area. This will be interesting to know why some households send their children to school instead of engaging them in *beedi* work at home. Many households might be doing just the opposite, engaging them in home-based *beedi* work. Interestingly, however, we find children combining work and schooling children may combine with schooling and idleness. The households supply child labour. The decision as to how a particular child in a household spends his or her time in different alternative options is made by the household itself. We assume that a typical household in the study area chooses amongst five mutually exclusive and collective exhaustive alternatives available to them.

These alternatives consists of (1) Full time schooling and no work, (2) Combining schooling and work, (3) Full time work and no schooling, (4) No work and no school, and (5) Part time work and idleness. Hence work means taking part in family-based *beedi* work. We are interested to know about what are factors that influence or cause the participation of children in *beedi* work. Specifically we are interested to know about factors that enhance the probability of a reference child to be placed in one of the five options stated above. This kind of household decision making process pertaining a child's belonging to any category warrants a multinomial choice model. The form of the choice equation and the method of estimation depend on the distribution assumption on the errors. Assuming that the errors have a logistic distribution, the appropriate technique for the estimation of the choice equation is the multinomial logit. The probabilities in the multinomial logit model are given by.

$$\text{Prob }(Y_i/x_i) = \frac{e^{\beta} j_i^x}{1+\sum_{k=1}^{j} e^{\beta} k_i^x}$$

$$\text{Prob }(Y = 0) \quad \frac{1}{1+\sum_{k=1}^{j} e^{\beta'} k_i^x} \quad \text{for } j = 0, 1, 2, 3 \qquad (1)$$

where x is the vector of explanatory variables and the co-efficients β', are normalized to zero. Normalizing the co-efficients of one of the choices to zero identifies the multinomial logit model. The co-efficients in our model are difficult to interpret because they only provide information on the effects of independent variable on the odd ratio. To interpret the effect of the independent variables on the probabilities of each choice, we calculate partial derivations.

$$\frac{\partial p}{\partial x} = P_j(1-P_j)\ \beta\ P_j\ P_k\ \beta_{xk} \text{ where } j,\ k = 0,\ 1,\ 2,\ 3 \tag{2}$$

Hence P is the probability of participation in each alternative.

The log-likelihood can be derived by defining for each individual, d_{ij} = 1 if alternative j is chosen by individual *i*, and O if not for the J-l possible outcomes. Then for each *i*, one and only one of the d_{ij}'s is l. The log likelihood is a generalization of that logit model.

$$\ln L = \sum_{i=1}^{n}\sum_{j=0}^{j} d_{ij} \text{ In Prob } (y_i = d_j) \tag{3}$$

SITUATING CHILDREN IN FAMILY FEATURES

Children are born to and raised in families. Family as a grass root social unit is more of social institution than an economic organization that produces as well as uses labour power. Family is composed of members related with each other by biological connection. Family may be a nuclear unit which is very tiny and consists of parents and the off springs. Grand parents and cousins are non-members of this unit excepting infrequent visits on certain occasions. Child well-being is intimately connected with family structure which means that a child from nuclear family may receive a few benefits and also suffer on many counts for the particular family setting. A child in nuclear family is evidently better placed by way of better nutrition, medical care and education. Family size facilitates better child care and investment on children as smaller size results in higher per capita income provided that family income does not fall. Family expenditure on children obviously goes up because of fewer children to take care of. Joint family system does not permit the adult earner to spend only on their offspring. They have to take care of other children in the same family who are not their biological descendents. Joint family or extended family is a bigger institution in India that is based on earthen values and principles. Sharing of prosperity as well as of adversity is the edifice or principle of the system. There are many things in common between joint family system and the primitive communism of our ancestors. Primitive communism is a phase in the evolution of human civilization that did not allow a accumulation of private wealth. Every single member will work according to his ability and will get according to his need. Joint family system appears to be one such commune where incapables need not suffer as a consequence of their incapability. They would get everything that is needed for minimum human existence. It does not matter whether they earn or not. The head of the joint family, the patriarch, who happens to be the senior most members, is at the helm of affairs of the family. Generally members can not raise personal wealth. Income of individual members is deposited to the head who handle the family finance. He decides on spending in the sprit of altruism. The weak members are placed on equal footing with strong members. Such a system of family setting is analogous to a huge tree having many branches and sub-branches. The joint family system entails all kith and kin extending to distant cousins sharing a common family ethos and values. The number of family members is thus quite large in comparison to nuclear family. The members of the joint family share the distress equally and divide the happiness equitably. It means that: Poverty is evenly distributed and affluence is also evenly distributed. Children are beneficiaries in many aspects, of this extended bonding. The emotional support and collective care of the extended family act as psycho-social development input. Children of the nuclear family miss this collective support. Nuclear family emerged in the course of migration to urban areas in search of better living and in a bid to avail better opportunities of life. Migration to cities may also be caused by dire economic necessity. Whatever is the reason of leaving the joint family and take the uncharted course to a new and uncertain life in cities, children are prone to miss the collective support. Death or disappearance of either of the parents in a nuclear family brings disaster to the children. The protective shield of both parents to child is significantly weakened as a result of the mishap. Nuclear families settled in the city are cut off from the root of their ancestry in the far away villages. They are vulnerable in the absence of connectedness, present in the extended family structure. Loss of father is sure to have an adverse impact on children, particularly on boys. They have to take up job to support their sagging famiiy. Death of father heralds stoppage of income flow for the family where father was a major breadwinner. Boys rather than girls are put to income earning activities outside home.

The nature of work determines which gender among the children would replace father as earner. Girls are equally likely to undertake work if the courtyard of the home is the work site. Prevalent customs disallows girls, among certain communities to go outside for work. Education is the first casualty when a boy goes out for work to ensure two square meals a day. There are other occupational hazards to which the boy is exposed. Long hours of work imperil his health. Work with sharp tools and implements enhance the likelihood of physical injury. Lack of affordable health care support in the incidence of work-related accidents can cause childhood morbidity. Physical maltreatment and mental abuse by the employer can severely demoralize the child. Thus death of father can trigger a chain of violation of rights of the child. The childhood is derailed in the unsavoury eventuality of such death. The state must come forward in such tragic cases to protect the child from neglect and abuse. The nuclear family that loses is sole bread winner must not be allowed to sink in poverty. Income generation programme for such distressed families must get highest priority of the local government. This intervention could save the child from many such dangers.

Death, dissertation and disappearance of mother caused more harm to daughters than to sons in a nuclear family. Death of father brings about more economic harm than that of mother, excepting a few cases where mothers are already in work to supplement family income. Girls are more likely to take up domestic chores in the absence of mothers. The gendered division of work among family members prevails. Females take part in household work which is generally light in nature. They cook food, prepare vegetables, maintain sanitation and hygiene, wash utensils and take care of siblings and aged. Males in contrast undertake hard work which includes taking care of animal husbandry, out side wage work, on field farm work if the family owns cultivable land. When there is no adult female and that is quite obvious in a nuclear family girls have to fill the vacuum left behind by the departed soul. The immediate casualty in the life of the girl is the stoppage of schooling. She has to undertake all responsibility as her mother used to take up. Everything is lost out in her life all on a sudden. The kitchen work is extremely hazardous. The girls of tender age have to handle with fire and they are exposed to smoke. Her care and protection disappears over night. Thus a single parent family poses immense harm to children.

FAMILY STRUCTURE AND CHILDHOOD ADVERSITIES

We need to investigate the possible connection between family structure and childhood situation for our study area. We have come across three types of family structures in the study villages: single parent, nuclear and joint. Advantages and disadvantages of these three types of family constitution have been already outlined in the previous section. Single

TABLE 6.2
Family Structure in the Villages

Structure of the family	*Frequency*	*Percent*	*Cumulative Percent*
Single parent	35	1.3	1.3
Nuclear	927	34.8	36.2
Joint	1698	63.8	100.0
Total	2660	100.0	

Source : Household Survey in Murshidabad in 2008.

parent families are relatively few in our study area. They are altogether 35 children who hail from single parent family and they constitute a meagre 1.3 per cent of total children. A total of 927 children belong to nuclear families. The majority of them, as high as 1698, belong to joint family.

Family is synonymous with household in this analysis. Membership to kitchen or sharing a kitchen by the individual member is the differentiating factor. The joint family constitutes of a little conglomeration of splinter family units who collectively share the single kitchen for all of them. This may also be a small collection of single families bound by close kinship survive on food prepared in the common kitchen sharing a common kitchen by all members of the extended family implies participation by all members in the all housekeeping activities. Continuation of such way of collective living is an indication of the presence of mutual understanding and sense of solidarity among all members of the big family. Children are in safe heaven in a joint family system as they do not miss the protection in the absence of biological parents. There is still a predominance of joint family system in the village landscape. Urban living is rather associated with nuclear family system. Urbanization which creates employment in industries and in service sector encourages migration. Thus migrant families that constitute a huge share in the urban population are evidently nuclear. Thus the village landscape is dotted more with joint family structure. The villages in India still retain some of the features of India's traditional social organization that foster collective living and community bonding.

We have tried a different kind of connection between family structure and food security pertaining to children. Children may skip food in certain situation when the family faces the severest food crisis. While adult members, sometimes, skip food in a particular day to feed the hungry mouths of the children. Regular access to food by the children is one of the most significant measures of children well-being. Food and nutrition are basis necessity for survival. Adequacy of nutritious food protects children form childhood malnutrition, preventable diseases, disability and many other childhood ailments. We need to see the connection of food availability of children and the structure of the family they belong.

The purpose is to discern any positive connection between family structure by passing poverty and the childhood hunger and starvation.

TABLE 6.3
Children Skipping Food and Structure of Family

	Structure of the family			*Total*
How many times	*Single parent*	*Nuclear*	*Joint*	
0	21	635	1115	1771
2	0	10	20	30
3	1	5	30	36
4	9	52	129	190
5	3	41	69	113
6	0	73	188	261
7	1	22	30	53
8	0	49	79	128
9	0	0	2	2
10	0	33	35	68
12	0	7	1	8
Total	35	927	1698	2660

Source : Household Survey in Murshidabad in 2008.

One interesting revelation from this cross tabulation is that food crisis for children are relatively acute in single parent family. We find that 60 per cent of children belonging to single parents did not skip food during last two weeks proceeding the day of the survey. We understand that food may be an important measure of child well-being. We did, as far as practicable in our field survey, put in much effort to talk to the children in private. Misreporting or under reporting can be ruled out in such an ambience where adults are no where around the child respondents. The information furnished by a particular child may also be verified by either of the parents present during the interview. This cross verification of information on as many items as possible can ensure accuracy of data. Thus in this particular instance, we took recourse to this technique. While a good number, 60 per cent of single parents did not miss the meal even for a single instance. The rest 40 per cent of children in this category of family had to skip food.

By contrast, a lower percentage of children, 31 per cent, in nuclear families had to skip food for some time during the preceding fort night. Thus children of nuclear families are more food-secure than the children of the single parent's families. Child care, especially child nutrition and food seems to be dependent on, to some extent, on the presence of both parents. Interestedly children of the joint family do not seem to be better placed in comparison to nuclear family children in having meals. Around 34 per cent of the children in joint family had to skip food, any time. Still they are more food secure than their counterparts in the single parent category.

FOOD ADEQUACY OF CHILDREN

We had meticulously observed dietary behaviour of the people of the study area. The culinary habits, recipes, the frequency of intake do not differ from those of the rest of the state. There is hardly any variation of Bengali food habit. Food here is defined as principal meals which consist of two square meals in a day, one during the lunch and the other during the dinner before going to bed. Our point of interest was the major meal not any other light food or snacks in between principal meals. Many children, as our survey finds, have to go without square meals a day instead of two.

We find that 68 children that constitute 2.56 of total had to skip 10 meals during the last period of 14 days during which they are supposed to take 28 meals. On the whole 889 out of 2660 a little more than one-third had to miss meal at least for once.

We have five child status relating to work and schooling. Full time child worker among the five categories is one most vulnerable state of children. They have to engage themselves

Chart of Children Skipping Meal

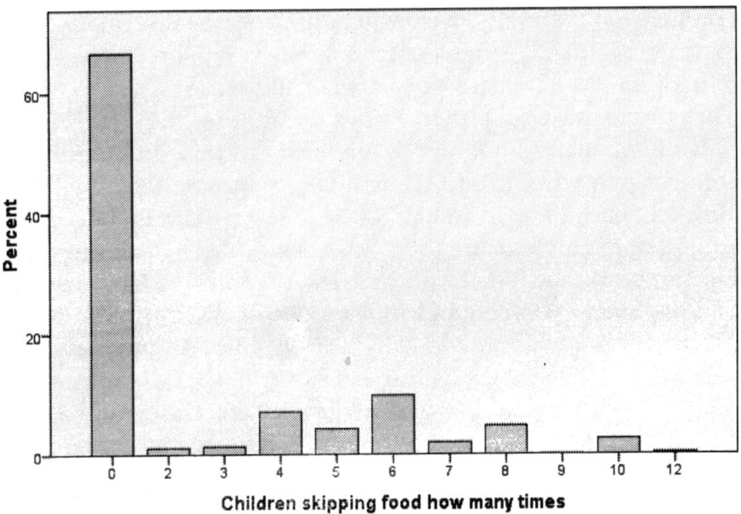

TABLE 6.4
Family Structure and Child Labour Participation

Structure of the family	*Child is not full-time worker*	*Child is full-time worker*	*Total*
single parent	33	2	35
Nuclear	830	97	927
Joint	1534	164	1698
Total	2397	263	2660

Source : Household Survey in Murshidabad in 2008.

for very long hours in tobacco work at home leaving no time for school and play. We may try to connect the incidence of full time working of children with the structure of family they belong to. We are interested to know particularly whether a certain structure of family has something to do with the engagement of children in full time work. The table displays that incidence of full time work is least at 5.71 per cent in single parent families.

The prevalence is highest at 10.46 per cent in nuclear families closely followed by 9 per cent in the case of joint families. One obvious reason for relatively smaller magnitude of child labour in single parent families is reluctance on the part of single parent to send their children for work outside. The single parent, either father or mother has to remain outside for many hours for wage work. In this situation if the children join work to supplement family income they might, in all likelihood, have to remain outside home. The home, in this situation, remains unattended. Any one of them must carry out kitchen work and others do household chores to keep the pot boiling. Single parents tend to keep one or more child at home to take care of household. Nuclear families do not have the constraint to keep their children at home. Either of the parents, mostly mothers take care of domestic work. Mothers do adjust their work schedules to take part in *beedi* work at home. Easy access to paid work is the reason that pulls all working hands in this work. There is hardly any mother in the study area who does not take part in this remunerative work. Hours and load of work, however, may substantially vary. This work for many families is the means for survival. There are some instances that we came across during our field visit that purchase of luxury items, in place of necessities, is the motive behind joining this work. For example, purchase of a coloured TV sets or new jewellery can be motivating factor.

EDUCATIONAL PARTICIPATION AND FAMILY STRUCTURE

Our next issue of interest is exploring any possible connection between family structure and educational process as well as outcome for children. Many children among our child population of 2660 are not in school. They are not in school now which does not mean that they were never in school. Many of them were in school but had dropped out in course of time in the past. Most unfortunate among the broad category of out of school are those children who had never enrolled in schools. Our survey finds that out of 2660 children, 438 are out of school. Thus around 16 per cent of children in our study villages are deprived of schooling. We may start with finding connection between access to schooling and family structure. The objective of this exercise is to find whether any particular type of a family can significantly influence school participation of children. Apparently children born to joint family are more likely to attend school as they do not need to partake in domestic chores that significantly prohibit school attendance. Other members in the joint family can free the children from the work by taking up themselves those responsibilities. Thus jointly family settings obviously create a favourable condition for children's school participation.

The favourable condition that suppose to be working in favour of schooling does not seen to make any mark in our study villages. Our survey reveals that 6 per cent of nuclear family children do not attend school while the magnitude is 5 per cent for joint families. There must be other reason than prevalence of favourable condition of extended family to explain school participation. School participation is rather interestingly high in single parent family which obviously lack the favourable condition in other family settings. One factor that works beyond family structure is the location of the school. This means that children tend to continue in school despite many other adversities if the school is housed in the close vicinity of their homes. This locational advantage favourably work by saving time as well as spending less energy on strenuous walking to distant schools. Academic environment, specific to a school can also make a difference. Children sometimes feel comfortable and they enjoy the teaching learning process in schools. This positive factor outweighs the negative aspect of the absence of encouraging condition in singular parent family. This reason along with others may cause the situation where only 8 per cent of children of the single parent families do not go to school. Mid-day meal scheme has been found in many research studies to have positive impact on school attendance. Thus cooked food served during school hours to children might have an overriding impact.

Table 6.5
Family Structure and School Participation of Children

Structure of the family	*Not in School*	*In school*	*Total*
Single parent	3	32	35
Nucler	169	758	927
Joint	266	1432	1698
Total	438	2222	2660

Source : Household Survey in Murshidabad in 2008.

School attendance is the basic imperative for learning. Children must go to school regularly. This is an essential part from the side of the pupil. Frequent truancy may result in school drop-out at the end. Learning process is derailed when children bunk school. We have explored this aspect and have tried to link this behaviour with the family structure. We have

Table 6.6
Family Structure and School Attendance of Children

Days of attendance	*Single parent*	*Nuclear*	*Joint*	*Total*
0	0	0	1	1
3	0	0	1	1
4	0	1	3	4
5	2	4	11	17
6	3	14	45	62
7	0	62	84	146
8	7	184	366	557
9	9	238	398	645
10	9	217	456	682
11	2	36	64	102
12	0	2	4	6
Total	32	758	1433	2223

Source : Household Survey in Murshidabad in 2008.

focused on last two weeks preceding the date of survey as measure. We are interested to know how many days a particular child had attended school during last twelve working days.

School absenteeism is a regular feature across the three types of families. Al though we find only one child who did not attend even for a single day during last twelve days. Only 6 children out of a total student size of 2222 had remained present on all days during last twelve days. Majority of students had attended 10 days and this trend is almost uniformly distributed. Thus we fail to find any significant correlation between structure and school attendance children remain present on most of the days of the work.

TABLE 6.7
Academic Performance of Children and Family Structure

Score	*Structure of the family*			*Total*
	Single parent	*Nuclear*	*Joint*	
A	2	54	75	131
B	15	438	758	1211
C	11	226	484	721
D	4	40	115	159
Total	32	758	1432	2222

Source : Household Survey in Murshidabad in 2008.

Students are expected to learn in the educational process. They learn literacy from the very beginning to face and flourish in the literate world. Literacy thus opens the access to knowledge and key to development and skill. Numerical ability and social studies are equally important for the student who aspires to gain knowledge. Academic achievement is thus the reflection of gain in learning. Students are expected to learn whatever was taught to them through schooling. Educational process involves investment which should result in positive return. Education is now accepted as investment for human resource development. Governments see it as opportunity for future growth of the country by producing educated and skilled citizens. Poor countries can not go too far in spending public money for expansion and improvement of education. The resource crunches forbid them to do so. Still what ever they spend on public education, particularly on elementary education should be met with positive outcome. Children must learn in successive grades of schooling. They must receive proper training, gain knowledge, creativity and understanding through the entire process. The entire investment or the spending of public money goes down the drain if they do not learn properly. It would be a wasteful expenditure for a poor country if the benefits are not forthcoming. Regular assessment of competency is an integral part of education delivery system. We have also tried to link the performance of children in the survey area with the family settings. Children of the single parent have performed worst in this measure of educational outcome. Around 12 per cent of children in this family setting have obtained 'D' grade, the lowest score in the ladder of performance. The same is 5 per cent for the nuclear families and slightly higher at 8 per cent for joint family children.

RELIGION AND CASTE AFFECTATION

The study villages are predominantly Muslim in congruity with the demographic pattern of the district. Muslim comprises of 17 per cent of the total population of our study area. The two districts on both sides of the river Ganges, namely, Malda and Murshidabad are similar on this particular aspect of demographic configuration. The triad of Muslim population, mass poverty and home-based *beedi* enterprise persisting in both the districts is the subject of enquiry of the present exercise. Hindu comprises of the remaining 23 per cent of the total population. We did not come across any other religious communities in the area. The pre-eminence of Muslim in the demographic configuration of the district as a whole can be traced back to the historical past that dates back to Mughal India. Murshidabad was the seat of administration of Mughal rulers in the eastern part of the country.

TABLE 6.8
Caste Affiliations of Children
Caste Category

Social Category	*Frequency*	*Percent*	*Cumulative Percent*
General	2279	85.7	85.7
SC	362	13.6	99.3
OBC	19	.7	100.0
Total	2660	100.0	

Source : Household Survey in Murshidabad in 2008.

Unlike many back ward and poverty stricken areas of our country, the people of our study mostly belong to upper caste or the general category. This situation is very unique in case of India's general scenario where poverty and low caste move in the same direction. The district of Murshidabad is enlisted in the most backward district in India by the measure of the number of poor people. The other district that have made their way in this exclusive club of distressed regions are either tribal or having a majority of presence of lower caste and backward communities. Poverty and lower caste nexus is broken in this instance because Muslims are enlisted as general category, barring a very few community among them who are included in the Other Backward Caste (OBC) very recently. Thus caste reservation, on the whole, does not apply to the Muslim community in India. The reason for exclusion of Muslim in the caste reservation is religious. Caste hierarchy is anathema to Islam which does not believe in segregation of people on the basis of any distinctiveness pertaining to gender, colour, and place of birth or occupation. Caste reservation exclusive to Hindus caste system is integral part of Hindu society.

Reservation for certain type of opportunities including government jobs for the under-caste and tribal people is provided in our constitution. This is positive discrimination aimed at accomplishing equality among citizens of India. Poverty is widespread among scheduled caste and scheduled tribe population in India. Some of the benefits accrue to the underprivileged population on caste consideration. They receive some special benefits under antipoverty programs, employment schemes and school admission in addition to job reservations of all types. Muslims despite beings poor can not avail these opportunities and incentives as a consequence of their socio-religious status as general category. The under privileged Muslims thus join the rank of upper caste Hindus who are relatively affluent than the lower caste people. Thus affiliation to general caste category, the choice not made by them, deprives them of many of the benefits. This missing positively adds to their poverty and destitution, Muslim children by virtue by of their belonging to general caste, can not avail of many incentives like stipends and free books meant for poor SC and ST students. It seems that their poverty does render them perfect beneficiary for such incentives schemes but their religious membership prevents them from receiving them. A little more than 85 per cent of our children in predominantly Muslim habitations belong to general category. Scheduled Caste children comprise of only 13 per cent.

CASTE AFFILIATION AND CHILDREN'S STATUS

Educational participation is one of the indicators of child well being. Education prepares the child to face the world. It teaches life skills and survival skill to children. Learning takes place in school. Thus a child out of school is misplaced. She invariably misses the opportunities for development. She joins the rank of illiterates and unskilled. The child is sure to step in to a very bleak future, a gloomy world of failure and neglect. Her upbringing as human resource is nipped in the bud. Schooling equips the child with necessary skill and power to lead a dignified life. Her skill would contribute to nation building. Thus a child by not attending school, is sure to become a burden on society in stead of being a net contributor to national economy by his skills and knowledge.

We have tried to investigate any possible connection between caste affiliation of children and their school participation. Children are divided in two exclusive groups: current students and out of school children. The Table 6.9

TABLE 6.9

Caste Category and Children's School Participation

Children	Caste category of the child			Total
	General	SC	OBC	
Out of School	374	58	6	438
In School	1905	304	13	2222
Total	2279	362	19	2660

Source : Household Survey in Murshidabad in 2008.

presents a story that is exclusive to this region and inapplicable in normal circumstances. People belonging to general caste are well ahead of scheduled caste in economic well-being. Under privileged people in India are historically victims of caste oppression. Special development programmes currently under way for these communities are meant for bringing them at per with general category. Government has not been able to accomplish this task of bringing about parity. Economic adversity, illiteracy and lack of opportunity still pose a huge barrier. Relative affluence still marks the difference between scheduled caste and general caste population in general school participation of children is dependent on family's economic standing along with other supply side and demand side factors. Obviously in general scenario, children of general caste families are more likely to attend school in large number than children of scheduled caste families. Here in our study villages, we find no difference in school participation of children along caste lines which is 83 per cent for general caste and 83.97 per cent for scheduled caste population. Caste connection seems to fail to differentiate in school participation and the reason is that general caste population comprises of Muslims who are as poor as their counterparts in the SC population.

For both caste categories, SC and general, the similar degree of schooling deprivation of children is evident, 13 per cent for both. Other Backward Community (OBC) has very thin presence in these areas. Interestingly, school participation is lower at 68 per cent for them.

TABLE 6.10
Caste Category and Full Time Work Participation of Children

Full time work participation	*Caste category of the child*			*Total*
	General	*SC*	*OBC*	
Child is not full time worker	2048	334	15	2397
Child is full time worker	231	28	4	263
Total	2279	362	19	2660

Source : Household Survey in Murshidabad in 2008.

Full time work participation of underage children is an indicator of childhood adversity. The child who works for very long hours in such a hazardous occupation evidently has no choice. She is compelled to join the work with a view to augment family income. Her childhood is lost in the company of adults who work from dawn to desk to comply the target of production on a particular day. Tobacco processing by the tender hands of the children is extremely hazardous. The exposure to tobacco dust for long hours is no less than deleterious passive smoking on which complete ban is being contemplated in many countries. The tobacco-related diseases are on the rise. The victims, as usual are mostly women and children. Participation of child labour in this hazardous occupation in tobacco amounts to shocking violation of child rights. We have taken up an interesting task of finding any connection between caste affiliation and child labour participation in our area of study. We find as expected that child labour rate is higher at 10,13 per cent in case of general caste and 7.73 per cent in case of SC children.

Children of the general caste are supposed to enjoy childhood in a better way than their counterparts in other caste category. This happens in normal circumstances but not in a context where astounding majority of population is Muslim and poverty is widespread among them. Thus poverty ultimately explains the extent of child labour in a circuitous way. The predominance of poor Muslims in the population reverses the long established positive connection between caste and economic adversities. This particular aspect of disconnections would be dealt with in subsequent chapters.

FAMILY HEADING AND FULL TIME WORKING OF CHILDREN

Participation of children in paid work is the decision of the family. The head of the family decides on the use of child time taking in to account the survival of the family instead of welfare of the child itself.

TABLE 6.11
Family Heading and Full Time Work of Children

Children's Full time work	*Head of the family*		*Total*
	Father-headed	*Mother-headed*	
Child is not full time worker	2283	114	2397
Child is full time worker	239	24	263
Total	2522	138	2660

Source : Household Survey in Murshidabad in 2008.

A family evidently get on well when it is headed by father rather than mother. In gendered society male person always stands a better chance of job than the female. Employers would always prefer to employ male in rural jobs particularly in agriculture in view of greater physical capacity to take up on-field jobs. Male can take strains, take the load, brave the inclement weather and can work for long hours. The male preference for employment in agriculture is further encouraged when wage differential is absent in rural job market.

The onus of heading a family passes on to mothers in dire situations when father is missing. Father may disappear for ever. Paternal death brings a blow to the family and heralds the untoward phase of hardship in their lives. Death of father to children amounts to vanishing of protective shield over their heads. They are exposed to prickling realities of the world. Father may in many instances leave his family to settle elsewhere. Thus childhood adversities go up manifold when father is no where around to stand by their side. Mothers step in to the vacuum created by the departure of her husband. Thus mother headed family is the creation of disaster. Mothers take up double duty to keep her family on tract. She continues her duty in the kitchen and perform household chores including taking care of young siblings. The other duty she assumes is more vital for existence. She needs to take up job to provide two square meals a day to her children. Thus weakening of financial standing of the family is the first outcome of the loss of father. Poverty and related childhood adversities are obviously more intense in mother-headed family than father-headed family. The negative fallout of the death of father on the family can be significantly mitigated if the family is already endowed with adequate productive assets and wealth as cushion against all odds. Death of any adults in such predicament of relative affluence causes emotional loss than economic misplacement.

Economic adversity befalls on the family in the wake of the unforeseen disaster. Family has to grope for coping up with unwelcome eventualities. Children do partake in labour activities and support families even when father is present and earning. In other words presence of father is not always a guarantee for childhood free from labour. Our study finds that 9 per cent of children belonging to father headed families are working on full time basis. The incidence just goes up almost two fold at 17 per cent in case of families headed by mother.

CHILDREN SIZE

The individual child in each family of our study area is the focus of our analysis. Childhood is a social construction and the perception about childhood varies across social contexts. But there is no controversy about what part of human life constitutes childhood. The beginning phase or formative segment of human life is childhood and adulthood begins after that. Age separates between childhood and adulthood. Thus there is an age limit under which all human beings are children. That age limit is country specific. A country can set 20 years as upper age limit for consideration as children, while that limit may be 14 or 15 years in other countries.

However the participation about childhood in general and age specification for identification in particular are subject to variation across nations. The perception is formed by particular history, culture, tradition and economic strength of a reference nation. The last feature has a major part or role to play in fixing the upper age limit. The state of the economy and prosperity significantly determines how long the young members of their population will be considered as children. An affluent society, in most likelihood, will fix at a higher age bracket. This is because childhood is a period of dependence. This is a formative phase of life that needs protection, care and proper grooming. The society is supposed to invest in their education and health. Children are not supposed to contribute to family income through participating in child labour. Thus for how long a society will take care of their budding citizen is factor that depends on economic strength of the nation. A poor country is evidently will not favour to continue this care and investment for a protracted period. Thus they would like to set a lower age limit. The Universal Convention of the Right of the Child at the United Nations General Assembly in 1989 accomplished a remarkable task of setting a uniform upper age limit 18 years for all children on this plant.

Thus a child, according to this convention is a human person below the age of 18 years. In India, we are yet to normalize the children age in all laws and statutes on children. Child Labour (Prohibition and Regulation (Act) of 1986 is a case in point. This law defines children as person below 14 years. Thus this law prohibits exploitative labour of children below 14 years of age.

Our focus in this study is child labour activities of children, thus we have considered children below 14 years of age and above 6 years of age. The same age group coincides with the period of elementary education. Number of children within this age bracket is an important variable in our study. More children provide more earning hands. This is true for families living on the margin and also true for cases where child employment is easily obtainable. Thus families would

Total No. of Children

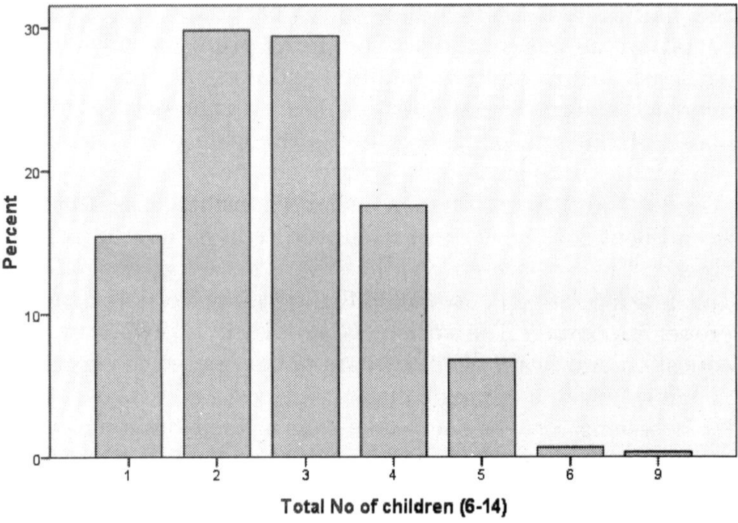

like to beget children to ensure steady income flow and better living with more amenities and comforts. The low cost of child rearing is also a factor in inviting more kids in to the family.

We have excluded all children below 6 years of age. There is no instance of working of any child below 6 years. We are interested in revealing working and schooling activities of children their nature and determinants in a poverty-stricken area of West Bengal. We kept those very young out-of-the-way. The six villages under study shelter 2660 children from 6 to 14 years. The table presents the frequency distribution of each child by the number of his or her brothers and sisters. Sharing with them the same kitchen and parental compassion, we find that 15 per cent of the children are only one child in these families. Around 30 per cent of the children in a total size of 2660 belong to families with two children in the aforesaid age group. The same percentage of children lives in a family of 3 children. Only 6 per cent of them are in the company of 5 children.

TOTAL FAMILY MEMBERS OF THE HOUSEHOLDS

The survey villages are populated by 18,354 persons. Thus children form 6 to 14 years comprises of 14.49 pr cent of the total population. The average family size is 6.90. The maximum size of the family we have come across is 20 and the minimum is 2. The average family size is evidently large at 6.90 higher than the normative size of 5 considered for a reference Indian family. Family poverty, family consumption expenditure and family income are calculated on the basis of 5 members comprising a reference family. Only 19 per cent of children in our study villages belong to a family of 5 members. Thus 30 per cent of children belong to families of either 5 members or less than that. It is therefore obvious that the rest 70 per cent of our children belong to families comprising of more than 5 members.

Family size is an important issue in the causation and effect on poverty. Poverty and family size can move in the same direction if dependency ratio is higher in the family. In other words, the number of dependents, comprising mostly of young children, aged and ailing members are more than the members of earners. The number, however matter less than the quality of employment which is reflected in the accrual of earning from the job. The rural areas can not provide the high paying job that involves handsome payment for unskilled or semi-skilled job. Agricultural job does not provide any handsome pay for the worker. Workers are paid, in most cases, a wage below the stipulated minimum. Therefore, larger family size can aggravate family poverty if number of earners falls short of number of dependants. We will look into the impact of family size on children's well being in our study area in the next chapter.

7

Parental Characteristics and Child Labour

We have also considered a few parental attributes that have bearing on children's status relating to labour and education. Household poverty is a dominant supply side determinant of child work. The next important determinant is parental illiteracy which leads to lack of demand for education (Wiener, 1991, Bhalla 1995, Burra 1995). Adult literacy has a positive impact on children's schooling. The strong effect is found in nearly all studies based on statistical inference (Rosenzweig and Evenson, 1977, Kanbargi and Kulkani 1991). The usual assumption is that parents having few years of schooling experiences would likely to send their children to school. Educated parents would understand the value of education. However, the perception of positive value of education depends on the possibilities of accrual of return. If the parents obtained the positive return through higher wages, better life standard and social esteem they would certainly attach immense value to education. They would send their children to school at any cost. Educated parents can afford to pay for school fees as they are better-placed in financial standing compared to their unlettered neighbours. However, education measured by a few years schooling experience may not always ensure positive return. It depends on the conditions in the labour market and the accrual of income.

Parental education particularly of fathers' education reduces the incidence of child labour indirectly through higher income and improved living standard. Poverty and large number of feeding mouths can compel parents to send children for work. This compulsion does not persist, in families those are relatively better-off. Education of fathers might have brought about the economic betterment. Therefore parental education is child labour reducing and parental illiteracy is child labour augmenting. Child labour exploitation is detrimental to child health, child education and child development in general. Thus parental education improves child well-being through preventing labour use of children. Parental education also minimises child idleness. The latter is pervasive in rural areas where employment opportunities for children is either skimpy or altogether absent. In such a situation, idleness increases manifold if schooling fails to attract these children. In other words, children who are not working may not be attending school. This is a worrisome situation where children were denied entry to labour market and they themselves do not respond to the beckoning of the school. Children may be reluctant to go to school if the school is far away. They would be disinclined to take lengthy and arduous walking daily. School environment might be repulsive. But many children do not go to school even these conditions are favourable. Educated parents are ahead of others in encouraging these children to go to school.

MOTHER'S EDUCATION AND CHILDREN'S WELL-BEING

Education of mothers is more beneficial for children's development particularly of girls. Several studies have documented the overwhelming impact on children. Girls children tend to see their mothers as role model to emulate in their own life course. Mothers, with few years of schooling background, will definitely send their daughters to attend school. Mothers equipped with primary education can immensely help their children in preparation of schools lessons and supplemental tuition at home. Unlettered mothers can not help their children in this way. Schools are generally swarming which virtually offer no individual attention and monitoring for each pupil. This gap can be filled without spending for private tutor when the child's own mother is equipped enough to lend that tuition support to their kids. Thus mother's education is associated with both quantity as well as quality aspect of schooling.

The other most remarkable positive impact of maternal schooling is on family size. Studies have established that education can help couple to take informed fertility decision. Educated mother can assert choice in reproductive behaviour. Education is empowering. A few years of schooling can be enlightening for mother to understand the adverse effect of begetting too many children. Poverty and family size are related in such a way that both are causes as well as effects. Poverty causes family size to grow. Parents perceive that many children generate many 'earning' hands through child labour participation. In poor countries the number of children swells on account of expectation of male child. Male child is always preferred to female child in poor families in India. Poverty generates insecurity and vulnerability which in turn causes larger size of children as cushion. Larger children size also deepens poverty by reducing per capita consumption expenditure where family income is given and constrained by lack of alternative income augmenting avenues. The cost of raising children goes up and competes with other items of necessary consumption within meagre family budget. Educated mothers can restrict the size of the children through asserting reproductive autonomy and informed fertility behaviour. The assertive power can emanate through convincing capacity gained through education and exposure to knowledge and understanding of benefits of small family. Secondly, the efficacy of contraceptives in preventing child birth widely advertised in the print media is an important piece of information which an educated mother, evidently can comprehend.

Mother can effectively interact with multipurpose health workers who routinely appear in their courtyard to discharge their duties as maternal and child health guides. Educated mothers can promptly and intriguingly learn the technique of contraceptives from the health workers. There is no dearth of empirical study to support this positive impact of maternal education on restraining of family size. Child nutrition is another area that receives the benefits of maternal education. Mothers with few years of educational background can discharge child care function well. Integrated Child Development Scheme (ICDS) is national programme currently in operation in virtually all villages in India. The programme is meant for children below six years of age. They provide early childhood education, supplementary nutrition and undertake immunization programme. An educated mother can come close to the functionaries of these child centres of their localities. They can articulate their specific needs and can seek assistance in providing nutritious food to their children. Immunization is most important child survival strategy. It can reduce infant mortality and child mortality in a significant measure. Educated mother can ensure timely administration of immunization doses and vaccination. Thus the benefits of mothers' education on the well-being of child are enormous.

PATERNAL ATTRIBUTES AND CHILDREN

Father rather than mother is a dominant actor in children's life course. This dominance is not only implicit particularly but he performs role as driver who holds the steering wheel. The onus of steering the family out of all adversities rests on him. He decides all matters in altruistic stance for the best interest of the family. His actions and inactions have a bearing on the life of his children. His earning capacity affects the well-being of children. If the father is a poor earner and the meagre income is the only source of living, children's well-being is the first casualty. Low income is the cause of multiple adversities in store for children. Food insecurity may befall on the family and children might not access adequate food and nutrition. Children may fall prey to frequent illness as a result of malnutrition. Poor parents may not afford expensive medical treatment in a condition where public health delivery system in not only inadequate but also deficient in quality. Child mortality, one of the best measures of childhood deprivation, would evidently go up in families where income flow is shockingly inadequate. However, meagre income earned by fathers may also be supplemented by income earned by mothers. But the incomes from both parents are not common.

Let us start with literacy attainment of fathers in our study area. Adult literacy particularly of parental literacy has a tremendous beneficial effect on children. Illiteracy is darkness while literacy is light that not only benefits the person itself but also illuminates the entire family. This is one of the measures of human development. A literate adult can easily access the information available in written form. Literacy thus empowers person in not only accessing the written information but also keep in assimilating them for their own uplift. A literate farmer for example can read and comprehend the written guidelines for optimum and balanced use of fertilizers in the field. A few econometric studies on productivity impact of farmers' education have come out with the interesting revelation that education makes a difference

Whether Father can Read and Write?

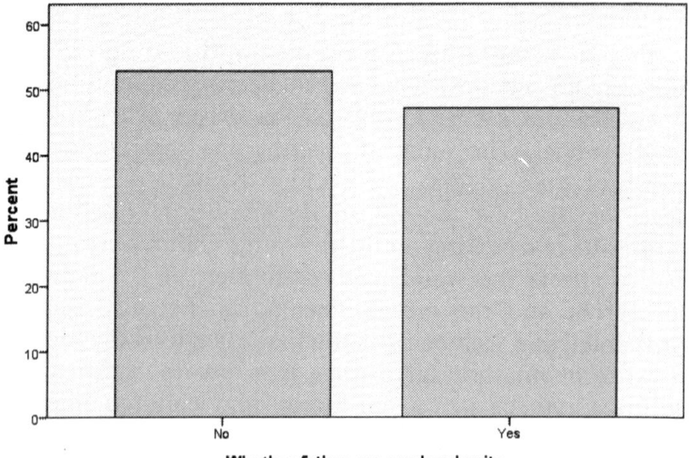

and it pays dividend by increased productivity and higher income. Literacy is a key to survival and prosperity in the increasingly literate world. Illiterates are thus far off the opportunities.

Literacy is an outcome of at least four years of schooling. The true meaning of literacy is learning of three R's: reading, writing and arithmetic. Literacy programme undertaken a few years ago under National Literacy Mission was crash course programme for the unlettered citizens of India.

We did not develop any structured measuring instruments to gauge the attainment of literacy of fathers. A piece of paper was handed over humbly to fathers of each family, on candidly expressing our objective of this task. They were asked to write their names and the names of the villages they inhabit. This was a crude measure of their writing ability. We did not opt for any other sophisticated and lengthy process of testing owing to our time as well as budget constraints. Similarly, a simple technique was applied to test the reading ability. They were very humbly requested to read out a few lines from a news item that appeared in the Bengali Newspaper on the day of visit. Engaging all of them to this

Occupation of Father

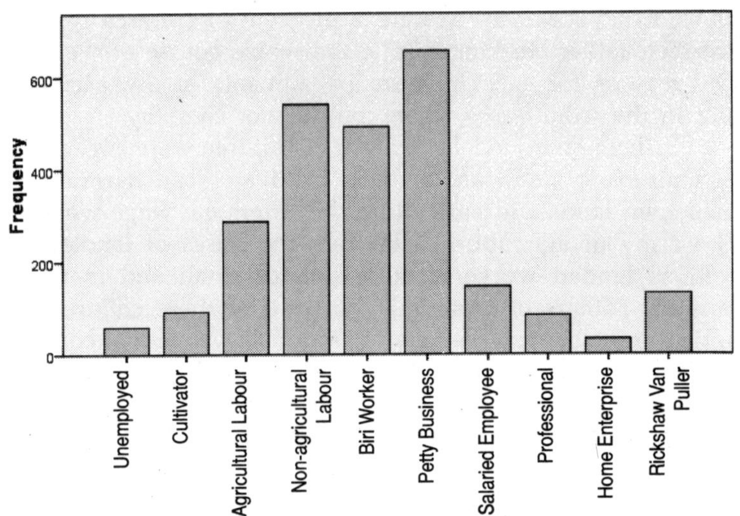

testing task was daunting in the beginning. Few of them were reluctant to show up in front of the strangers. But repeated persuasion yielded positive result. Thus in spite of crudeness of our testing tool, our measure, to certain extent, reveals the extent of literacy among the fathers of the children in our study area. We could find that 47 per cent of the fathers are literate, leaving 53 per cent of them doomed in the darkness of illiteracy.

The occupations of father, its nature and earning opportunities have a significant influence in the enjoyment of childhood by the children. Fathers are engaged in multiple occupations. One is not tied to only one occupation throughout the year barring government job. Agricultural work is seasonal. Though mono cropping has given way to multi-cropping but the latter is conditioned by availability of irrigation. The district as has already been explained in the last chapter suffers from inadequacy of irrigation. We have assigned each father to a particular occupation on the criterion of 'dominance' syndrome. Fathers might be employed in more than one category of occupations during the reference year. The dominant occupation is taken up which implies that he was employed for most of the days in the year. This conceptualisation of occupational groupings resonate the National Sample Survey categorization of 'Principal' and 'Subsidiary' activities. Around 2 per cent of children did not see their father working during the whole course of the year. The reasons for such idleness are ailments, frailty, accidents and in the worst cases where job did not come by.

Fathers of around 14 per cent of children were engaged in agriculture as dominant activity. Cultivators are farming on their own lands and agricultural labourers are wage workers. The army of agricultural labourers comprises of landless as well as landed workers comprising of small and marginal farmers. Fathers of around 11 per cent of these children are agriculture labourers. Fathers of around 18 per cent of children are Beedi workers in home-based units. Petty business includes retailing and vending. Ice cream sale during summer is lucrative business. Pieces of ice candies are kept in a box which takes tour in many villages on a bicycle. The box is put and tied to the rear seat of a bicycle. The small ice cream shop on wheel visits all hamlets in the neighbourhoods. Playing music from a tiny music system, kept in the bicycle with great care, is a ploy to attract children. The music played from the cycle in an otherwise silent locality is a way of telling the people of his arrival near their doors. Village women always aspire for a pair of glass bangles as a piece of inexpensive jewellery for them. Bengal and the district of Murshidabad do not manufacture glass bangles. Traders bring them from Moradabad in U.P. to sell here at profit. The bangles change hands from whole sellers to retailers before they are finally placed into the hands of village women. The modus operandi and the vehicles used for sale at every door step invoke curiosity to any visitor. There are a good number of bangle sellers in our study villages whose area of operation spreads far beyond the perimeters of their villages. The other types of business that goes in to the category of petty business are grocery, tea stall, vegetable vending, small stationery unit, cycle and rickshaw repairing units, fruit sale, buying used and abandoned metal utensils and rubber sleepers from households for onward sale of them at a profit to the stockist and such others trivial means of livelihood involving purchase and sale of stuffs. Salaried employees are significantly present in our study villages. This group comprises of government jobs, public sector and private sector jobs that entail fixed salary at the end of the month. Fathers of around 5 per cent of our children are engaged in this type of relatively safe, comfortable and secured means of living. Villagers also need various service provisions in addition to their primary requirement for food and shelter and much other stuff for comforts and luxuries. We have included all the varieties of professionals who are self-employed and sell their professional services to the villagers who need it. The village doctors or paramedicals, for example, fall in this group.

Professionals also include village priest for Hindu families. Barbers, washer men, midwifes, private tutors also join this category. Non-agricultural labourer encompasses a wide variety of wage work in construction, road repairing, work in shops, restaurants, cycle repairing shop, poultry, blacksmiths, shoe making, are examples of diversified means of living in our study area. The rural transport is the mainstay of communication. Around 2 per cent of fathers are engaged in self employed rural transport service in van and rickshaw pulling.

TABLE 7.1
Occupation of Father Child and Child Labour

Occupation of father	*Full time Work participation*		*Total*
	Child is not full time worker	*Child is full time worker*	
Unemployed	49	10	59
Cultivator	89	3	92
Agricultural Labour	247	41	288
Non-agricultural Labour	506	34	540
Biri Worker	426	66	492
Petty Business	603	53	656
Salaried Employee	141	5	146
Professional	82	2	84
Home Enterprise	28	5	33
Rickshaw Van Puller	111	20	131
	2282	239	2521

Source : Household Survey in Murshidabad in 2008.

Fathers' occupation can significantly influence children's participation in full time work through poverty reducing impact of high income jobs. We have cross tabulated between occupation categories of fathers' and children's full time work status to find out any possible connection between them. Unemployment of fathers increases the likelihood of children's joining of full time work. We have found 59 children whose fathers are currently not in employment. The eldest child in the eventuality of such odd circumstances takes the onus upon themselves to save the families from slipping down to the depths of despair. They join work whatever they obtain in exchange of their labour. We find that incidence of full time work by children is 17 per cent, the highest among all categories, for the children of unemployed fathers. Cultivators are relatively affluent in the agricultural community in the villages. The agricultural labouring class belong to the same community. Cultivators own land and seek their livelihood from their own productive assets. They do not go out to seek wage work like agricultural labourers in the same community. We find here that incidence of full time work by children stands at only 3 per cent for the fathers who are cultivators. Evidently the compelling circumstance where child labour is the only recourse to survival is absent or very thin in these comparatively better-off families in the rural landscape contrastingly. Child labour on full time basis is high at 14 per cent for children whose fathers are agricultural labourers. Children are following fathers' foot steps in joining agricultural wage work, to supplement family income. Full time child work is least at 3 per cent and 2 per cent respectively for children whose fathers are salaried and professionals. On the whole, the revaluation points out an indirect positive connection between better job or livelihood and better childhood prospects characterized by absence of very little presence of full time labour of children. The paternal job, as such does not make any impact but it definitely does through qualities of job gauged by their earning accrual.

Illiteracy of mothers of the children in our study area is widespread. Around 78 per cent of mothers cannot read and write. The prevalence of overwhelming female illiteracy is the shocking outcome of governmental neglect for quite long time in the area of human development. Pervasive female illiteracy is also an indicator of socio-economic backwardness of the area they inhabit as well as of the community they belong to. The area under study is predominantly Muslim and these unlettered mothers, in majority, belong to this minority community. Poverty and adult illiteracy, especially of female illiteracy, always coexist universally.

Child labour is always poverty driven that work on push factor to cause it. Adult illiteracy is also cited as important causal factor the power of influence may not be as strong as of poverty. Poverty and adult literacy work in tandem to cause and perpetuate child labour. There are number of studies to support this linkage. The widespread female illiteracy along

Whether Mother can Read and Write

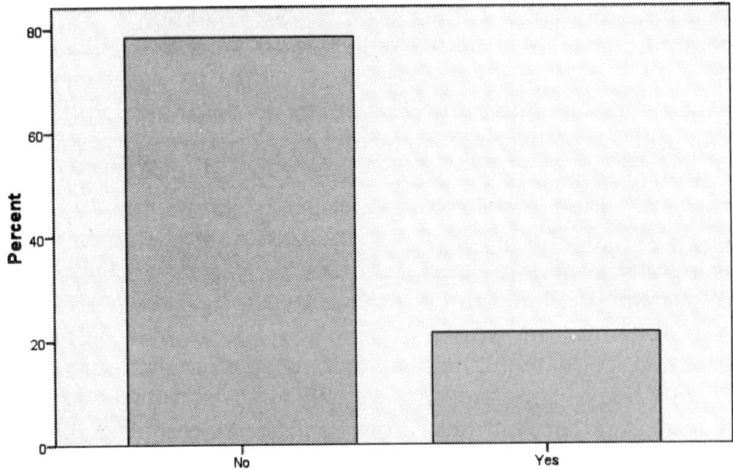

with household poverty breeds a condition, in which the home-based *beedi* manufacturing, not only persists but also prospers. Mothers join the work in overwhelming number.

TABLE 7.2
Maternal Literacy and Children's School Participation

Mother can read and write	*Out of School*	*In school*	*Total*
No	389	1687	2076
Yes	37	532	569
Total	426	2219	2645

Source : Household Survey in Murshidabad in 2008.

Full time schooling obviously pre-empts full time child work. The former is enabling for the child while the latter is disabling. There are many factors that work collectively for continuation of schooling by the children. Regularity of schooling and attending all class room transactions are beneficial for children. Learning achievement of pupil depends, to certain extent, on these aspects. We have undertaken an interesting exercise in this section that reveals the impact of maternal literacy on school participation of children. The positive impact of mother educational background on children's schooling behaviour has been documented in many empirical studies. We also find here the similar positive effect. Around 81 per cent of children are attending schools whose mothers are unlettered. School participation rate goes up 93 per cent for children whose mothers can read and write. We could discern an upward jump of more than 10 per cent in schooling evidently impelled by maternal literacy.

TABLE 7.3

Distribution of Mothers' Occupation

Mothers' Occupation	*Frequency*	*Percent*	*Cumulative Percent*
Unwell	2	.1	.1
Cultivator	2	.1	.2
Non Agricultural Labour	3	.1	.3
Biri Worker	2524	94.9	95.7
Petty Business	9	.3	96.1
Salaried Employee	9	.3	96.4
Household Work	95	3.6	100.0
Total	2644	99.4	
Missing	16	.6	
Total	2660	100.0	

Source : Household Survey in Murshidabad in 2008.

The home-based *beedi* enterprises in the study area sustain on women's and children's labour. The occupational distribution of mothers points out at the overwhelming participation of mothers in home-based *beedi* work. Around 96 per cent of all mothers perform this task as family labour. Participation of mothers in other occupations is very insignificant.

8

Economic Well-being : Where do the Households Stand?

A large number of children in our study villages have joined the family labour force. They are either withdrawn form school or they had never enrolled. Schooling deprivation brings a permanent full stop to their growth and development. We have come across an exhaustive list of five situations for these children. Full time work in beedi units by children is the worst of all five situations. One end of the spectrum is the position of full time students, the ideal, perfect and sought after state of children. The other end is marked with worst situations of full time working by them which are unacceptable, dehumanizing and harmful. Between the best and the worst states, lie different positions less harmful but less than ideal state. These different positions are away from the coveted perfect childhood which each child is entitled to have on this planet. The harmful effect of work in tobacco units on children needs no elaboration. Medical Research world wide has found, through clinical observations that exposure to tobacco not only as smokers, active as well as passive, causes respiratory troubles, lung diseases including tuberculosis, breathing difficulty and many other debilitating diseases. Children run the risk far more than the tobacco users or consumers because their exposure to tobacco dusts is prolonged.

The question that haunts us, the curiosity that brought us here in the company of rural households and the inner urge to look for the answer is why children take part in family-based tobacco processing units in these villages. The answer is gradually unfolding itself. We have studied the local economy to look for the explanation of the perpetuation of child labour in these selected areas. A vibrant local economy delivers affluence, creates opportunities, generates jobs and holds out a bright future. The local economy, as it appears, holds less promise for future and carries with it all symptoms of stagnant and backward settings. Industries in formal sector, that could absorb a significant segment of local work force, is conspicuously absent. The traditional crafts that had commanded extensive market in India as well as abroad, were pride to boast for the people. Crafts and metal works by the gifted local artisans are struggling to survive in the ambience of immense adversities. The competition from cheaper synthetics, imported from China is threatening their survival. Government does not come forward with incentives to protect and promote these local crafts. Service sector occupations are very thin by their presence. Agriculture with falling land-man ratio is the mainstay of livelihoods for the people. Infrastructure deficiency baulks the productivity growth. The non-agricultural activities are not robust enough to take in the surplus population in agriculture.

People thus fall back on *beedi* binding as the last option for livelihood. It does not seem that they are oblivious of severe harmful effects of handling tobacco dust for long hours. Poverty compels in large number of cases, to take up the deleterious job, allowing for very few exceptional cases where grabbing of more consumer durables is the overriding reason for joining the work. The reason for overwhelming presence of this harmful activity in this part of Bengal has already been explicated in the earlier chapter. Poverty is unquestionably the dominant reason and it is the same everywhere and at any time where child labour persists. However, research studies on causality of child labour have documented the presence of many other reasons in addition to poverty. Adult illiteracy is a major reason that positively comes, after household poverty, by way of influencing power on children time use pattern. Educated parents are more likely to send their children to school rather than engage them for paid work. Maternal education is stronger as factor in influencing children schooling, particularly of their daughters. However, the potency of adult literacy in reducing child labour is contested by many scholars and activists. Unlettered parents have been found to send their children to schooling if they are persuaded and are sensitized through collective action.

Household poverty generates push factor which can not singularly generate child labour. Pull factor must be present side-by-side. The perfect marriage between these two factors produces child labour. Presence of push factor can cause idleness of children. Idle children neither go to school nor join any remunerative work. The issue of 'no where' children has been subject of intensive research, an issue of concern and an indicator of child deprivation. The problem persists in rural areas rather than in urban areas because the latter offers various informal and ill paid jobs for children. Agricultural activity is dominant in the rural area which is characterized by seasonal unemployment for adult workers. Non-agricultural economic activities are far from being vibrant. They are very thin and even altogether absent some where. The rural economy stands and flourishes on two pillars: agriculture and non-agricultural industrial activities. They work in unison, supplementing each other for mutual growth. The surplus work force in agriculture is absorbed in upcoming non-agricultural occupation in course of the gradual expansion of the latter. However, the absorption is not universal. Agricultural in many places, bear the brunt of overpopulation, low productivity, low capital formation, and many other ills and manifestations of backwardness. Thus the idleness of many children in rural areas in the direct outcome of the lack of pull factor, where labour market is dysfunctional and incapable of creating jobs for all including women and children. While poverty pushes the children to work for wages, employment opportunities for children should be present to engage the children. The factors, push as well as pull, must simultaneously work to generate and perpetuate child labour.

HOUSEHOLD POVERTY

Poverty still cripples millions of people in India even after sixty long years of independence from the shackles of colonial power. Our colonial master did nothing to eradicate poverty of her subjects. Poverty deepened during the entire stretch of two hundred years of colonial rule. Agriculture that provided livelihoods for the teeming millions was squeezed by the colonial master and their Indian accomplices for their financial gain. The peasants who toiled on the field to produce crop that filled their coffers were mistreated. The resources produced by land did never bounce back to it for the development of this gift of nature and for the improvement of the lives of the people who tills the land. Colonial agriculture was starved of investment during the long stretch of a double century of colonial rule. Poverty of today's India owes much to colonial neglect of agriculture, the mainstay of our economy and livelihood.

The connection between household poverty and child labour is beyond disputation. A large body of empirical studies across the globe have confirmed this connection. Poverty primarily causes child labour in conjunction with other social-economic ills. Concentration and prevalence of child labour in certain locations of the globe is the testimony to this connection. Child labour persists in those geographical locations where poverty is endemic. Those grey locations in the world map are South Asia, Sub-Saharan Africa and parts of Latin America. Children are pulled to low paying work in agriculture as well as in urban informal sector to supplement family income. Adult's earnings, taken together, are insufficient to put family wheel on track or to provide two square meals a day for all the members, children are engaged to help families to tide over the crisis of income shortfall. Thought of initially as expedient action for the interest of the families to put the burden of running the family on the tender shoulders of children, but this overture ultimately heralds the onset of the working life of children. Once put in work place, they are not withdrawn and they fail to revert back to normal childhood. Thus poverty that results in low income generates child labour. Persistent poverty of a family also induces discontinuation of schooling of children. Children from poor families are withdrawn from school and are sent to work places. They are also withdrawn from schools to work on family farms.

Although farm work is seasonal in nature but frequent absenteeism from school often leads to permanent withdrawal. Poverty is also cited everywhere as a dominant reason for school drop-out. Schooling is not altogether free, in true sense of the term. Even free education turn out to be expensive for many families living on the margins. There are many fees in addition to tuition fees which poor parents have to cough up to allow their children to stay on. There is evidently a limit beyond which a family can not go; withdrawal follows just after this point when they are pushed to the wall. Children may join paid work to help family if employment opportunity for them is plenty in the vicinity of their homes. Poor parents migrate to cities along with their children in search of livelihoods. They find employment in upcoming construction sites, in road building, in factories and in a wide variety of informal sector jobs where they become victims of inhuman exploitations. Indian cities are best examples of exploitation sites of millions of migrant rural workers. They are unlettered and unskilled. They have no organised voice of resentment. They have no platform to organise protest against their employers. There is nothing like labour rights, condition of work, safety at work places, hours of work and stipulated minimum wages. They eke out their living on the mercy of their employers in the city.

The city authorities are oblivious of their presence in their areas. They live an anonymous life in the city landscape. They live in makeshift dwellings and continue living until city planners bulldoze and flatten their ramshackle homes. They are illegitimate citizens and this illegitimacy emboldens their employers to exploit to the maximum extent possible. The real estate developers get scot-free when workers die in the workplace as a result of neglect towards safety. Compensation and insurance are hard to come by in such tragedies. All members of the families including children join work to make a living. Children of the migrant families join work for two reasons: easy availability of work in the cities and inadequacy of adult income to survive in the cities.

Many poor families in the villages do not migrate to cities for some reason. The children who stayed back in the villages do not always find employment excepting helping family farm or family business, if there is any. They remain idle for most of the time; idleness is a problem in many places which needs immediate policies and action. Universal and free education, in letter and in spirit is the solution. Schools must be affordable accessible and enjoying.

The relationship between poverty and child labour is not unidirectional which means that while poverty causes child labour likewise the perpetuation of the latter also perpetuates child labour. The intergenerational cycle of poverty and child labour persist that does not break itself over a considerable period of time. How does it happen is an interesting question in development economics. When a child starts her life as a child labourer, one immediate visible consequence is her derailment of schooling. Her human capital formation process is thwarted. She remains unskilled labourer throughout her working life. Sometimes the little skill, the children pick up in course of work for a long period, is of no avail. This on job skill gained by them in latter course of life as adult workers never raises their productivity and enhancement of wages. Thus child labour connotes unskilled labour, lack of training, missing of educational opportunity, low wages and consequent poverty trap. Low wages and low income of family cause higher fertility in expectation of more earning hands of the children. Thus child labour practice is passed on from one generation to other and poverty is also passed on in the same way. Generations of families can not come out of the shackles of poverty and destitution created by lack of human capital formation that would improve skills of the workers and raise income.

We need to reflect on what constitutes poverty and how does it affect human well-being. Persistence of child labour in a country, in a particular region within a country or even in a sub-region within a regional boundary, or in a particular section of population within the sub region are all indicators of persisting economic ills. If child labour is the mark of unwellness, then absence of child labour is the mark of human progress and prosperity. Poverty is the horrible lived experience of certain section of human race, identified as poor. Life circumstance of the poor people is described as a situation of poverty. The poor suffer from multiple bottlenecks in their daily living experiences. They do not get enough food for healthy living. Food provides nutrition, supplies energy in the form of calorie for effective functioning of body. They take diet well below the recommended dietary allowances. Inadequate dietary intake triggers malnutrition for all ages affecting children in a massive way. Child malnutrition is one of the prominent manifestations of household poverty. Family fails to provide nutritious food for children that would help in developing bones, muscles and tissues of children in their growing stage. Malnutrition results in growth stunting and wasting of children, exposing them to severe bacterial infection, and variety of childhood disease. They do not acquire the natural immunity system to fight the disease and thus they easily fall prey to these afflictions.

Child morbidity is always associated with poverty and inadequate health care support. While household poverty inhibits the access to market for health care by the poor, the absence of state supported medical care or presence of low quality medical support system of the state accentuate rather than mitigate the widespread child morbidity. Infant and child mortality are related to household poverty. Reduction of infant mortality has been set as a goal to be achieved by developing countries. Massive investment and donor assistance have been directed to bring down the rate through augmenting child nutrition, prenatal care and immunization. India's infant mortality rate is alarming and its magnitude is considerably high in states afflicted by poverty on the one hand and massive human development failure on the other. Thus, household poverty and vulnerability induces child malnutrition, child morbidity and child mortality including infant mortality. Thus, poverty reduces the survival chances of the offspring. For poor families accessing adequate food for the entire members is a formidable challenge. Left to market, to fend for themselves, the poor are sure to experience starvation. The government must come forward to protect these vulnerable citizens for whom market has kept them out. Government formulates anti-poverty programme for theme and vows to implement them as soon as possible to stem the tide of further slipping down to the depth of poverty.

Elimination of poverty is the priority agenda of all developing countries. Many of them generates own resources through fiscal measure for massive public investment for poverty eradication programme. A few in the company of developing nations supplements internal resources with donor assistance to fight poverty. Sub-Saharan African countries depend on external assistance for antipoverty programme. Donor countries are insisting on institutional reforms as condition for giving away the aid. Anti-poverty measures may take different shapes and dimension depending on the perceptions of the gravity of the distress and nature of intervention needed to mitigate at a particular point of time. Creation of wage employment for adult members of the poor families is one such form. India had tried this form in her earlier plans. Food for work programme is an example of this genre. Provision of productive assets for the poor was also tried in the Seventh Plan period to create income and employment opportunities for them. Integrated Rural Development Programme (IRDP) was introduced to fight poverty through the mixture of low cost bank credit and government subsidy for creation of productive assets that would yield stream of income after an initial gestation period. Micro credit and self-help groups currently underway in India are some form of collective initiatives of poor women for income earning micro enterprises in the villages.

The National Rural Employment Guarantee Scheme (NREGS), India's largest employment programme currently underway, aims at abolition of rural poverty. This scheme differs from any other scheme of the some ilk of the past on one aspect. Government is compelled by the act to provide unskilled employment for 100 days within the village for at least one adult member of a family seeking employment. The enactment of this legislation on employment is a significant advancement of people's right to work. Rural people are now empowered to claim the jobs and the local government is bound to provide them within a stipulated time period. The job seekers would get unemployment allowances in case of failure by the local government. This massive employment program is envisaged to fulfil two objectives: one is the creation of wage employment and resultant income generation. Enhanced income would raise the purchasing power of the villages. The other outcome, expected from this employment scheme is creation of rural infrastructure by way of installing minor irrigation scheme to augment agricultural productivity, land development, construction of rural road for improved rural connectivity, development of fisheries, construction of school building and social forestry. The scheme is widely applauded for its success, to much extent, in eliminating poverty in many places. However, the success is not universal and the statistics of implementation in many districts in India is not at all cheering.

Government furnished report card for each state in India on the performance of the scheme in creating days of employment for any particular year. Many states have miserably failed. The average days of employment created is no more than twenty in a year. Serious anomalies in the distribution of job cards have been reported in media. Government has been trying for last several years a different route to reach rural households to assist them in tiding over the acute food crisis as a result of lack of purchasing power. Instead of providing wage employment for the rural poor, government is providing food security through a wide network of public distribution system. This is a measure to mitigate nutritional poverty. One of the anti-poverty measures work through food subsidy where identified poor can buy foodgrains at subsidized prices. The poor can avail, rice, for example at Rs. 3 per kilo under a weekly quota. The provision of mid-day meal to school going children is one such measure of food intervention. Each student in the primary school is entitled to get cooked food during school hours. Government is contemplating to extend the scheme to upper primary class. This provision also evidently enhance food security for families unable to by food at he market price.

Anti-poverty programmes must target the poor. Therefore, the task of identification of poor is most crucial and challenging. Wrong identification can render the programme ineffective. The benefits may go to non-poor in the eventuality of wrongful selection. In India, the Planning Commission is charged with task of constructing poverty line for the country as a whole. The poverty line is the threshold income level below which all people will be marked as poor and therefore are eligible for receipts of anti-poverty benefits. The Planning Commission calculates the head count of poor on the basis of consumer expenditure survey carried out by National Sample Survey Organization in its various rounds. The survey records the spending of respondent, family on various food and non-food items during the last reference period which may be the last week, last month and last year. They calculate, on the basis of the information furnished by the households, the number of households that fail to make into a minimum consumption spending that defines the poverty line for the ongoing plan period in the total sample. The head count incidence of poverty is thus measured for each state and for the entire nation. The budgetary allocation of fund from the central government for each state and union territories for anti-poverty programme is made on the basis of number of poor supplied by planning commission.

Planning Commission furnishes the poverty ratio for each state but does not identify the poor households. The onus of identification is passed on the respective state governments. The Ministry of Panchayat and Rural Development is assigned the task of locating the poor households in the villages. The District Rural Development Cell (DRDC) is the nodal body in each district in India that take up the task of implementing, co-ordinating and monitoring of all central government's anti-poverty programmes. This district body gets the job done by the three tier Panchayat machinery, the vibrant grass root local governments that epitomize participatory democracy for the rural people. These local bodies, comprising of Panchayat and Municipalities are now empowered more, in the wake of 73rd constitutional amendments. Eradication of poverty at the village level is the primary responsibility of Panchayats. Therefore, persistence of child labour in tobacco processing in the selected villages is an indicator of unpardonable failure in the area of human development.

Panchayats now oversee, plan and implement all human development programme in their respective jurisdiction. Child education, for example, is now incorporated in their agenda. They have to establish school in school-less villages within their territorial jurisdiction. *Sishu Shikhsa Kendra* (SSK) and *Madhyamik Shiksha Kendra* (MSK) are now managed and funded by Panchayats. These are alternatives to formal school where children who can not attend formal school for what so ever reason will be enrolled and to be retained. Panchayats as a grass root local governments are now assigned with the responsibility of implementing central sponsored anti-poverty schemes. The devolution of power and transfer of responsibility to the local body is a remarkable step towards decentralized democratic governance. This is undoubtedly a laudable step towards participatory functioning replacing bureaucratic discharging but the local institutions are not always capable enough to deliver goods. They are beset with infrastructure insufficiency and shortage of trained manpower and they are alarmingly laden with loads of tasks pertaining to almost all aspects of rural life. There are a host of poverty alleviation programmes that come under ambit of the *Gram Panchayat*. They have to keep the record of the poor living within their functional territory. Each poor household is given a BPL card as its identity document for production in the moment of necessity. BPL households are entitled to subsidized prices of rice and wheat at the local PDS shop. They can avail medical care free of cost in the public health care system. They can enjoy many other facilities announced by the government from time to time. This is a coveted card and passport for many benefits for the underdogs in rural as well in urban areas. Obviously for the intrinsic power of the card, there is always mad race among the poor to grab one at any cost. When too many aspirants chase too few benefits, crisis is inescapable

The selection of BPL families thus succumbs to crisis. A section of poor excluded from the list vehemently resent. They give vent to their grievances and lodge their complaints in the appropriate forum, the village assembly, *Gram Sansad*. The

Ministry of the Rural Development stipulates that BPL list, prepared after the survey, must be placed at the village development committee for final approval. This practice, however, came into effect during 10th Plan period, from 2002 to 2007, when identification of poor began to be accomplished by household survey. Poor households were identified before the 10th Plan, but through a traditional procedure formulated by the central government. During the 8th plan for example, spanning the five year period from 1992-97, income up to Rs. 11,000 per annum per family was the criterion for identification of BPL families. During 9th plan period, from 1997 to 2000, a family whose annual income was less than Rs. 20,000 and not having more than 2 hectares of land, TV, Fridge, etc. was classified as BPL. From 10th plan onwards, the methodology of identifying poor household underwent sea charge income or per capita consumption expenditure was replaced by other number deprivation measures. There was a shift from a narrow definition of poverty to a broader definition of economic unwellness.

Income or expenditure can not be a comprehensive indicator of economic well-being. Income approach was being contested by well meaning economists, social thinkers and activists for quite a long time. The argument gained ground and the advocacy to expand the meaning of poverty intensified in the wake of the publication of human development report under the auspices of the UNDP during nineties. The Ministry of Rural Development of the Government of India in 2002 formulated a scoring sheet for each household comprising of thirteen criterions. The schedule to be canvassed by the grass root functionary was expected to reveal almost all aspects of life and livelihood of the people. Any household can score from 0 to 4 in each criterion. Therefore, any household can in total, can score from 0 to 52. It means that lowest mark in the scale of each criterion is 0 and the highest mark is 4. Thirteen criterions can be grouped into five board headings. Ownership and command is the first heading which incorporates land holdings, possession of consumer durables, apparel, and command over food. The second heading is living conditions which contain the type of dwelling house, and dwelling environment relating to hygiene and sanitation. The third is livelihood that contains the nature of labour employment and means of living. The fourth is economic hardship that encompasses extent of indebtedness, migration status and nature of assistance the household would like to seek. The fifth and the last category is human resource formation that includes literacy status of adults and schooling status of children.

The household survey schedule designed by the central government during 2002 to record the score on each of thirteen items or indicators did not please many economists. Apprehension loomed large that it would not reveal the intensity of poverty. The alarm was raised in many corners that the genuine poor would be excluded and non-poor could get in the exclusive club of the poor. Denial of access to the genuinely poor is similar to deprivation of entitlements to a large number of people who not only need support but also are incapable to assert their rights. However, state governments got a title liberty in bringing about a slight modification in the scoring methodology. States are free to decide on the total score as a cut-off limit below which all households will be designated as poor. The identified household will receive the BPL card in due course for claiming central government and state government benefits. West Bengal has used a scoring template that starts at 12 with a maximum of 60 a score of 32 being the cut-off limit to be eligible to get the BPL tag. The whole exercise was mired in controversy, resentment and street protest and went straight in to newspaper headlines. The ruling government was accused of partisan attitude in enlisting BPL households.

The present study looks into poverty of the households as the universal correlate of child labour. We have tried with different measures in a bid to bring to light economic adversities of the families eking out their living from a very deleterious means. Many families just keep body and soul together from the income earned through the harmful-job that imperils the health and physical well-being of all the members of the family. We are interested to know whether poverty is uniform in its intensity for all children households in our study area. Do the poor households engage their children in home-based tobacco processing? Do the non-poor households are sending their children to school instead of engaging them for work. The pertinent question that comes up obviously is that how can we separate the children households in the two categories of poor and non-poor. We did not conduct any BPL survey in line with thirteen score templates ourselves. Despite alleged discrepancy and inadequacies, we recorded their poverty status on the basis of possessing BPL card provided by the local Panchayats. We took recourse to other measure to gauge at economic standing of the households that goes far beyond income or consumption expenditure as measuring rods. The experimentation with other approach to get at the root of poverty will be taken up in the following sections. Mean while we can explore with the disbursement of BPL card among households by the local development authority. We do it deliberately as a gross measure for identification despite its suspected inappropriateness. The respondent families were asked whether they possess BPL card. We have gathered information of 2660 children on their BPL status. It has been found that 44.7 per cent of children belong to BPL families and rest, 55.3 per cent are non-BPL or APL families.

BPL FAMILIES AND CHILDREN STATUS

Children of designated BPL families are expected to be lesser goods buttressing the long held and widespread acceptance of poverty as a dominant determinant. We will cross tabulate children status with their BPL status i.e. their

TABLE 8.1
BPL Family and Child Labour

BPL Status	*Children*		*Total*
	Child is not full time worker	*Child is full time worker*	
Non-BPL	1361	111	1472
BPL	1032	156	1188
Total	2393	267	2660

Source : Household Survey in Murshidabad in 2008.

membership with BPL families. Full time child work the worst situation of children among five alternations situation in the study villages is an indicator of childhood adversity.

The table reveals that full time child work is around 13 per cent for BPL families compared to a lower level of 7.47 per cent for non BPL families.

TABLE 8.2

BPL Family Children's School Partcipation

BPL Status	*Children*		*Total*
	Out of School	*In school*	
Non-BPL	192	1280	1472
BPL	250	938	1188
Total	442	2218	2660

Source : Household Survey in Murshidabad in 2008.

School participation is 87 per cent for children belonging to APL families. The same rate comes down to 79 per cent for BPL families. There is thus a positive correlation between child poverty and childhood adversities. The latter is measured by two parameters: Full time child labour and schooling deprivation.

THE OTHER MEASURE OF POVERTY : ENGEL'S RATIO

Engel's ratio is a popular measure of economic well-being or relative affluence of a family. Engel's ratio measures the percentage share of non-food expenditure in total consumption expenditure of a family. Food is essential for survival for all living beings, the question of intake, however, depends on body sizes of them. The difference between food intake of an adult elephant and that of a tiny ant is just immeasurable. Food, clothing and shelter are primary needs for human beings. Animals need the first and not the remaining two. Food is source of our work energy. Human body needs functioning rest as well as immunity to fight afflictions of diseases. Food leaves immediate impact on the person who takes it. It mitigates hunger of the famished. This gain is psychological though. But psychological gain is immense but unobservable. Food provides vitamins, protein, carbohydrates for physical well-being of humans. A child needs balanced diet for her proper growth of bones and tissues. This food must have nutritive value to positively work on human body. A plateful of food is not the guarantee of nutrition which means that quality matters more than the quantity. Nutritionists, therefore, have been recommending balanced diet rich in food value. The availability of food, however, is not guaranteed to all citizens in India. Food security is an issue of concern. The poor not only lacks the purchasing power to acquire enough from the market but also are oblivious of the necessity of balancing of diet for healthy and productive living.

Our ancestors, the primitive men, occupied themselves with one and only task of collecting food from very harsh and adverse surroundings. Physical survival was the only concern of the primitive men on the earth. Clothing and shelter were no where near food as inevitable for survival and they were pushed to secondary requirement that concerned them very little. Thus for millions of years the primary concern of mankind was food, whereas shelter and clothing, as essential commodities came much later. Thus prioritization of needs for men is evidently related to stage of human civilization. Progress of humanity shifts the priorities over a very long stretch of time. Economic prosperity, associated with the progress of humanity over last thousand of years, has shaped and moulded consumption priorities. Human demand for non-food luxuries and non-food essentials for decent living is a development that had followed the era of industrial revolution in Europe. Economic prosperity did not visit this planet before the arrival of industrial production, scientific discoveries, colonization and the spread of knowledge and education in the western hemisphere. Thus until the era of industrial progress, food was the primary concern for mankind. In terms of spending by families food expenditure took away the whole, leaving very little or even nothing for non-food expenditure.

The western world showed the way in shifting or apportioning this consumption spending on non-food items as a result of their economic progress. This shifting from bare subsistence on food to better living by spending on non-food was conspicuously absent in the vast swathe of present day developing world. Therefore, what is true for a world region is also true for a nation and equally applicable down to individual households. Poverty restricts spending on non-food items. Put in other words, rise in income and consequent rise in purchasing power leads to greater consumption of non-food items. Rise in the standard of living is reflected in the rise of non-food spending.

Engel's ratio is thus a measure for relative opulence or relative destitution. Lower Engel's ratio is an indicator of relative affluence and the higher, one, obviously, indicators relative poverty. We have calculated the Engel's ratio for all the children households in our study area to look at the poverty from slightly different angle. BPL households were identified by the local authority. We did not repeat the same exercise based on the thirteen criterions and counting aggregate score for each households. The last section has deal with the official BPL status and the possible linkage of this status with children present position, relating to work and school.

TABLE 8.3
Engel's Ratio Class

Ratio Class	*Frequency*	*Percent*	*Cumulative Percent*
40.01 - 50.00	17	.6	.6
50.01 - 60.00	84	3.2	3.8
60.01 - 70.00	182	6.8	10.6
70.01 - 80.00	992	37.3	47.9
80.01 - 90.00	1381	51.9	99.8
90.01 - 100.00	4	.2	100.0
Total	2660	100.0	

Source : Household Survey in Murshidabad in 2008.

This table presents the frequency distribution of children as per Engle's ratio class. The richest among the children households are those whose Engel's ratio falls within '40 to 50' class. Very few children belong to this exclusive category of rural rich. Their magnitude is as low as 0.6 per cent which means that only 17 children out of a population size of 2660 belong to such families whose food spending is less than half of their total consumption spending. The next category by way of opulence as measured by Engel's ratio is 50-60 group. A slightly higher percentage of children at 3.2 per cent belong to this group. The highest concentration of children, as the distribution table reveals, is in 80 to 90 group. Almost 52 per cent of all children belong to this group. The next highest concentration is evident in 70 to 80 class of Engle's ratio. The group contains 37.3 per cent of all children. Families, spending almost all penny on food are extremely poor. They constitute a very microscopic segment of only 0.2 per cent of the total.

We can construct our poverty groups from the table of Engel's ratio distribution. If we consider 80 as out of Engle's ratio and therefore a gross replica of well-known 'poverty line' then children below this cut-off mark belong to poor families. We find that 52 per cent of children of poor. Thus, poverty as

Table 8.4
Children Schooling and Engel's Ratio Class

Engel's Ratio Class	*Children*		*Total*
	Children not in School	*Children in school*	
40.01 - 50.00	0	17	17
50.01 - 60.00	1	83	84
60.01 - 70.00	15	167	182
70.01 - 80.00	127	865	992
80.01 - 90.00	295	1086	1381
90.01 - 100.00	4	0	4
Total	442	2218	2660

Source : Household Survey in Murshidabad in 2008.

we have conceptualised and measured by spending proportion on food items is evidently higher than the incidence revealed in the government BPL survey.

We now explore the possible connection between poverty as measured by Engel's ratio and its impact on children's school participation. The richest group having lowest Engel's ratio has a 100 per cent school participation rate. The next richer group can boast of almost similar performance, missing only one child who does not go to school. The school participation rate is almost 99 per cent in this group. School participation comes down to 91.75 per cent in 3rd group of 60 to 70 Engle's ratio. It further comes down to 87.19 in case of 4th group, from 70 to 80 Engle's ratio. The downfall continues at the 5th group at the same pace. The rate now stands at 78.63 per cent. Not even a single child attends school in the last category.

Thus school participation and poverty of the households are inversely related. This connection has come to the fore in our study. Several empirical studies on determinants of schooling have found a very strong effect of household poverty on schooling deprivation. The next state of child deprivation is engagement of children in fulltime work. Not all the children are in full time work in our study villages. Many of them do part time work in tobacco processing at home during the period of school vacation, during leisure in the morning and in the evening in a gesture of helping their parents. This employment even for a few hours in a day without interfering with school attendance is not acceptable though. This certainly affects adversely on the health and well being of the children. Exposure to tobacco dusts even if for a few hours is injurious to health. Taking part in games is always beneficial for children. Work in the afternoon along with other adult member deprives the children of the pleasure of game and much beneficial effect associated with games and sports. Still this situation is better than full time work engagement of children where they toil and perish in the same way as the adults do. Therefore, we consider the worst situation of child deprivation as the first measure of childhood adversity in the present discourse.

TABLE 8.5
Child Labour and Engel's Ratio Class

Engel's Ratio Class	*Full time child workers*		*Total*
	Child is not full time worker	*child is full time worker*	
40.01 - 50.00	17	0	17
50.01 - 60.00	84	0	84
60.01 - 70.00	173	9	182
70.01 - 80.00	910	82	992
80.01 - 90.00	1209	172	1381
90.01 - 100.00	0	4	4
Total	2393	267	2660

Source : Household Survey in Murshidabad in 2008.

The richest group of families as evident from lowest Engle's ratio of 40 to 50 do not have any child labour. The immediate next group with a reduced opulence as reflected in 50 to 60 Engle's ratio group have similar showing. This group is child labour free. Child labour, by the nature of full time occupation exists by 4.94 per cent in Engel's ratio group of 60 to 70. The incidence of child labour goes up to 8.26 per cent in the relatively poor group with Engel's ratio ranger from 70 to 80. It further goes up to a very high figure of 14.22 per cent for poorer group of families with Engel's ratio from 80 to 90. The most destitute group of the highest Engel's ratio have 100 per cent work participation rate for children. We find that child labour begins to generate from the Engel's ratio of 60 onwards. We do not find a single child labour below that limit. We do further note that incidence of child labour progressively increases with gradual fall in the Engel's ratio. Poverty and child labour nexus is further established conclusively as a reality. Poverty however is viewed in this analysis as spending capacity on non-food items *vis-à-vis* spending on food.

CONSUMPTION EXPENDITURE AS A MEASURE OF POVERTY

Our next attempt is to look at the consumption expenditure of the children households. Monthly expenditure or weekly expenditure and even the expenditure on the day of the visit by the investigator are easy to get. This is the reason for its widespread acceptance and application in India for measuring income poverty. Income data is elusive to get by. Households survive on different sources of livelihoods. One household may cultivate a small piece of land, may do non-agricultural wage labour during lean period and can do petty business during any time of the year. Aggregating these forms of different livelihoods poses a grave problem of accounting and calculation. For example, income from agriculture is problematic to calculate if not totally impossible. Total expenditure including own labour cost has to be deducted from total proceeds of any crop. There may be wide variety of crop a farmer can produce throughout the year. Farmers do not keep written records of prices and cost for each crop. They have to recall whenever asked to furnish. Recall method runs the risk of recall lapses that ultimately produce incorrect data ineligible to be used in economic analysis. This problem of misreporting of income data, not only exist in agriculture. Incomes from all self-employment activities are beset with similar problem of calculation.

They have also run an equal risk of misreporting. Thus accuracy of data on income from self-employment is subject to serious constraints. Wage work is not so difficult to calculate if the market wage rate is uniform through out the year. One can collect the prevalent wage rate and can multiply the same with number of days of wage work. The data can be reasonably trusted if the respondents correctly recall his days of work during last year. Income from salary can easily be calculated in rural area. Salary income is extremely rare. Therefore, the convenience of a recording a flawless data of salary income is rarely experienced by investigator in rural area. Other than the problems of miscalculation, conceptual vagueness, recall lapses also stand in the way in getting at the income of the reference household. There is another one that overtakes all in creating problem to get at the income data and that is dogged refusal to share with a stranger the information about the magnitude of family income. This reluctance does not arise out of fear about income tax complicacy. Rural household tend to keep their income under wrap and more so to a visitor from outside. Data on income is, therefore, so elusive. Still we come across data on rural income in many instances. One can cast doubt on the accuracy of the rural income data on account of fallibility that can crop up as explicated above. Income although being the best measure of purchasing power and level of living of people is relegated to the secondary place.

Our end is estimating the incidence of poverty among the population, the means to that end may be, as one of many, income of the family in question. We can take to other route to arrive at the poverty estimate. That route is not infested with so many imperfection possibilities. Consumption expenditure during a last reference period for the entire household is one such less risky but comfortable route. Construction of Monthly Per Capita Expenditure (MPCE) Class is undertaken at a regular interval just after collecting household consumption expenditure survey. The latter task is performed by the National Sample Survey Organization (NSSO). Planning Commission of India estimates the poverty in India on the basis of household consumption survey data provided by NSSO. The commission estimates the magnitude of poor on the basis of a yardstick, popularly known as poverty line. The threshold income level per head below which all are poor and the commission is committed lift all of them above the threshold line and therefore remove poverty, once and for all. The threshold poverty line is per capita income that allows a person to command food that must minimally provided with 2400 kilo calories per day per person in rural area and the same is 2100 for urban area.

The rural poverty lines based on Consumer Price Index for Agriculture Labourers (CPIAL) and in a similar way urban poverty line is constructed on the basis of Consumer Price Index for Industrial Workers (CPIIW). NSSO collects data on consumption expenditure of sample households for entire country every five years (quinquennial). They compute MPCE class, proportion of sampled households falling in each of the expenditure category from raw data recorded in the schedule. Planning Commission takes hold of the analysis of the NSSO to ponder over the efficacy of anti poverty development program. They peruse our success and failure on fight against poverty. The commission plan for the next five years on allocation of fund for poverty alleviation programme with an eye on the magnitude of poor in India provided by NSSO. The latter is also conducting household consumption expenditure survey every year on this sample. The latest annual survey is 63rd round. The survey estimated that, in 2006-07, around one half (50.3%) of the Indian rural population belongs to households with Monthly Per capita Consumption Expenditure (MPCE) less then Rs. 580 at 2006-07 prices. The average MPCE for rural India was Rs. 695 and Rs. 1312 in urban India at 2006-07 prices. The corresponding average MPCE in 2005-06 (62nd round) was Rs. 625 and Rs. 1171 in urban India.

The 63 round report also brings to light a wide variation of Average MPCE across status in India. Going by the share of food in total consumption expenditure as a measure of rural standard of living, the report says that the share varies from 40% and 43% for Kerala and Punjab respectively to around 60% for Assam, Orissa, Jharkhand and West Bengal. A few words here about consumption distribution of NSSO rounds would not be out of place and outside the context. District level data on consumption was maid available from 61st round onwards. This has certainly facilitated micro-level comparative study on poverty and level of living. The respondents have to recall the expenditure data to share with the investigators. Expenditure incurred very recently, say, during last months on consumption items can come to mind easily. So 30 day recall period is adopted for one segment of the survey. This is called Uniform Recall Period (URP) consumption data for all items are collected for the last 30 day period. The other strand is Mixed Recall Period (MRP). In this segment of the consumption schedule, consumption data for last 365 days on selected five non-food goods, education, and institutional medical care are collected. Along with this data, food consumption for last 30 days is collected. According to 61st round (2004-05), the rural poverty ratio in India was 28.3 per cent using Uniform Recall Period (URP). However, the Mixed

Recall Period yielded lower ratio of 21.8 per cent for rural India. NSSO provides a soothing news on poverty reduction during the period from 93-94 to 2004-05. Based on an estimate using URP, poverty ratio in India was 36 per cent. It came down to 27.5 per cent during 2004-05.

Planning Commission constructs the poverty lines based on consumption expenditure survey, for the entire country and for each state for the rural area as well as for urban area. There is variation in poverty line income among states as a result of differences in consumption pattern, particularly of food and variation in prices of commodities. Poverty line for rural India during 2004-05 was Rs. 356.30 and for urban India was Rs. 538.60. For West Bengal, the state where our respondent households inhabit, the poverty line was Rs. 382.82 for rural area and Rs. 449.32 for urban area. The proportion of poor in rural Bengal was 28.6 per cent compared to 28.3 for rural India. The combined estimate, entailing both urban and rural area places West Bengal slightly ahead of national average. Poverty, measured as number of people below poverty line was 27.5 for the country and for West Bengal it was 24.7 per cent.

Planning Commission also published the average MPCE for each state also for all districts in the states. The list also provides the best MPCE district within each state. This has been possible due to the novelty of 61st round survey that recorded consumption data in such a way where district level data is generated. This innovation has facilitated in preparing rank of each district in terms of Average MPCE. This ranking exercise has brought to light that Murshidabad, in which we have carried out our survey, is the worst MPCE district in West Bengal. The average MPCE in Murshidabad was Rs. 428. On the basis of MPCE calculation Murshidabad is the poorest district in the state having a poverty ratio of 55.9 per cent.

We have also recorded and analysed the children's households. Our reference period for recalling consumption expenditure on all items, in conformity with NSSO Consumption schedule, was 30 days period proceeding the day of visit by us. The reference period was purposively shortened to minimize the possibility of recall lapses.

TABLE 8.6
Monthly Per Capita Expenditure Class

Monthly Per Capita Expenditure Class	*Frequency*	*Percent*	*Cumulative Percent*
Rs. 151- Rs. 300	516	19.4	19.4
Rs. 301- Rs. 450	1173	44.1	63.5
Rs. 451 - Rs. 600	609	22.9	86.4
Rs. 601 - Rs. 750	216	8.1	94.5
Rs. 751 - Rs. 900	68	2.6	97.1
Rs. 901 - Rs. 1050	37	1.4	98.5
Rs. 1051 - Rs. 1200	17	.6	99.1
Rs. 1201 - Rs. 1350	9	.3	99.4
Rs. 1351 - Rs. 1500	3	.1	99.5
Rs. 1501 - Rs. 1650	6	.2	99.8
Rs. 1651 - Rs. 1800	2	.1	99.8
Rs. 1951 - Rs. 2100	2	.1	99.9
Rs. 2101 - Rs. 2250	2	.1	100.0
Total	2660	100.0	

Source : Household Survey in Murshidabad in 2008.

The minimum MPCE is Rs. 161.54 and the maximum is Rs. 2150.00. The average MPCE is Rs. 446.62, slightly higher than the magnitude revealed by the planning commission in 2004-05 for the district.

Around 19 per cent of children belong to households whose MPCE is less than Rs. 300. The table shows us that 63.5 per cent of children belong to households where MPCE is less than Rs. 450. The highest concentration of household at 44% is found in MPCE class of Rs. 301-Rs. 450. The next class is Rs. 451-Rs. 600 where the frequency of children's households is 22.9 per cent. From this point frequency begins to fall drastically indicating very thin presence of relatively affluent class in our study area. Almost 86 per cent of children households belongs households whose MPCE is equal or less then Rs. 600. We find here the lowest expenditure class of

Rs. 151-Rs. 300 is extremely poor category. Almost 19 per cent of children belong to this destitute group. Going by the poverty line of Rs. 382.82 for rural West Bengal, as set by the Planning Commission roughly 25 per cent will be added to the group below official poverty line. Altogether around 44 per cent of children belong to poor households in our study area. The official poverty line is contested in many corners as it does not capture fully elements of deprivation. The report submitted by the National Commission on Enterprises in the Unorganized Sector, headed by Prof. Arjun Sengupta in 2004, observed that 77 per cent people in India survives on average expenditure of Rs. 20 per day capita. These people are not only poor but also vulnerable.

TABLE 8.7
Monthly Per Capita Expenditure Class and Children's Schooling

Monthly Per Capita Expenditure Class	*Children*		*Total*
	Not in School	*In School*	
Rs. 151- Rs. 300	137	379	516
Rs. 301- Rs. 450	212	961	1173
Rs. 451 - Rs. 600	74	535	609
Rs. 601 - Rs. 750	16	200	216
Rs. 751 - Rs. 900	2	66	68
Rs. 901 - Rs. 1050	0	37	37
Rs. 1051 - Rs. 1200	0	17	17
Rs. 1201 - Rs. 1350	0	9	9
Rs. 1351 - Rs. 1500	0	3	3
Rs. 1501 - Rs. 1650	0	6	6
Rs. 1651 - Rs. 1800	1	1	2
Rs. 1951 - Rs. 2100	0	2	2
Rs. 2101 - Rs. 2250	0	2	2
Total	442	2218	2660

Source : Household Survey in Murshidabad in 2008.

The Commission therefore, calls for redefinition of poverty line in India. It recommends heightening of poverty line that would include not only the poor but a huge population of economically vulnerable section. It we go by this expanded definition we find that a little more than 86 per cent of children in our study are economically vulnerable as their families belong to MPCE class belong to just equal or less than Rs. 600.

This is a very righteous attempt to connect children's belongings to MPCE class and their school participation. The table reveals a negative correlation between poverty and school participation. Poverty seems to discourage school participation. School participation is lowest at 73.44 per cent

TABLE 8.8
Monthly Per Capita Expenditure Class and Child Labour

Monthly Per Capita Expenditure Class	*Children*		*Total*
	Child is not full time worker	*Child is full time worker*	
Rs. 151- Rs. 300	430	86	516
Rs. 301- Rs. 450	1043	130	1173
Rs. 451 - Rs. 600	570	39	609
Rs. 601 - Rs. 750	205	11	216
Rs. 751 - Rs. 900	67	1	68
Rs. 901 - Rs. 1050	37	0	37
Rs. 1051 - Rs. 1200	17	0	17
Rs. 1201 - Rs. 1350	9	0	9
Rs. 1351 - Rs. 1500	3	0	3
Rs. 1501 - Rs. 1650	6	0	6
Rs. 1651 - Rs. 1800	2	0	2
Rs. 1951 - Rs. 2100	2	0	2
Rs. 2101 - Rs. 2250	2	0	2
Total	2393	267	2660

Source : Household Survey in Murshidabad in 2008.

for children of extremely poor family having MPCE class of Rs. 151 to Rs. 300. Improvement in economic standing or reduction of poverty as reflected in the higher MPCE increases the school participation of children.

The table shows that school participation goes up to 81.92 per cent for children of next higher MPCE class, i.e., Rs. 301 to Rs. 450. It further goes up to 87.84 per cent for higher next category of Rs. 451 to Rs. 600. It further goes up to 92 per cent for next higher class. From Rs. 901 to Rs. 1050 onwards we find that all successive MPCE classes have 100 per cent school participation of children.

We consider full time work of children and we will try to relate it with MPCE classes to which they belong as a measure of poverty. The purpose of this exercise is to see whether poverty pushes the children towards full time hazardous work. We need to see from our data set generated from the household survey how poverty as measured by MPCE can influence children's participation in labour force. As schooling deprivation is highest among lowest MPCE class of very poor category, the same is also true for labour participation on full time basis. Child labour rate is highest at 16.66 per cent for this poorest category. Similarly the incidence comes down at 11.09 per cent for the next higher MPCE class, Rs. 301 to Rs. 450. It again reduces to 6.40 per cent for the next class of Rs. 450 to Rs. 600. From Rs. 901 MPCE onwards, we do not find a single child working on full time basis in tobacco rolling. Therefore, the table further establishes the child labour and poverty nexus, that is omnipresent but with a rider that, poverty is not the sole cause.

STANDARD OF LIVING AND CHILDHOOD ADVERSITIES

Poverty as a degradable state of human existence comes up in the discourse on human distress where child labour is one such manifestation. Poverty always works on push factor side to cause child labour. Because poverty is associated with low income, the latter pre-empts them to access commodities and services required for minimum level of living. The minimum however is contextually defined and culturally conceived. It has cultural imperatives that vary across geography. It changes over time. A particular society constructs its own minima therefore; minimal living as any society in the advanced western world has set for itself, is quite dissimilar to what a poor and agrarian society in the eastern world has set. Likewise, the same minimum is subject to change and reshapes itself overtime. The minima that were accepted two hundred years ago in the same society no longer persist now. Attitude to and expectation from life has undergone a change during this prolonged period, the minima has changed in tune with social transformation. Food, shelter and clothing, in the early stage of advancement of human race, were necessities for survival. Minimal level was thus defined as accessing these bare necessities. Society did not accept any material possession beyond those bare minimum.

The bare necessities and threshold living was vaguely defined in the earlier conceptions. Food for example, is now planned and defined in terms of its nutritive value that must supply energy for physical functioning. How much energy a representative man requires for healthy physical living? What is a representative man? Where does the man live? Does the person live in a village or in a city? Is the person aged? Is she young? Many such multifaceted issues came up in setting nutritional norm of food intake and minimum physical living. Poverty occupied the centre stage of global concern in the wake of the Second World War that coincided with, during, the same time span, end of colonial rule in the vast swathes of Asia, Africa and Latin America. It does not mean, however, that poverty as a situation of human adversity had emerged in the aftermath of western colonialism on eastern hemisphere. Poverty is not a recent phenomenon, nor a post-colonial social evil. It has been persisting on earth for millions of years. We were ravaged by the onslaught of famines several times in our past. Millions of people died of starvation in almost all faces of the globe during last many centuries. Outbreak of dreadful epidemic had almost depopulated an entire region on the earth. Natural disasters had also brought enormous damage, destruction and devastation of a large part of our human race.

The saga of unspeakable human misery is speaking for itself the persistence of poverty and consequent vulnerability of human kind in our bygone years. We have heard of poor laws in Britain as well as in continental Europe in medieval period. Colonial India did not see a single attempt to remove poverty of her subjects. Sri *Dadabhai Naoroji,* the architect of drain theory of colonial exploitation, often had equated un-Britishness with imperial neglect of massive poverty in India. Our colonial masters overlooked the poverty question but our leaders started spearheading the national movement for liberation that had intensified during early twentieth century. They had envisioned a free India, not only from political subjugation but also free from endemic poverty and hunger. The planners of free India charted out a course of planned economic development for India that would ultimately aim at removal of poverty. Economic development was thought to be means and removal of poverty was the end to accomplish within a stipulated time period. Poverty as social evil began to be reflected upon, relooked and articulated. Poverty was defined in caloric norms by a new body constituted in free India named, Planning Commission. The concept of a representative adult emerged who need, on daily basis, a minimum level of calorie from the food he takes during the day.

Not all the citizens are adults; there is sizeable presence of children. Do the two categories need same amount of calories? The answer is obviously in the negative. Children do not need the same level energy what an adult does. Adults have to do hard labour generally which children do not do. Therefore, need for calorie must differ. The problem was overcome by introducing a new methodology what is known as adult equivalent scale to bring out symmetry. Nutrition experts were invited to recommend a minimum calorie norm.

The expert group, after a rigorous research, came to accept that work intensity and energy needs of the workers can not be same for both urban and rural area. Rural adults have to toil more than their urban counterparts. Here work implies all daily activities to support daily physical living of the reference adults. The expert group, taking cue from the nutritionists prescribed a minimum 2400 calorie for rural area and 2100 for urban area as minimum requirement. Thus an average person in India must take food, in a day that should contain minimum calorie of 2400 if the person resides in a rural area. The food must contain that minimum nutrition that goes in to what is called basic need, along with a minimum access to clothing, shelter and services without which a bare living with minimum attainment is not possible. Poverty line is thus a threshold income that permits the reference person to command these basic necessities. Planning Commission of India sets the poverty line in an interval of five years plan and end of the preceding one. Therefore, the threshold income or the poverty line income is subject to change to take into account the inflation as measured by consumer price index. The Head Count Ratio (HCR) is thus proportion of population falling below the poverty line income. Countries are free to set their own poverty line in accordance with their perceptions.

World Bank very recently uses 1 US Dollar per day per capita as a global bench mark. But international poverty line expressed in one currency is beset with problem of conversion. The bank also proclaims that 2 US Dollar per day per capita is a benchmark for measuring economic vulnerability across the globe. Construction of poverty line income to count poor is always subject to controversy and contestation. The displeasure is aired that governments tend to exhibit a lower incidence of poverty as a mark of the positive outcome of their development effort. Keeping poverty line a lower income level would obviously lessen the number of poor. However, Indian poverty line is updated by planning commission from time to time on the basis of the findings of consumption expenditure survey carried out by NSSO.

Economists, social thinkers, intellectuals, statesmen and activist were not happy with this confined interpretation of income or purchasing power. Can poverty be put in a tiny box of income criterion? Put in other words, can poverty be removed by meeting the basic needs that contain a bare minimum of food, clothing and shelter? Is physical living enough for meaningful living on this earth? These questions had haunted many minds in many corners. The basic need approach to qualification of poverty was not accepted. Poverty must be broadened to include to all aspects of human development. Development must not imply a narrowed down concept of rise in income and purchasing power of the people.

Development should not restrict itself to an outcome when a few millions of people are now earning income more than what required meeting the basic needs. Prior to 1990, development was conceived as rise in per capita income or per capita GNP of a country in question. Development policies of the developing countries were framed and implemented with an aim in mind to raise the per capita GNP. Countries were compared and their relative positions in world ranking were determined on the basis of per capita national income calculated on the basis of purchasing power parity. Countries which could cross a thresholds per capita income in US $ could step in to an exclusive class of developed world.

The shift from 'commodity space' to 'capability space' as a measure of human wellbeing had already gained currency during 1990. The argument that income is not the sole indicator of wellbeing gained ground everywhere. UNDP, the organ of the U.N entrusted with the task of facilitating economic development in least developed countries through undertaking various projects incorporated this expanded notion of development in their understanding of development. They began to focus on human development as the ultimate goal of economic development process. Growth in per capita income is the means to achieve the end of human development. The concept of human development encompasses three areas of development outcome: (a) capability to lead a long and healthy life, (b) capability to read an write as well as attainment of intellectual ability so that people can take part in social and cultural life in a meaningful way, and (c) capability to command over resources to sustain physical life, to have adequate nutrition and to have healthy living condition. UNDP constructed human development index for measuring an individual country's performance in promoting human development. Average longevity of the citizens of the country is taken up as an indicator of physical well-being. Educational attainment is measured by a combination of adult literacy rate and Gross Enrolment Ratio for children. Economic well-being is measured by per capita income.

The total human development score to be achieved by a country is the sum total of score on each of the there areas. Per capita income as a measure of human well-being that lost it's pre-eminence with the advent of the new scale. Many countries slipped down in the rank of human development score despite their very high standing in per capita income. Similarly, many low income countries surpassed others by their appreciable performance in human development front. Income can not alone reveal the qualities of life. Because quality of life can be enhanced by provisioning of public goods the access to which does not depend on family income or purchasing power? For example, say a piped water line passes through one side of one's residential dwelling. The resident can avail pure drinking water without much hassle than other who may reside far away from that water point. Thus quality of life, that to much extent depends on availability of pure drinking water to rule out any possibility of attracting any water borne disease, differs where income may not differ. Public provisioning of pure drinking water which people can collect without hassles can enhance the quality of life. We have constructed standard of living index as a proxy for economic standing of the families of our study area. Income of the households is not, only problematic to get by, serious recall lapses, miscalculation, suppressions and intangibility cripple the income data flow and accuracy.

Household amenities, productive and unproductive assets and ownership of luxuries are tangible. No one can hide those stuffs from the view of the onlookers. Therefore, suppression of facts associated with sharing income mainly form self-employed occupation can be ruled out comfortably in case of observing and listing of household assets. Quality and scale of productive assets of households reflect the economic standing of the households. The productive assets like land and livestock not only generate income but also work as collateral in the dire eventuality of incurring debts. Quality of housing does matter in the physical well-being of people. Dwelling houses built of brick and cement that we call "*pucca* houses" of relative affluence of the people. We have also considered quality of toilet facility available to the households. Hygiene, sanitation and life free from frequent occurrence of infectious diseases depend on the quality and type of toilets. Open defecation in the field poses several health hazards. Thus good toilet is a mark of better living. Cooking inside the living room is detrimental to health. A good living condition requires that there should be separate room for kitchen. Thus having a kitchen is a feature of better living by households. Ownership of durable goods is a sign of economic strength.

Box

Construction of Standard of Living Index

House type	:	4 for *pucca*, 2 for *semi-pucca*, 0 for *kachha*
Toilet facility	:	4 for own flesh toilet, 2 for public flush, or own pit toilet. I for public pit toilet, 0 for no facility
Source of Lighting	:	2 for electricity, 1 for Kerosene gas, 0 for other source
Main fuel for cooking	:	2 for electricity, LPG, 1 for coal, or Kerosene, 0 for other source
Sources of drinking water	:	2 for pipe, hand pump, 1 for public Tube-well, 0 for others
Separate room for cooking	:	1 for yes, 0 for no.
Ownership of irrigated land	:	2 if households owns at least some irrigated land, 0 for no irrigated land
Ownership of livestock	:	2 if owner livestock, 0 otherwise
Ownership of durable goods	:	4 each for a car or tractor, 3 each for a moped or scooter, motor cycle, telephone, refrigerator or colour television, 2 each for a bicycle, electric fan, radio, transistor, sewing machine, black and white television, water pump, bullock cart, 1 each for a matters pressure cooker, chair, cot, table, clock

We have emphasised on quantity as well as on quality while constructing Standard of Living Index (SLI) for our survey households. We have assigned weights to all items where higher value items will draw higher weights. The different weights for different items are presented in the box above. Each household is thus allotted a score which is sum total of individual score on all items taken up for construction of standard of living index. The following table presents the frequency distribution of children according to their affiliation with a particular standard of living group.

TABLE 8.9
Standard of Living Index Range

Index Range	*Frequency*	*Percent*	*Cumulative Percent*
0-10	324	12.2	12.2
11-20	847	31.8	44.0
21-30	760	28.6	72.6
31-40	409	15.4	88.0
41-50	185	7.0	94.9
51-60	75	2.8	97.7
61-70	35	1.3	99.1
71-80	4	.2	99.2
81-90	21	.8	100.0
Total	2660	100.0	

Mean : 24.67, Standard Deviation : 14.0.49.
Source : Household Survey in Murshidabad in 2008.

Around 12 per cent of children belong to extremely poor households having SLI score of less then 10. We find that 72 per cent of our child population of 2660 belongs to families having of a SLI score less than 30. SLI range from 31 to 50 can be said to be of middle category in wealth ranking. We find that 22 per cent of children belong to this category. Likewise SLI ranging from 51 to 90 can be placed in relatively rich category. Here we find that 5.1 per cent of these children belong to this exclusive wealthy category.

We have considered two states of childhood adversities: full time work participation and full time schooling participation of children in the present analysis. It would be interesting to note the connectedness between standard of living score and the adversities for children. Let us start with schooling non participation.

Table 8.10
Standard of Living Index Range Children Schooling

	Children		*Total*
Range	*Not in School*	*In school*	
0-10	120	204	324
11-20	164	683	847
21-30	107	653	760
31-40	38	371	409
41-50	9	176	185
51-60	2	73	75
61-70	2	33	35
71-80	0	4	4
81-90	0	21	21
Total	442	2218	2660

Source : Household Survey in Murshidabad in 2008.

School participation rate is 62.96 for children of destitute families having standard of living score up to 10. The immediate better category is 11-20 group whom we mention as very poor class. The schooling participation of children has gone up to 80.63 per cent comparatively better than the earlier class. The middle group of households whose standard of living score ranges from 31 to 50 has recorded a substantial improvement in school participation that stands at 93.50 per cent. The rich households comprise of score from 51 to 90. The school participation of their children is 97.03 per cent. From score of 61 onwards and up to 90 comprising of the upper layer even in the rich class, school participation is 100 per cent.

Full time child work is the worst form of childhood adversities. The table present the connection between economic standing of the households measured in achievement of standard living score. Full time work participation rate is highest for destitute category, the lowest rung in the score

Table 8.11
Standard of Living Index Range of Child Labour

Range	*Children*		*Total*
	Not full time worker	*child is full time worker*	
0-10	250	74	324
11-20	750	97	847
21-30	695	65	760
31-40	387	22	409
41-50	177	8	185
51-60	75	0	75
61-70	34	1	35
71-80	4	0	4
1-90	21	0	21
Total	2393	267	2660

Source : Household Survey in Murshidabad in 2008.

group. The incidence is 22.84 per cent. The phenomenon of poverty and child labour nexus is further established in this exercise. Slight improvement in living condition, scaling from "destitute" to "very poor" category reduces the child labour incidence. Full time work participation rate is 11.45 in case of 'very poor' group. The 'poor' group is slightly ahead of very poor group in economic standing having a higher asset base. The scores from 21 to 30 are considered as constituting 'poor' category. Full time child labour rate is 8.55 per cent for the 'poor' group. Child labour rate is 5.05 per cent for middle group. As usual, there is only one child working on full time basis from the rural rich group. The incidence is negligibly at less then one per cent.

9

Food Insecurity and Child Labour

The connection between poverty and child labour seems to be omnipresent and indisputable. Poverty has to persist in the childrens' households for occurrence of child labour because adult incomes are evidently inadequate to sustain the family. Poverty thus generates push factors that cause child labour but this factor on its own, singularly is incapable to cause child labour. The pull factor has to be present simultaneously to generate this. Both these factors have to work together. This is just analogues to a proverbial saying that two hands are equally needed for a clap. The availability of job for children within neighbourhood is pull factor. The pull factor is visibly present in a situation where child labour legislation does not come in to play and secondly unskilled, low paid and flexible work schedule, must characterize the job available for children. This pull, whatever is its strength can be resisted by families who do not need children's income for running the family wheel. They would rather send these children to school. They would certainly incur cost for this action. They bear with the cost in an expectation that education for the children is a kind of investment that would yield positive return in future. One resource that the child misses by joining work instead of school is the skill. An unskilled labourer remains entrapped in perpetual cycle of low wage and poverty.

Thus child labour seems to have intergenerational cycle. The first generation child labourers are more likely to promote second generation child labourers. This is inescapable because child labour is associated with lack of skill, low income, higher fertility and lack of education and these are passed on from one generation to the next. The cycle is a hard nut to break unless government comes forward to take up the task of breaking the cycle through massive investment in elementary education. Pull factor that works in tandem with push factor meets no resistance from the families that survive on the margin of social existence haunted by the unvarying fear of shortage of food. The food economy and its dynamics, therefore, come in the discourse on child labour. Food insecurity as an obverse of household vulnerability is a new entrant in the discourse. But the inclusion of this has added a new dimension to the analysis and search for appropriate policies to contain child labour. This insertion is not an attempt to go beyond poverty to search for its cause. Rather it is a noble attempt to bring to light a forgotten aspect of poverty that mediate between the latter and the child labour in a context where local economy does not offer opportunity, to transcend the subsistence living. Food insecurity as a subject of deeper understanding has drawn attention from scholars and activists. This new discourse places food at the centre place of household economy.

FOOD AS A COMMODITY

Food is basic requirement for survival without which physical well-being is threatened. Therefore, for the humanity as a whole food, clothing, and shelter are primary need for which our ancestors had to strive in the nascent stage of civilization and at the beginning of our march to material prosperity. When our basic needs were met, new demand cropped up to lead a better life. This was a beginning of humanity's progress towards material advancement in the wake of new discoveries, invention, use of capital and technology. Demand began to shift from essentials to luxuries, production and supply of the newer goods responded quickly to the newly created demand. Economic activities began to expand. The subsistence or primary economy that had confined itself in production and exchange of basic goods was overwhelmingly added by industrial economy and later by service sector economy. This is usual course of material advancement and the trajectory of development for each society and for each region of the world. In the earliest stage of human life, accessing food was primary concern for all. When money and exchange was yet to emerge in the life of men, our ancestor would invest most of their time of the day in gathering food. After the advent of production and exchange, a major part of income was spent on food. Unfortunately this spending pattern is not the thing of the past. There are millions of people in the present world who retain the same practice because development and prosperity had eluded them. There are enormous areas in South Asia, in Sub-Saharan, Africa, in Latin America that still lead the primitive living characterized by hunt for food. Thus food insecurity is one manifestation of poverty. Food for all is still a dream; we are many miles away from that cherished goal. The goal is getting further away in days ahead as food production is severely threatened by environmental factors. The climatic change as a consequence of global warming is posing a serious threat to the ecosystem in the foodgrain producing regions of the world. Flood and drought are showing their fangs by turn. The most alarming among these adverse developments is the dwindling acreage for food crop cultivation. More and more of cultivable lands are put to use for production of high value commercial crops. Cultivation of plant on a massive scale for production of bio-fuel has also taken away a large tract of land usually used for raising food crop. The world is now alarmed of the depleting reserve of underground fossil fuel. The threat of decreasing crop production is also added by recurrent crop loss in the field as a result of pest attack. Loss of foodgrain during transportation and storage is quite substantial. The fear of food insecurity looms large now. The world community has taken the issue seriously now.

The United Nations although charged primarily with the promotion of global peace and security devoted itself in thought and action to avert impending food crisis. The World Food Programme under the auspices of the United Nations was launched during nineties. Food security rather than military security catapulted to primary concern of the UN. The member-states were persuaded to prioritize production and distribution of food grains. The Food and Agricultural Organization (FAO), the global body for development of agriculture, jumped in to action at the behest of the UN to campaign for modern agricultural practices for heightened production and productivity. Mono-cropping is now replaced by multiple cropping. Irrigation coverage has considerably expanded in India. Watershed programmes have been taken up in dry land agriculture. The World Bank has come forward to lend support to state governments in India in installing river lift irrigation, deep tube well, shallow tube well and other micro-irrigation projects to boost agricultural production. In India, agricultural productivity had witnessed unprecedent growth during eighties and nineties but it had failed to keep the momentum in later years. The reason for this fall in growth rate, as many point out, is the decline in public investment in agriculture in the later half of nineties. The availability of food in per capita terms, which had increased by 1.2 per cent per annum during 1980, came down during the subsequent decade by 0.28 per cent.

FOOD, POVERTY AND NUTRITION

Sociologists say that Food is a social commodity. They lament that social context of food, as a commodity, has never caught serious attention of scholars. Sociology has brought forth social distances in a caste-based society where class caste nexus still exists overwhelmingly. Food, therefore, is ascribed different values for different social contexts. The ascription of differential values, however, was overlooked in the earlier sociological studies. Economics, however, see food as a commodity having intrinsic utility. The latter is described as a quality inherent in any goods or services that satisfy human wants. There are two types of goods we demand and we use for daily consumption: economic goods and free goods. We do not pay for free goods, air we breath for examples. We pay for economic goods because, they have to be produced by combination of human effort, use of natural resources, capital and technology for which a certain amount of cost is incurred. The price of any goods is therefore average monetary cost of production plus a margin of profit. Food is economic goods as its production involves cost, direct as well as indirect. Food, like any other economic goods, is not abundant as air is. This has a limited supply because the inputs all put together, including land, is limited in supply. Price is thus reflection of relative scarcity.

FOOD PRODUCTION

The availability of food at a certain point of time in a year or say, the amount of food stock does not depend on the crop output of that year. Surplus food grains of the previous years stored in go downs. Government keeps the record of production of various food crops for each year. There is Agriculture Price Commission in India at the national level to study the actual cost of production of each crop. It also fixes the remunerative price, taking into account the average cost of production and the extent of profit margin as a reward for the farmer's enterprise. Agriculture is always subject to vagaries of monsoon in India. Any disruption in the course of monsoon, belated arrival or early departure, can adversely affect our major food crop. Irrigation is yet to lessen our monsoon dependence. Installation of irrigation project is not so costly in budgetary terms; it is far more costly environmentally. Thus food production depends on a host of factors a part of which is natural and a major part is, of course, man-made. Agricultural policy of the government is one such measure in the arena of and made factors. Fixing of Minimum Support Price (MSP) by the government is crucial Credit policy; particularly the policy on rural credit is an important factor in influencing farmer's decision to raise certain crop. The Rural banks must reduce the cost of credit to farmers. Post-harvest sale is another issue that also haunts the farmers. A favourable crop output is thus an outcome of positive showing of these factors.

WHAT IS THE UTILITY OF FOOD?

Food production in a year plus previous food stock together makes available food stock for the citizens of the country. However, food security which implies access to food all the time for the people has nothing to do with production or availability of food stock. It has been well documented, notably by Professor Amartya Sen's seminal work 'Poverty and Famine' that famine had ravaged many countries or many locations of country in the past at a time when food production was normal. The famine strikes the poor as they loose their exchange entitlements suddenly. Thus famine is the result, not of the decline of food crop production but of the result of sudden loss of purchasing power of the millions of poor. Thus food crop produced in the agricultural fields, after processing, does not reach the plate of meal for millions of poor. There are various factors that come in between the tea cup and the leap. Market price and affordability come in between. Loss of purchasing power, thus obviously deprives the poor of dietary intakes that results in semi-starvation and even starvation, if the access is denied for a prolonged period. Food insecurity thus looms large over a vast segment of underprivileged population. Hopefully government has come forward to protect these vulnerable through various food-based intervention programme. One of such programs is *Antyodaya Anna Yojona* for the aged, ailing and feeble.

The other is Targeted Public Distribution System (TPDS) for people below poverty line who cannot afford to buy food grains at the prevailing market price. Under the scheme each poor household as identified by the local government will be provided with 25 kilo of rice or wheat each month at the subsidized price of Rs. 3 per kilo. Mid-day meal programme for primary school children across length and breadth of the country is a massive nutrition programme. Each student is served with cooked meal every day in school. The programme aims at achieving two goals at the same time: nutritional support for children and encouragement of school attendance and retention.

Food is thus essential for human existence. Food provides fuel of body engine. Human body needs energy for physical activity and food is the source of energy. Quantity of food does not matter much as quality of food does. Food must be nutritive and balanced, safe and palatable for easy absorption in the body. The food must contain proteins, vitamins, carbohydrates, minerals and other micro-nutrients for healthy living. Food adequacy implies nutritious diet without which human beings are susceptible to various infections diseases as a result of the loss of immunity. Child malnutrition is alarming in India. Infant mortality in India is the result of malnutrition of pregnant and lactating mother. The two square meals in a day must be rich in nutritive values. This is a challenging task for India.

POVERTY AND FOOD INSECURITY

Poverty and food insecurity are inseparable with each other. Poverty is the inability of the poor households to access adequate food. Low purchasing power always restricts the access. Poverty in India is defined in terms of poverty line which is a bench mark, expressed as per capita income. The poverty line income must allow for every member of a household to access food that must provide 2400 calorie for rural area and 2100 calorie for urban area. The difference in calorie requirement is due to differential energy requirement for physical activities. One can not dispute that agriculture wage work, even all works related to agriculture is much more laborious requiring higher level of burning of calorie. The urban work is rather less laborious therefore requires comparatively less calorie. Nutritionists therefore, have recommended two calorie norms for two different settings. It is presumed that persistence of poverty is an indication of an abysmal presence of calorie inadequacy among underprivileged population. Unfortunately, in India the trend is upsetting and disquieting for planners and policy-makers.

Poverty reduction in recent times does not commensurate with increase in calorie intake. Calorie deprivation continues to be high despite poverty reduction.

Economists are looking for reason for this unusual and undesirable outcome. They argue that poverty estimate in India is based on national average derived from household expenditure data provided by NSS. The recall period for the household respondent varies from last week to last year. Reporting errors cannot be ruled out in the mixing of reference period. There is widespread variation in taste, preferences, choice, attitude and prices relating to consumption basket. The average poverty estimate therefore does not take into account this wide divergence. There is a possibility that there is shift within the consumption basket, a shift from cereals to non-cereals, from food to non-food, has taken place. Therefore, growth of caloric intake lags behind poverty reduction. Using the quinquennial NSS data for 15 major states that account for about 95 per cent of the country's population, one can see that the per capita caloric intake has declined in rural area during the period from 1984 to 2005. Undoubtedly the cereal price rise has adversely affected the calorie intake of the bottom 30 per cent of the households since the price elasticity of cereal is close to one. One strand of arguments, spearheaded by a group of economists in India does not find any reason to worry about the decline of cereal consumption.

Following the line of reasoning, Professor *Hanumantha Rao* (2000) holds the view that decline in cereal intake cannot be taken as an indicator of deterioration in human welfare. The fall in cereal consumption was more than compensated by increased consumption of non-cereal foods. Thus per capita calories intake did not toe the line of decline in cereal intake. Interestingly, the relationship between poverty and calories intake amongst states in India is not robust. Poorest states in India, like Orissa and Rajasthan exhibit lower population of caloric deficient population. A few richer states as measured by lower head count ratio of poverty have higher proportion of caloric deficient population.

However, in recent years, policy-makers and planners are more interested in nutrition outcome rather than on caloric intake as indicator of human development. Caloric intake is problematic to measure whereas nutritional outcome is easily observable. Anthropometric measures are now widely accepted as indicator of nutrition. Body Mass Index (BMI) is used to measure the extent of malnutrition. Infant Mortality Rate and Child Mortality rate are now accepted as indicators of human development. The Millennium Development Goal (MDG) had taken up the task of reducing IMR by 2015.

FOOD INSECURITY AS ENTITLEMENT FAILURE

Professor Amartya Sen, the noted noble laureate and exponent of entitlement approach for dealing with the issue of poverty and famine. He described the latter as a worst culmination of persisting and widespread hunger of a large number of population. Famine had ravaged many countries in the past. He pointed out that famine occurred not solely due to sudden fall in food production. In fact, he pointed out with the help of historical evidence that in many cases, famine had hit a certain region in a year when food production was normal. He attributed the loss of command over food by a section of a population as entitlement failure. The landless agricultural labourers who comprise a formidable section in the rural population have command or ownership over their own labour power. This is called 'entitlement' which is socially accepted, legally agreed and can be exchanged for certain other thing such as "wage" for example, in the market economy. This "exchange entitlement" is a socially accepted system. The agricultural labouring class may suddenly experience exchange entitlement failure which implies that they no longer command enough food at going market priced. Exchange Entitlement or E-Mapping as conceptualized by Professor Sen is a possible set of commodity bundles a person exchange. Starvation occurs when the E-mapping does not contain enough food.

A landless agriculture labourer may face food shortage if the wages she receives in exchange of her labour power stay behind the escalating food prices. The food price may go up if there is sudden rise in demand. Thus higher food price will not altogether drive out her from the market but she has to carry home lesser amount of food than what she needs for her entire family. Food inadequacy leads, if persists for long, to temporary hunger. Poverty is also explained in the frame of entitlement approach whereby a section of population cannot command sufficient commodities in exchange of their own commodities, labour for example, to lead a decent life. Thus poverty is also entitlement failure and if the failure is transitory then the poverty or commodity depravities is also momentary. On the other hand, if the failure lasts for a long period, the poverty is said to be chronic. The same is true for food crisis or insecurity. One of the features may be transitory while other is chronic. The policy intervention need not be same for both the situations.

Starvation is a symptom of a sudden fall in household food supply. This is a sign of inadequacy if not an indication of total lack of food. When food inadequacy persists, the households tend to adjust, among themselves, with the lesser amount of food. Members adjust themselves in this crisis situation by adopting "one square meal" a day instead of "two square meals". Adult members may skip one meal in a day as a gesture of sacrifice for the sake of children and the aged. The earners may not like that the dependents in their households should bear the brunt. This is an ideal situation where altruism persists, in the absence of which, sufferings looms large over children and elderly. Sufferings on gender lines can not be ruled out. Studies have shown that there is pervasive discrimination against females and girl children within the households in nutritional provision. Food crisis obviously aggravates this adverse predicament for them. Food-based intervention by the government is hailed as step towards social protection for vulnerable sections of the population. *Antyodaya Annapurna Yajona*, is a food programme for the aged people in the rank of the poorest of the poor. A few state governments, West Bengal for example, has recently taken up a project called "Sahaya" under this new scheme cooked meal would be distributed to the identified poor at a particular time in each day. Among the ongoing food programmes, mid-day meal scheme for primary school going children is the largest one in the country by the sheer magnitude of its beneficiaries. No other programme of this genre in any part of the world can match India's noon meal programme by way of its size, effect and management. During the initial years, all school going children were provided with twice kilos of either rice or wheat per week. Children themselves used to collect their quota from the PDS shop nearest to their homes on production of the attendance certificate furnished by the school. This dry ration scheme continued until the Supreme Court ruling in response to public interest litigation. The apex court directed the central government to introduce cooked meal every day to each student within school campus instead of dry ration. The latter did not fulfil the purpose for which this grandiose scheme was mooted. The objective was two fold: supply of nutrition and encouraging school enrolment and retention. The latter did pick up significantly but the former did not because the dry ration added up the existing food supply of the underprivileged families. Low income families evidently were benefited by this food scheme but the children, for whom the scheme was implemented, got little due to large number of feeding mouths. Introduction of cooked meal scheme however ensures adequate nutrition to a large number of school going children in India. School participation, in recent years, has remarkably improved. Despite various deficiencies and loopholes in the present arrangement of mid-day meal, this is a positive step towards nutritional security for millions of children in India. Child malnutrition is still a formidable challenge in India.

RIGHT TO FOOD

Right to food is yet to emerge as guaranteed rights in our county. But right to life guaranteed under Article 21 of our constitution implicitly incorporates right to food for all citizens of our country. Right to life implies right to live with dignity and right to protection against starvation and malnutrition. The weak, infirm and ailing persons can never lead the lives that are meaningful and productive. Lack of access to nutritious food in adequate amount can derail a person's ability to taste the fruits of life. Physical well-being is a basic condition for accessing the opportunities for growth and development of every human being. Food should not only be balanced and nutritious, but also needs to conform to the culinary habits and cultural traits of the person concerned.

Enforcement of right to food for all Indians as constitutionally guaranteed rights is confronted with supply side concern. Domestic production of food grains is an issue of prime concern. A country as large as India cannot opt for bulk import in an era of escalating global food prices after providing for huge import bill for petroleum products. Food-grains have to be produced domestically in adequate quantity to ensure availability of food grain throughout the year. We are still lagging behind many developing countries in productivity. Augmenting of productivity is primary task. Our agricultural activity in general and crop output in particular is constrained by the vagaries of monsoon. Delay in arrival monsoon in rice producing zone adversely hit crop prospects. Excessive rain also brings flash foods in low-lying fields resulting heavy crop loss. Flood is not the only retarding enemy of crop output, there is other monster that stands in the polar opposite of flood by its very nature. The latter threat is drought. Thus the outburst of nature's fury in the form of flood or drought can hold back crop production and that in turn, results in crop shortage.

The new government at the centre is contemplating a bill to be placed in the parliament for making right to food as legal enforceable rights. The right of food is mooted in line with right to work currently under way in rural India. The flagship rural work programme is known as National Rural Employment Guarantee Scheme (NREGS). The scheme provides for 100 days of employment for any adult member of the rural household. The scheme primarily aims at enhancing rural income and also building rural infrastructure for creating opportunities for future growth. But accepting right to food as a fundamental right by the government is not only a remarkable step towards advancing human rights but also a policy announcement that calls for huge budgetary provision and shift of policies. The government needs to reformulate agricultural policy with an aim to boost food production through provision of cheap credit, incentives and structuring minimum support prices (MSP) in a bid to encourage farmers. The recent trend of use of land for producing cash crop is worrisome. Farmers are swayed by the prospects of hefty profits in cultivating commercial crops. The market for such crops is highly volatile and runs the risk of failing prices. Thus agricultural policy must alert enunciate the land use pattern, incentives, easy flow of credit, infrastructure support and remunerative price. Food security will remain as distant dream if policies do not come in place focusing augmentation of food crops.

PERCEPTION OF FOOD ADEQUACY IN WEST BENGAL

Perception of food adequacy is a measure of food insecurity not as a perfect yardstick but as a crude indicator. The question pertaining to perceptive adequacy is a subjective disclosure by the head of the household. Subjective disclosure is not tallied with physical verification of momentary stock of food a household commands. National Sample Survey Organization in India is the collector of food statistics. They conduct consumption expenditure survey to measure poverty over a period of time. They undertake thin sample study each year and large survey every five years. The last survey on perceived adequacy of food consumption was taken up in 2004-05. The report presents data on perception of Indian households by daily availability of enough food during last 365 days in rural areas as well as in urban areas. The purpose for the whole year recall period is to identify those crucial months or days of the year when food insecurity reaches its peak. The similar exercise was carried out in 1993-94. We are, therefore, now in a position to study the change over a period of a decade. It was found that percentage of households where all members reported enough food throughout the year rose from 94.5% to 97.4% during the period.

The latest report is truly revealing and interesting. The percentage of households not getting enough food in some months of the year was the highest for ST households at 3.7 per cent followed by SC households (3.3) per cent in rural area. The percentage of households not having enough food every day in some months was the highest in West Bengal (10.6) per cent followed by Orissa (4.8) per cent and the lowest in the states of Haryana and Rajasthan. In rural areas, the agricultural labour households reported highest proportion of perceived seasonal inadequacy of food. Farming households, those who predominantly seek their livelihoods from self-employed agricultural occupations exhibit lower proportion in the perception of food inadequacy. There is wide variation among social groups in the perception. Food inadequacy percentage is highest among scheduled tribe communities. The latter stands at the bottom of the social ladder and suffers insurmountable socio-economic adversities. The next in the group is scheduled caste community where 3.3 per cent of them perceive inadequacy of food. The survey also focused on beneficiaries of government food programme to gauge their perception. Two types of programme are currently under way: one is *Antodaya Anna Yojona* and the other is Targeted Public Distribution Programme for BPL families. It came to light that food insecurity haunts Antodaya card holders more than it does to BPL card holders.

FOOD INSECURITY AND CHILD LABOUR : EARLIER STUDIES IN INDIA

We take up in this section, a review exercise of a few studies on the relationship between food insecurity and child labour. These studies were mostly undertaken by eminent scholars during beginning of the new millennium at the behest of the World Food Programme under the U.N.O. The latter was alarmed, concerned and interested in discerning the ill-effects of imminent food crisis threatening the humanity at large and poor in particular. The ill-effects specifically include the swelling of child labour and child malnutrition. The battery of research studies on this issue included both empirical survey as well as studies based on secondary data. The study entitled "Food security and child work in Rural India authored by G. Daly, D. Bhattacharyya and B.P. Dash is an exercise of different genre. They have meticulously used secondary data to bring home their argument that food insecurity and child labour move together in same direction. They find that food insecurity and child deprivation in general co-exist at least in India's rural landscape. They had used food insecurity map of rural India prepared by World Food Programme. One could easily locate food deficient areas, of varying degrees, in the map. They prepared a similar map, in line with food insecurity map, child labour infested regions of India. The latter map was super imposed on the former to see whether child labour zone overlap with food insecure zone.

Interestingly and expectedly it did. The locations in India having food crisis are those, sheltering highest magnitude of child labour regionally speaking. They recommend massive food-based intervention by the government to eliminate child labour. Another excellent paper in the series is food security and child work in south India, "Determinants and policies by S. Mahendra Dev and C. Ravi (2002)". The two scholars have noted substantial beneficial effect on food-based intervention on school going children in the states of Kerala and Tamil Nadu. The mid-day meal programme of the two states has succeeded in bringing down malnutrition among children. Food-based intervention has thus reduced school dropout, has increased retention and thereby has succeeded in bringing down the incidence of child labour. The authors have noted astonishingly that the same did not happen in the neighbouring states of Karnataka and Andhra Pradesh. The latter has the ill-famed distinction of having the highest percentage of child labour among Indian states. Another paper exclusively focuses on Bihar, infamous for massive failure on many human development indicators, such as, adult illiteracy, child labour and child malnutrition. The paper titled 'Child Work in Bihar, A Leeway for Household Food Insecurity" authored by Piush Anthony is an excellent piece for reading and reflecting on. The paper brings to light efficacy of food-based intervention programs in combating child labour.

The state in question belongs to BIMARU region of the Hindi heartland of India, posing a formidable challenge to India's growing prospects of being a great power in not so distant future. The region seems to be indelible spot in the 'progressing' face of India. The region is marked by extreme economic inequality, social exclusion, gender bias, poverty, caste repression, unequal power relation and many other social ills that do not go well with India's image as a largest democracy of the world. Child labour is substantially high in

Bihar. The author points out that the higher incidence of child labour has linkage with lack of access to schooling. Food insecurity is another obverse of household poverty that perpetuates child labour. The empirical survey of 12 villages across the state brings to light the pervasiveness of 'kind' wage in stead of cash wage in agriculture work. Children are provided with one square meal a day in exchange for a day's work. Mid-day meal scheme, as the author points out, is yet to be popular in Bihar as a measure for encouraging school participation. Child labour has also a caste dimension. The lower social group endure recurrent food insecurity as a result of their income volatility.

Child labour is also at a higher scale where food insecurity overcast this social existence. An excellent paper named "Hunger Illiteracy and Child Deprivation in a Tribal Region: A study of Jharkhand" by Nira Ramchandran and Anup Kr. Karan (2002) needs attention. The uniqueness of this study lies in it focus on a tribal state, newly born, carved out from erstwhile state of Bihar. The present study is based on extensive household survey over 12 villages selected from three representative districts of the state. Seasonality of food insecurity has come to the fore in their study. Adequacy of food prevails in the post-harvest period that last for few months. Monsoon is the period of severe food crisis when agricultural wage work is hard to find. Most households face two to four months of food shortage with at least two months of near starvation level. The food insecure households fall back on children for income support. The study finds that child labour is high among food insecure households. Underlying the explanatory factors discussed in the foregoing research studies undertaken by prominent scholars in this field, there is a common thread of food insecurity that envelops all of them. The impact of school feeding programme on school enrolment as well as on retention is discernible. Food insecurity not only causes child work but it also prevents school participation.

PERCEPTION OF FOOD INADEQUACY IN OUR STUDY VILLAGES

We were tempted to elicit information on food security in

the villages where child labour persists in a significant way. The nature of labour by the children, as has already been disclosed, must draw serious attention from all corners, particularly from the government: one at the centre and the other at the state level. Child labour, as a whole, is unacceptable but there are few categories among the employment which are more dangerous than the others. Work with tobacco dust to make local cigars *(beedi)* fall in this 'dangerous' category. This work imperils health. Respiratory system is severely affected causing lifelong breathing trouble and asthma. Lung infection and even affliction with tuberculosis have been reported. This work engagement, from the young age, shortens one's life span. Frequent ailment, as a consequence of prolonged exposure to tobacco dust, reduces the life chances. Mortality is relatively high in this region. People have no other alternatives of livelihood. Demand side factor as well as supply side factor act together to generate and perpetuate child labour in tobacco work. Poverty and consequent low income certainly work on supply side of this occurrence.

Poverty reduces purchasing power that results in lower commands over goods and services in the market. In the absence of any supplemental subsidy to bridge the supply gap, by government or by donor agencies driven by philanthropy, the deficient families have to cope up with reduced amounts of all these. The supply of consumption goods, particularly of food which includes cereals pulses, vegetable and other items for consumption that collectively make a 'square' meal would be evidently inadequate. The adverse outcome of inadequate diet is nutritional deficiency. However, the impact may be even among all members or may be skewed favouring a few at the exclusion of others. This distribution will depend obviously on intra-household allocation of food. Thus poverty that predominantly causes child labour also may cause food insecurity. But food insecurity is not always resultant of poverty alone. It has to be coupled with lack of social safety net, neglect of the poor and vulnerable and absence of public provisioning of food for the people who cannot afford it in the market. Thus poverty can deny access to food if food-based intervention programme for the poor does not stand in the way to rescue. Public Distribution System for provisioning of food for the needy at subsidized prices can keep off poverty through expansion of food security net.

FEAR OF INSUFFICIENT FOOD SUPPLY

Fear of insufficient food supply haunts many families. We had surveyed in the study villages. Food insecurity has multifaceted manifestations; the fear of inadequacy is one of them. We did notice that households tend to maintain a stock of food grains, cereals and pulses that would run for at least a fortnight. BPL card holders collect their quota of rice or wheat from the PDS centres at a price considerably less then the prevailing market price. Sometimes PDS quota falls short of their requirements that go up with increasing number of feeding months. In that eventuality they turn to market to tide over the deficits. Perishable goods can not be preserved. Vegetables and fish that make a wholesome meal for Bengali have to be bought on regular basis. Quality and amount of these stuffs obviously vary. Purchasing capacity ultimately decides both. We were interested to know whether the households ever were haunted by the fear of inadequate food any time during the preceding month. A large number of families in course of our interaction have shared with us their feelings of inadequacy. When the reserve, particularly of food-grains, depletes fast, and the purchase cannot be undertaken to refil the stock, uncertainty befall on such families. The fear may be unfounded, we did not rule out the possibility. Households might have enough food stock but may suffer from unnecessary fearfulness. The possibility as it appears is extremely remote. We need a deeper probing to reveal this.

Does the fearfulness relate to household poverty? Poor households are already identified by the government agency on the basis of BPL survey, based on thirteen parameter provided by the department of Rural Development. BPL households are identified by the local government followed by distribution of multipurpose BPL card to them. They procure the weekly quota of foodgrains at subsidized price on production of BPL card at the nearest PDS centres. They are enlisted to many other facilities such as free health care, education incentives, provided by the government.

TABLE 9.1
BPL Family and Fear of Insufficient Food Supply

BPL Status	*Fear of insufficient food supply last month*		*Total*
	No Fear of insufficient food during last month	*Fear of insufficient food during last month*	
Non-BPL	783	689	1472
BPL	375	813	1188
Total	1158	1502	2660

Source : Household Ssurvey in Murshidabad in 2008.

Around 44 per cent of the households belong to BPL category. The Table 9.1 connects membership of BPL to the presence of fear of insufficient food supply. We find that around 56 per cent of children belong to families haunted by fear of food inadequacy. Out of a total of 1188 BPL children, 68 per cent had fearful experience of food inadequacy. In context, 45.88 per cent of non BPL children had such experiences. Non-BPL families comprise of multiplicity of economic standing. A significant number of them are very much close in economic characteristics to many of their counterparts in BPL category. They could not make the grade to be included in the exclusive list of the poor. It would be grave folly to understand that all non-BPL are equally well-off financially. Many of them might have excluded on objective judgment as per government criterion. The exercise of listing is also, in many cases, mired by subjective consideration. Affiliation to ruling political party, which media reports on various occasions, did place ineligible candidates in the exclusive list. Thus fear of impending food shortage also afflicted non-BPL families. Fear is intense among BPL families. This connection at least testify the commonsense notion that fear arises from the inability to command required food stuffs for all members of the family. Even the provision of subsidized food sale could not altogether remove the fear among the BPL households.

We do not rely only on BPL listing to carry on the exercise of relation the food inadequacy fear with penury of the households. BPL listing is subject to severe criticism as it does not convey the actual magnitude of poor in a certain locality. Firstly, the methodology of selection is contested by leading economists. Secondly, the government is bound by the poverty cap fixed by the Planning Commission. This constraint limits the counting of actual poor. Thirdly, wrong identification and unjust inclusion or exclusion in the coveted list is highly probable. Favouritism and nepotism are sure to creep in the process in view of retention and expansion of vote bank of the ruling dispensation at the local level. We, therefore, take it up as a crude measure. Still we find, using the crude measure of poverty, the influence of economic adversity on fear of inadequate food supply.

We have thought out our own measure of economic standing of the households. We have constructed Standard of Living Index (SLI) for the entire households covered within the

TABLE 9.2

Standard of Living and Insufficiency of Food

Standard of Living Index	*Fear of insufficient food supply during last month*		*Total*
	No fear of insufficient food during last month	*Fear of insufficient food during last month*	
Destitute	23	299	322
Very poor	238	616	854
Poor	316	437	753
Middle	447	150	597
Rich	134	0	134
Total	1158	1502	2660

Source : Household Survey in Murshidabad in 2008.

survey. Each household is assigned a total score obtained by it on the basis of economic endowment. Households are then classified on the basis of five categories in ascending order of score: destitute, very poor, poor, middle and rich.

Destitute children comprises of 12.10 per cent of child population. As expected, almost 93 per cent of them had a fearful experience of food shortage. The next higher group in standard of living ranking is "very poor". The proportionate share of this group is 32.10 per cent in total. Fear of shortage has come down to 72.13 per cent in this group. A decline of 21 per cent is evident with a small improvement in economic well being. The immediate higher group is 'poor'. The fear is gradually disappearing with rising status. In case of 'poor' household 58 per cent felt insecure about food. From 'poor' to 'middle' the decline is very fast, only a quarter of the households in the 'middle' category have reported their negative experience about food inadequacy. We do not find a single household in 'rich' group having had experiences perceiving food inadequacy.

The fear of food inadequacy, thus, can not be rejected as on unfounded psychological inhibitions. It's legitimacy is further established when we cross-tabulate between fearing households and households-relative economic standing. Poverty thus causes the fear. Improvement in standard of

Table 9.3
Food Shortage Fear and Children's School Participation

	Children		*Total*
Fear	*Not in School*	*In school*	
No fear of insufficient food during last month	101	1057	1158
Fear of insufficient food during last month	341	1161	1502
Total	442	2218	2660

Source : Household Survey in Murshidabad in 2008.

living followed by rise in purchasing power has eliminated the fear.

Our child population is divided between two groups: one belonging to fearing families and the other group belongs to non-fearing families. We find that 43.54 per cent of the children hail from non-fearing households. Within this 'bold' group' 91.28 per cent is currently enrolled in school. The fearing households do not fare well on this score. School participation rate for them is 77.30 per cent. Schooling is one of the most prominent indicators children' well-being, along with many other childhood attainments. A childhood without debilitating ailments is one of such perfect state of beings as children. Households haunted by the threat of food depletion and an imminent possibility of going without food for members have negative implication for school attendance for children. Food shortages, actual or imminent, seem to impede school attendance. But this proposition seems to be unlikely, particularly for the primary school going children. Because cooked midday meal is now almost universal. Thanks to government initiative in food-based intervention to encourage school enrolment and retention across the country. Many studies have noted the wonderful impact of this scheme. Thus, children who are not attending school and have left once and for all are in most likelihood; belong to upper age bracket from 11 or 12 years onwards. They are supposed to stay in upper

TABLE 9.4

Fear of Insufficient and Child Labour

Fear	*Children*		*Total*
	Child is not full time worker	*child is full time worker*	
No fear of insufficient food during last month	1094	64	1158
Fear of insufficient food during last month	1299	203	1502
Total	2393	267	2660

Source : Household Survey in Murshidabad in 2008.

primary grades for which free meal at school is yet to come by. Government is contemplating to include this group under the food programme. These grown up children aged 12 and above in the "food fearing" households may cease to go to school to help families in different ways available to them. Joining labour force to help their families is one such option.

The table presents the distribution of full time child worker between two types of families under consideration: one is "fearing" and the other is not. Only 5.52 per cent of children in the fearless households have been found to take part in full time work. For fearing households the participation has gone up to 15.62 per cent.

RUNNING OUT OF FOOD

The last section has dealt with a particular aspect of household food insecurity that manifests itself in threat ambience. The horrifying feeling that food may be deficient for household members is more subjective than objective security of actual stock. But this subjective judgment is no less important in understanding the construction of food security arrangement. Fear engulfs those households incapable of affording enough stock of food as a result of shrinking purchasing power. Poverty and fearful experience seems to be inseparably bound. The experience of semi-starvation by household members during the span of a reference period of 60 days is another indicator of persisting and prickling food insecurity. Did a section of population have such horrible experience of a day ever for few days without any food during the last 60 days? We did count the days of such transient starvation. Children were thus classified in two exclusive categories of belonging to families. One category of families did not face this crisis situation and the other did. We calculate that 37.4 per cent of children belonging to families did not go through the painful experience and 62.6 per cent miserably did.

Running out of food even if for a day is the manifestation of economic distress for the suffering family. Food crisis, as it appears, is not widespread and overwhelming in this study area. But still it persists and that is unacceptable. This is not

TABLE 9.5
Days Running Out of Food

No. of days	*Frequency*	*Percent*	*Cumulative Percent*
0	991	37.3	37.3
1	12	.5	37.7
2	6	.2	37.9
3	29	1.1	39.0
4	155	5.8	44.8
5	300	11.3	56.1
6	236	8.9	65.0
7	533	20.0	85.0
8	184	6.9	92.0
9	12	.5	92.4
10	178	6.7	99.1
11	5	.2	99.3
12	14	.5	99.8
15	5	.2	100.0
Total	2660	100.0	

Source : Household Survey in Murshidabad in 2008.

the issue of food inadequacy. This is not the situation where the meal one takes falls short of what is taken as a full meal. This is an uncomfortable situation when stock of food dries up and members in the households undergo starvation. Not all the members simultaneously starve; a few of them have to. Generally the adults, in a gesture of altruistic attitude, sacrifice for the sake of the younger ones. They do not want to see that the younger ones remain unfed. Females generally take the pain. They serve meals to males including children but they themselves go on fast. Intra-household allocation of food is the subject of enquiry for development economics. Many studies have confirmed the gender discrimination within the households in dietary intakes and consequent nutritional outcomes. Unevenness in the distribution of food within a family is the replica of the persistence of gendered inequity in the larger social sphere. Girl children suffer more *vis-à-vis* the boys. Investment in education as well as in nutritional care is not equal among children.

The table exposes that a meagre 0.2 per cent of children are members of such families whose food stocks had run out for 15 days during the span of last 60 days. These distraught families, very few though in our study villages, expose the hidden sufferings of many underprivileged families in many parts of India that do not come in to public glare. This table presents the frequency distribution of days of suffering caused by starvation. Going without food for a day in the time span of 60 days for a negligible 0.5 per cent is an insignificant issue to worry us. Twenty per cent of the children belong to families who had missed their food on 7 days during the same time span. Fasting, not on one's own volition even for a few times is an indicator of deep-rooted malfunctioning of the system on which we live and face our lives. The persistence of such discomforting social malady also speaks of malfunctioning of our social institutions that have failed to discharge their responsibilities. The state has miserably failed to provide food security network for all its citizens particularly for those who are defenceless in the eventuality of food shortage. Our study finds that around 63 per cent of the household had undergone starvation in varied degrees.

Does the food scarcity ravage all families irrespective of household poverty? The questions need to be addressed. Households are already grouped in binary classifications of BPL and non-BPL. This job is already done by the government

TABLE 9.6

BPL Status and Running Out of Food

	Running out of food		*Total*
	BPL status	*No*	*Yes*
Non-BPL	712	760	1472
BPL	285	903	1188
Total	997	1663	2660

Source : Household Survey in Murshidabad in 2008.

agency. We may use the government listing, for the time being, to explore the association between phenomenon of food crisis and the poverty at the household level

We find that 76 per cent of BPL families are exposed to food crisis. They had faced a miserable situation of running out of food, however, in a varied frequency. Comparatively a lesser magnitude of 52 per cent of non-BPL families has had such painful experience. Thus the connection between poverty and running out of food is evident. Poverty and consequent low purchasing power restricts their entry to food market. The affordability is obviously constrained. The families debarred from the market for food are expected to be saved from food crisis by the targeted public distribution system. The persistence of crisis overwhelmingly in the BPL families speaks for itself the serious shortfall in the delivery system. Large scale corruption has already crippled this system in the absence of accountability transparency and monitoring. The statistics on BPL is likely to be erroneous. The genuineness of BPL data is subject to contestation from many corners. Despite this known limitations of the government data on poverty stricken households, we find a reasonably positive connection below poverty and food running out.

UNEMPLOYMENT AND RUNNING OUT OF FOOD

We have also explored the presence of the horrible experience of food stock in the households plagued by occasional unemployment. Employment does not come by year round for many families. We have considered employment of the head of the households. The survey finds that 29.51 per cent of the household heads were employed throughout the year and the rest of them had to remain idle for some days in the year.

The days of unemployment varies from 30 days to 210 days during the reference year. Unemployment for four months has hit 26.57 per cent of household heads. This is closely followed by unemployment for three months afflicting 17.63 of household heads. Although tobacco work, the mainstay of livelihood for the families, is not seasonal employment is also not assured for each day of the year.

TABLE 9.7
Days of Adult Unemployment and Running Out of Food

No. of Days	Running out of food		Total
	No	Yes	
0	638	147	785
30	2	4	6
60	134	288	422
90	101	368	469
120	93	614	707
150	29	197	226
180	0	44	44
210	0	1	1
Total	997	1663	2660

Source : Household Survey in Murshidabad in 2008.

Unemployment is caused by disruption in the delivery of raw materials by the *Beedi* companies for whom the home based workers work. As the payment is linked to the production of finished output to the companies, the discontinuation of raw material supply obviously keep the workers idle. Companies do not stop the supply of raw materials deliberately. That action is not supported by their goal of marketing and harvesting of profits. The delayed delivery is caused by actors on the far end of the entire production process. Raw materials have to be brought from far off places outside the state of West Bengal. Therefore, causes remain outside the control of the local actors. Unemployed heads fail to seek other variety of employment in the neighbourhood. Agricultural wage work is hard to come by. Non-agricultural work is either conspicuously absent or very thin in presence. They do not have land sufficient enough to pursue farming. Thus unemployment for some months of the year seems to be unavoidable. Still food deletion has visited 18.72 per cent of households in our study villages. It appears to be unusual and improbable but it has certainly happened that employment does not seem to result in comfortable payment of wage. Thus quality of employment matters more than the quantity of employment.

But families having had bitter experience of unemployment had also undergone food crisis in heightened intensities. Heads of the households that did not find employment for 30 days of the last year are rather better placed in relation to others. Still 66.66 per cent of them went through food depletion. For households that suffered 60 days of unemployment, food stock depletion had stricken 68 per cent of them. Again households that have to bear with 90 days of unemployment, starvation had befallen on almost 79 per cent of them. Starvation has gone up to 86.84 per cent for households whose heads had to remain unemployed for 120 days in the last year. Food insecurity has further deepened for families whose days of unemployment of heads are higher than the earlier cited days.

We have our own measure of living standard of the households as indicator of economic standing as estimate of poverty. The purpose is to verify whether the two correlates of food stock depletion conform to our measure of living standard.

TABLE 9.8
Standard of Living Index and Running Out of Food

Standard of Living Index	*Running out of food*		*Total*
	No	*Yes*	
Destitute	7	315	322
Very poor	151	703	854
Poor	270	483	753
Middle	436	161	597
Rich	133	1	134
Total	997	1663	2660

Source : Household Survey in Murshidabad in 2008.

'Destitute' as we have conceptualised is the poorest of the poor category in our classification of our households according to standard of living score. They must receive any social protection in the first go. When benefits are inadequate to cover all the poor in a region, government must target them as priority recipients. They do not have any asset base to seek their livelihood from the productive assets. Wage work is the only source they can access for living. Income poverty is not the only vice that afflicts them. Ill-health is most common sight. Diseases of different types befall on them frequently. Debility has lessened their ability to work for wage. Dependency ratio might be very high. This is a phenomenon of too many feeding mouths and very few earning hands. The constraints of the local economy have been already highlighted in the earlier chapter. Tobacco work is inescapable here and the diseases generally associated with prolonged exposure to tobacco are hardly resistible. Disease deepens poverty as public health care system meant for the poor is not extensive enough to stop the poor from private spending on health care. The category of 'poor' is not a homogeneous pack; there is wide variation among them. Penury is horrible for few while the same is not so for others. Our category 'destitution' is the description of inhuman living condition characterized by distressed living condition.

Our revelation also reinforces the conclusions of many exploratory studies that extreme poverty and food deprivation always move together. The former evidently causes the latter. We find that almost 98 per cent of people in this destitute category did not find food to eat during the reference period at least in one occasion. Is the horror of food depletion same for all categories of poor? Is the bite less piercing for the poor whose penury is also less? The table furnishes the answer to the question posed as above. Very poor category is just above 'destitute' in the hierarchy of poor. The former is slightly better off than the latter. Food stock running out was experienced by 82.31 per cent of people among this slightly higher category. The 'poor' category is better than 'very poor' category as the latter's 'adjective' describe the depth. The same horrible experience to food crises was faced by 64 per cent of people in 'poor' category. The same has come down to 27 per cent for the middle category. The improvement is visibly sharp. No one in the 'rich' category did face any food crisis in the reference period. Their relative opulence could easily surmount the food crisis.

INADEQUACY OF FOOD INTAKE

Running out of food in the household is the severest form of food deprivation that is synonymous with transient starvation. We come across a different type of crisis that relates to insufficiency of food obviously less severe than the situation where one member or a family unit can not access food on many occasions. A full meal must be balanced and should be in adequate amount. The situation turns distressful when a person have to be satisfied with just half or a little more than what she eats usually. Our study reveals that 63 per cent of the children families had to finish their meals that were inadequate in quantity.

Food Eaten by the Family Members was Inadequate

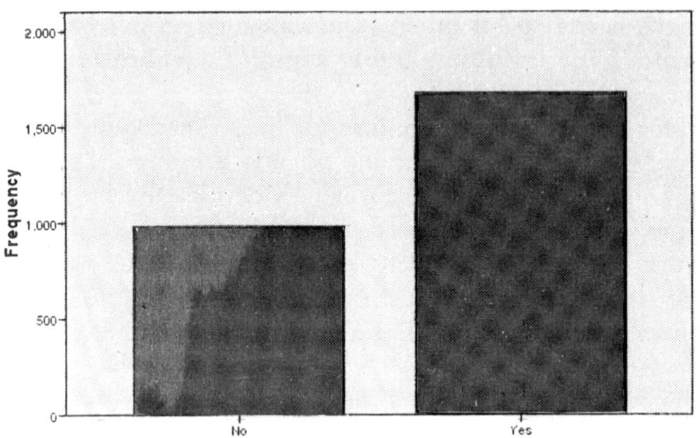

Food eaten by the family members was inadequate

When food crisis ravages households, the latter have to bear with this distressful predicament until the crisis is over. Households tackle the food inadequacy in different ways. The coping mechanism is interesting to wit and reveals many aspects of intra-household allocation of food. However, the solution of food inadequacy is not accomplished by sourcing the amount of shortfalls, to meet the deficits, through loan or informal credit. Households have been found to seek solution of the problem through rearrangement of food distribution temporarily. Adults skip food for the sake of the younger children.

TABLE 9.9
Adult Skipping Food for the Sake of the Children

How many times	*Frequency*	*Percent*	*Cumulative Percent*
0	992.0	37.3	37.3
2	6.0	.2	37.5
3	20.0	.8	38.3
4	138.0	5.2	43.5
5	199.0	7.5	50.9
6	216.0	8.1	59.1
7	385.0	14.5	73.5
8	224.0	8.4	82.0
9	61.0	2.3	84.2
10	327.0	12.3	96.5
11	2.0	.1	96.6
12	61.0	2.3	98.9
15	29.0	1.1	100.0
Total	2660.0	100.0	

Source : Household Survey in Murshidabad in 2008.

Adults did share with us the coping mechanism of skipping food, one meal each time, during noon or at night but not the both of the meals. The table above presents number of times the adults skip their meals to allow children, particularly, to enjoy full meal. We find that around 37 per cent of adult did not do that at all. There are two reasons for such action or inaction. One, the particular household did not face food inadequacy at all. Two, the adults were, very exceptionally non-altruistic in attitude and action within family. It needs deeper probing to ascertain which reason among these two works for this phenomenon. We find one per cent of adult skip food fifteen times for the sake of the children. This is the highest instance of adult sacrifice of food for the sake of the children.

Table 9.10
Food Inadequacy and Child Labour

	Children		*Total*
Food eaten by the family members was inadequate	*child is not full time worker*	*child is full time worker*	
No	934	48	982
Yes	1459	219	1678
Total	2393	267	2660

Source : Household Survey in Murshidabad in 2008.

Almost 37 per cent of these children belong to 'food adequate' or 'food solvent' households. The rest 63 per cent of total, belong to households frequented by inadequacy on several occasions. We are interested to know whether children of the 'food inadequate' households tend to join labour force in a bigger way than the children of the food adequate households. Child labour participation, which we conceive here as full time work engagement, is 13 per cent for food inadequate households. The same is only 4.88 per cent for 'food adequate' households. Thus food insecurity and child labour nexus is further established in this exposition.

10

Education in Human Development Process

The efficacy of schooling as a weapon to fight child labour is beyond contestation. But one may understandably ask 'what type of schooling is prescribed as solution'. Are all the schools of same grade? The possibility of different types of schools differentiated on the basis of various attributes, such as school hours, quality of classroom transaction, delivery mechanism, attitude and orientation of teachers, infrastructure and many other physical conditions can not be ruled out. In India, there is simultaneous presence of formal schools as well as of informal schools. Schooling schedule is fixed in formal school while in informal school the same is flexible. School hours are stretched in the formal schools while these are short in the informal schools. An informal school comes up as and when necessary to serve a particular segment of children abandoned by the formal school system. To put the matter straight, formal schools have eluded them and their magnitude is still overwhelming. Platform school for the underprivileged platform children sighted in India's major railway stations is one such example of such informal arrangement for delivery of elementary education.

Sceptics raise the issue of inefficacy of such informal schooling arrangement in eliminating child labour. They argue that formal schools maintain school hours sufficiently stretched to avert child labour engagement of the pupil. They find the solution in expansion, both horizontal as well as vertical, both qualitative as well as quantitative, of formal schooling and not emphatically schooling as such. They point out that governments in each child labour prone nations in developing world specifically tend to establish informal schools to pull children caught in labour engagement and put them in educational process. They take to short-cut and inexpensive route quite oblivious of its limited impact of this measure. Sometimes, these initiatives are undertaken to respond to the concern and pressure of the international community. Donor countries of the west insist the recipient countries in Africa to act very quickly on eradicating child labour through provisioning of universal elementary schooling. Formal schooling system is shockingly inadequate in poor countries owing to resource constraints on the hand and the lack of political will on the other. Poor spending on elementary education by poor countries in Africa and in other regions of the world is the cause as well as effect of mass poverty over there.

Human history, however, is replete with instances of many nations where compulsory elementary education was introduced by the states braving the insurmountable constraints of poverty and low income. South Korea and Japan are glaring examples of remarkable accomplishment in providing universal elementary education. They did not wait for economic growth to empower the respective states to allocate adequate financial resources for compulsory education of children. This example was emulated by many of their South-East Asian neighbours. The initiative, taken hundred years ago, yielded amazing result. They are now coined as East Asian tigers because of their industrial might. They have been posing serious challenges to western economic hegemony and their monopolist position in selling industrial products across the globe. These Asian giants are gradually expanding their pie of the global market of electronics goods. The car-makers of Japan have made a mark surpassing many western models in quality, beauty and sophistication. This was made possible through national priority on human capital formation. Universalization of primary education was the edifice on which human capital formation process had ensued. The widespread notion that the delivery of education would follow economic development was belied by these countries. Human development and economic prosperity do not move hand in hand. The former, in many instances lag behind the latter.

Back home in India, we have example to buttress the view that relatively poor states, measured by per capita state domestic product, have shown better result in literacy in general and elementary education in particular than many states that are better-off economically by the same measure. Education is an investment that calls for financial ability of the government. Expansion of school network, provision of school infrastructure, teachers' training, teaching aids and many other supply side factors have to be provided by the state. The extent of financial allocation significantly determines these provisioning. But adequate supply side arrangement is not the guarantee for universal enrolment and retention. Demand side factors are equally important to work in conjunction with supply side provision. Child labour can be eliminated through universal elementary education that is effective, joyful, accessible and entirely free. Informal school is a lackadaisical measure to stop child labour. The flexible nature of teaching and learning, variable teaching hours, untrained and unmotivated teachers, weak administration, lack of accountability, and attitude of quick fix solution collectively makes the informal arrangement of schooling virtually useless in addressing the issue of child labour. The insincere states just feign to jump into action that meets with no tangible outcome.

FORMAL SCHOOL VERSUS INFORMAL SCHOOL

Formal school system is the key to success not the informal school. The potency of formal schooling in combating child labour is not only a conviction but it was put in practice in the states of southern India, infamous of harbouring massive proportion of child labourers. The M.V. Foundation took up the challenge during 1980s to eliminate child labour in the state through mediating between schools and child labour families in a view to ensure enrolment and retention of children in school. They took up their project, first in *Ranga Reddy* district in the state of Andhra Pradesh for experimentation of their noble scheme. They had translated their belief into action in the field to find the result. It was impressive. The success story of M.V. Foundation in addressing the issue of child labour in child labour prone districts of Andhra Pradesh through encouraging and invigorating formal schooling is now every one's knowledge. The effort is appreciated everywhere. The success is cited as model to replicate in places where similar problem persists overwhelmingly. They do not take recourse to punitive measure in partnership with the government to compel the parents to send their children to neighbourhood schools. The volunteers of the foundation visit each household of the vulnerable areas to gain knowledge about their living conditions and their attitude towards children's education. The volunteer's home visits were rewarding for the *Foundation* as it had to deal with parents and communities. The foundation workers began to visit the families repeatedly to convince them about the usefulness of child's education and also about the harm of idleness and child labour. It was revealed in course of the project in the district that poverty cannot singularly be invoked as a reason for remaining out of school for thousand of children. The school system had miserably failed to pull them. The system needs overhauling to attract children as well as to fascinate the unwilling parents. The foundation vowed for ensuing universal primary education for all school age children in the experimental district. Massive numbers of children were out of school as they had either dropped out or not been enrolled in school. The foundation introduced bridge course for them to prepare for entry in formal primary school according to age. The bridge schools are manned, managed and founded by the *Foundation*. The foundation stands as a mediator between the state formal school system and the children of underprivileged families.

How can education be a tool to combat child labour? The

first one is to compete for time in a day for an individual child. Full time work that derails the development process of a child comes in direct conflict with the full time schooling. The latter overtakes the former if urge and compulsion for labouring can be lessened to facilitate full time schooling. Only formal schooling arrangement can accomplish this task conditioned upon quality, affordability and accessibility of formal schooling. Informal and flexible learning arrangement stands no chance in combating child labour. This was preached by the Foundation as well as practised by them. The second one is the consequential benefit of education towards eliminating child labour. The outcome of the first measure is direct and immediate where as that of second one is indirect and time taking. The second method works through human capital formation process. Child labour begets poverty which in turn perpetuates child labour. The nexus of child and poverty is unbreakable and inter-generational. Education imparts skill and produce human resources. Child labourers are engaged in unskilled and low paid job. Education can only prepare and train them for skilled and better paying jobs. Higher wage rate would reduce poverty and child labour with higher parental perception towards positive return to education.

EDUCATION FOR ALL

During the end of the last millennium, the humanity began to ponder over our future, our past failure and course of action in the new millennium. The Millennium Development Goal (MDG) was set to achieve within stipulated time. The last century had witnessed enormous opulence as well as massive poverty in the human race. The gap between rich and poor is widening within the countries. The disparity among nations is growing in a way that generates fear that poor nations in the south are on the verge of decimation. Poverty, malnutrition, hunger and many other forms of debilitating social ills have almost crippled a significant chunk of population of the contemporary world. Poverty has to be fought collectively. Reduction of poverty needs global action. The MDG under the auspices of the U.N.O. sets many other human development goals alongside eradication of poverty. Education for all is one such goal to achieve. Endemic illiteracy is a curse on humanity. Education has eluded a vast multitude of people, particularly the children in developing regions. Unequal education opportunity has deepened poverty and discrimination on the basis of gender, caste and class. The social divide in India is historically deep-rooted through perpetuation of hierarchical caste structure. Incidence of poverty has significantly come down in post-independent India. The removal is faster in recent years. The post-nineties India has been witnessing significant reduction in head count ratio of poverty. The planning commission is releasing official statistics that speaks of government's success in fight against poverty. The report emboldens the planners to predict that with the present rate of reduction in the magnitude of poor people; the time is not very far when poverty will be a thing of the past.

Sceptics, however, oppose tooth and nail this heightened jubilation of victory. They raise serious doubts over methodology of calculation of the poor. They adopt alternative methodology that entails wider notion of poverty to get at the correct estimate. They bring out poverty figures that far exceed the official estimate. The disagreement on poverty estimate between Planning Commission and other non-government agencies including many scholars in India has been a serious issue in the public discourse. The gap in the magnitude of poor does not seen to disappear or at least come down unless there is an agreement among all on what constitute, poverty and who qualifies to be 'poor'. We need to move forward from 'nutritional' poverty to holistic concept of decent living as human beings. Despite this irritating disagreement on figures, the incidence of poverty has come down since the dawn of independence. The pace of decline might not be that fast as the government takes pride in claiming. But there is no disagreement on the unwelcome reality that development outcome is not evenly distributed across regions and social categories in India. The slow pace of poverty reduction among scheduled caste, scheduled tribe, ethnic communities, hill tribes, minorities, women headed households, even after six decades of our journey in the path of planned development, speaks for itself serious neglect of equity and social justice.

As freedom from poverty and hunger is yet eluding millions of Indians so is education even at this juncture of time. Literacy has gone up quite substantially during the period of planned development. Enrolment in elementary schools in India has gone up remarkably in recent years. School network has expanded significantly compared to what was there in the beginning. Number of educational institutions has increased manifold. But a significant section of population is left out in the process of educational expansion. Gender discrimination is one side of the lopsided development outcome. Female illiteracy is still quite high among minority, schedule caste, schedule tribe and among many other marginal groups.

The Indian constitution under the directive principles of state policy insists on free and compulsory education for all children up to fourteen years of age. Our constitution that contains this pledge towards our children came into effect in 1949. Article 45 that spells out the promise remains a sweetened announcement without having any legal teeth to bite the offenders. In a sense, it was accepted as inescapable duty of the state to provide education to all children in India until passing of 93rd amendment of the constitution that endows legally enforceable rights to education for children in India. This is a big leap forward. It heralded a new dawn and opened a new chapter of India's destiny towards prosperity, inclusive development and social justice. We have witnessed flurry of activities, taking up of programs, meetings and conferences, escalation of budgetary, provision, inviting western donor agencies, seeking financial help, guidance and technological assistances during last two decades in India. This sudden awakening after a long period of inertness is evidently the response to the global call of Education for All. The Millennium Development Goal for all nations under the UN system pledges to remove hunger and mass poverty. The goal also obligates states to remove illiteracy, gender discrimination and strives towards universal education for all children.

DISTRICT PRIMARY EDUCATION PROGRAMME (DPEP)

Primary education in India is crippled with many shortcomings. The most visible miserable state relates to its accessibility. Millions of children have no access to primary education as a consequence of their socio-economic situations. Access is also denied to many children for their condition of habitation. Children of the remote areas severed of any communication link, children of the hill tribes, of deserts as well as of forest fringes make up this distraught lot. The immediate task would be the horizontal expansion of primary school network that could cover these difficult geographical tracts. This was an uphill task that involves massive public expenditure. The next snag that afflicts primary education system is the problem of drop-out. The other problem that closely follows is the poor quality of education. Thus the war has to be fought on three fronts: universal enrolment, universal retention and quality education. The British Government, through its overseas development agency, came forward in the early ninety to assist the government (centre as well as states in India) to tackle the problem jointly. They provided the major share of the cost for the proposed overhauling of the delivery system of education. During 1994, DPEP come into effect in selected districts of India. The selection was done on the basis of the situation of female literacy.

The districts in India that shelter very high magnitude of unlettered females were accorded priority in introducing DPEP. The initial phase of DPEP in India, in selected educationally backward districts, measured by the extent of female illiteracy became a catalyst for change in a system that was beset with inertia. This was, in major share, a foreign funded project to overhaul the system to usher in a new era of universal quality primary education in India. Indian government was not absolved of the financial sharing, nor were the state governments kept out of public spending on the project that came up within their respective territories. The unique feature of this new programme is its decentralized planning. The district level is the highest stage to prepare plan on the basis of intensive survey carried out at the household level, at the school level as well as at grass root government's level in the villages. Plan for each district in a state could differ as a result of different requirements and settings. The budget across districts would vary on the basis of differential quantum of needed investment. The districts having large number of inaccessible areas would need more fund for establishing new schools.

DPEP came in to effect in 1994 in India's selected districts on experimental basis but it soon assumed a pioneering role in sensitizing, strengthening and overhauling the system that faltered miserably. Its thrust areas are three-fold: expanded accessibility, pedagogic innovation and community participation. DPEP recognises that horizontal and vertical expansion of primary education is stupendous task that should not remain within the exclusive perview of officialdom. It must be a popular movement where people, who are impending beneficiaries of the programme, are involved in every phase. DPEP for the first time seeks co-operation from NGO's. Government effort cannot reach all locations and all selection of population. NGO's are welcome to bridge the gap. DPEP brought in an innovative idea of people's participation. Village Education Committee (VEC) and Ward Education Committee (WEC) are popular forums that came into being as part of DPEP. This was down to top rather than 'top to down' approach. These committees are nodal body at every village or at every municipal ward that are intimately involved from the process of planning down to implementation. Thus DPEP is a clear deviation from the long drawn practice of delivery from centralized authority that kept out the beneficiaries those are important stake holders.

Schooling network was shockingly inadequate. Quite a large number of villages did not have primary schools for their children. Distance thus triggered discontinuation. Inadequacy of numbers was certainly a problem on one side. But the problem is more intense in the existing arrangement of schooling. Facilities in the school were staggeringly deficient. Overcrowded classrooms were appalling sights. Schools were starved of teachers, particularly of trained and motivated teachers. DPEP for the first time diagnosed this ailment in the system and began to put emphases on deployment of teachers in the first go to be followed by in-service training and orientation programme for all of them. A large number of para-teachers were engaged in the existing schools to maintain the optimum pupil-teacher ratio. Schools began to come up in 'school-less' villages specifically in unserved and in remote areas. However, most remarkable accomplishment of DPEP is the introduction of joyful learning module for children. This is not an easy task to engage children who are first generation learners used to repulsive teaching-learning method. The school curriculum should be attractive and comfortable for the children who did not have any pervious exposure to early childhood education. DPEP could realize the necessity for innovation in classroom transaction and improvement in pedagogy to retain children in school.

Murshidabad in which our survey villages are located was selected as the first phase recipient of DPEP. The districts that were left out in the first phase were included in the second phase. DPEP was later subsumed under *Sarva Shiksha Abhiyan* (SSA) the flagship programme of the central government. DPEP is thus a precursor of SSA that significantly helped in formulating the new programme sharing many experiences during a long course of journey since 1994.

SARVA SHIKSHA ABHIYAN

DPEP was meant for universalization primary education for children of the primary schooling age from 6 to 10 for a full course of four years. In many states, primary schooling years run for five years that target children from 6 to 11 years. Upper primary education that goes up to eighth standard is thus left out in the focus of DPEP. SSA was taken up for all children from 6 to 14 years. This is India's first effective initative, launched at the turn of the new millennium, to give shape to its promise during the adoption of her constitution. Article 45 in the Directive Principles of State Policy spells out that state will provide free and compulsory education to all children. Although this constitutional provision was not legally enforceable in the court of law but it was expected to act as guiding spirit.

Provision of elementary education is now a bounden duty of the state in India after the 93rd amendment of Constitution. It took very long years for the state of India to accept education of children as rights for them which make the government obligated to provide for free and compulsory education to all children. Right to education was inserted into

Article 21 under fundamental rights of our constitution. This is a remarkable step towards promotion of human rights in India. SSA was taken up to fulfil the Constitutional duty of the state. India was positively responding to the global call of Education for All in many international forums under the auspices of the U.N. Pressure from such global assembly began to mount on India to go ahead for immediate action on universal elementary education. The Millennium Development Goal (MDG) set by the U.N. on the eve of the next millennium would remain unreachable if India does not commit herself in conformity with the global call for eradication of poverty, hunger and illiteracy from the surface of the earth. SSA came up in the backdrop of the domestic as well as global situation. Constitutional obligation at the domestic level and conforming MDG at the global level led to the birth of SSA that not only subsume the existing DPEP but also transcends it by way of its coverage and commitment.

The SSA sets its mission to accomplish within a stipulated period. It pledges to (1) to enrol all children (aged 6 to 14 years) in state primary school, in Education Guarantee Centres, in alternate and innovative school by 2003. (2) To ensure five years of primary education to all children by 2007. (3) To focus on quality and holistic approach. (4) To bridge gender gap and social gap in primary education by 2007 and in elementary education by 2010. (5) To ensure all children accomplish eight years of elementary education by 2010. These are lofty targets but achievable if political will and financial resources spontaneously come by. There has been remarkable spurt in gross enrolment ratio in recent years but the goal is still elusive. We have still many miles to go to reach universal enrolment and retention. We need to address some basic issues embedded in the socio-economic milieu that hinders significantly. Those obstacles are to be removed before we strive for universal elementary education within shortest possible time. There is distinct departure from DPEP on two courts. Firstly, SSA coverage is wider than DPEP because SSA targets children from 6 to 14 years old for whom it pledges to provide elementary education. Secondly, unlike DPEP it covers the whole nation from the very inceptions.

SSK AND MSK

Sarva Siksha Avijan is now Sarva Siksha Misson. It draws gains and hands-on experiences form the working of DPEP. SSA has learnt one lesson form the DPEP that bureaucratic control and dominance of officialdoms can thwart the tempo and can derail the process. SSA could be an addition to the battery of schemes currently underway in the department of Education of the state government. It was not annexed with the department which is already burdened with regular tasks. SSA came under and empowered and registered society at the state level. It would work in tandem with the education department but not as a scheme delegated to it. The SSA authority at the state level is autonomous and it obtains all sorts of co-operation from different departments of the state government. Department of Panchayat and Rural Development builds rural infrastructure for implementation of SSM. Sishu Shiksa Kendra (SSK) is the child education centre, a prototype of primary school, to come up in each school less habitation. SSM recognises that a child must have physical access to school within one kilometre of her residence. Teachers are named as Shiksha Samprasarak in the SSK. Panchayats are entrusted with the task of establishing SSK, maintaining buildings and recruitment of teachers, selected from the same locality, as far as practicable, and payment of salaries to them.

SSK is meant for primary school going children who could not attend the formal primary schools of the government. It basically caters to the needs of disadvantaged children who are left out of the mainstream schools for variety of reasons. Economic hardships and the compulsion of child work stand in the way. Distance to traverse to reach the school may be exhaustive that leads to absenteeism and discontinuation. SSK has succeeded in bringing school almost at the doorstep of the children doing away with the distance that was a formidable barrier. SSK enrols the children who were either dropped out or had never been enrolled in school. Madhyamik Shiksha Kendra (MSK) serves the children who could not avail upper primary grades for various reasons. The responsibility of management of MSK primarily rests with the Panchayats. This local government has to provide infrastructure and construct buildings for the schools. There is a management committee for each MSK to supervise and govern institutions. The local authority at the panchayat level undertakes a household survey within its territorial jurisdiction to identify children who are left out of mainstream school. Enrolment drive is undertaken at the beginning of each academic year. Each MSK tries to make sure that no children are left out at least within its catchment area. Teachers are recruited by the local Panchayat.

As DPEP had witnessed considerable success in its mission of overhauling the primary education delivery system in India, SSA can also claim similar success in expanding of elementary education. Enrolment has gone up significantly in elementary level. Dropout rate that went too high, particularly in the upper primary stage before the inception of SSA, has come down satisfactorily. Participation and involvement of community in the affairs of school are forthcoming overwhelmingly. This is an important positive outcome of the SSA that people who are the major stakeholders are participants. SSA is thus an attempt to fulfil the constitutional obligation of providing education to all children. Children are now rights holders not the passive recipients of educational service provided by the state. Parents are now attending parents-teacher meetings in large proportion after the launch of SSA. But the goals set to achieve under this mammoth scheme is further sliding away. Universal enrolment is yet to be achieved. Gender gap is yet to be removed but the gap has substantially narrowed down in recent years. SSA deserves the credit for this. It would be unfair to belittle SSA efforts. It would be wrong to be too much optimistic. The goal set in beginning of SSA did not materialize at least, by the time it was expected to do. It might be a little discomforting but should not be up setting. When a government program is launched vouching for time bound implementation one hopeful aspect is its priority and urgency. We need a few more years to accomplish the task. Financial provision has to be enhanced. Observers of the state of elementary education in India have raised concern that budgetary provision, expressed as percentage of GDP on elementary education, has shockingly come down in recent years. There has been a persistent demand from all corners to raise education budget to 6 per cent of GDP. Elementary education must get the proportionate share. Although SSA is a national programme, state governments have to share a part of expenditure on its implementation. During the 9th five years plan, at the beginning of the programme, the central government used to spend 85% of the total expenditure and the respective state government used to spend remaining 15 per cent. The share of states went up and that of the central government came down during 10th five year plan. The central share was 75 per cent and share of the states went up to 25 per cent. During 11th five year plan, the sharing arrangement is fixed at 50:50. Many state governments are reluctant to accept the huge financial liabilities. Educationist is alarmed at this burdening of financial responsibilities on resource-poor states. They raise their voice against abdication of most critical task by the central government.

MID-DAY MEAL SCHEME

National Programme of Nutritional Support for Primary School Children is now popularly known as Mid-day Meal Scheme. It was launched in 1985 on India's Independence Day. The programme is in operation throughout the country. The program when mooted, aimed to kill two birds with a single stone. One was to encourage school attendance and the other was to provide nutritious food to the primary school children. Malnutrition leads to debility that causes weak comprehension, cognitive disorder, lack of attention, frequent exposure to diseases, and many other inhibiting syndromes.

Poor children are worst sufferers by way of inadequate nutritional intake. They make a major chunk of rural children. They run the risk of missing school as a consequence of nutritional poverty. Therefore, the target of universal primary education can never be achieved in a situation where millions of children are half-fed, ill-fed and even go without food. Thus Mid-day Meal Programme was akin to appearance of angel in the lives of these disadvantaged children. It worked well barring a few cases of initial hiccups. During initial phase of the scheme, each primary school going child was given three kilograms of rice or wheat, free of cost in a month. The condition is that the child has to attend minimum 80 per cent of school days during the last month. The provision of food-grain under the scheme continued for many years despite allegation of corruption in PDS shop, poor quality of grain, delay in delivery and dwindling share of nutritional intake of the child in families living on the margins of survival.

The provision of uncooked foodgrain to children under mid-day meal scheme was scraped at the behest of the apex court in India. The court ruled in response to a petition submitted by the People's Union of Civil Liberty, that each child must be served with cooked meal daily at noon in the school campus. The Supreme Court's verdict is binding for all states and this system of service is in vogue now everywhere. Various studies have captured the wonderful impact of the noon meal scheme on enrolment and attendance. The scheme covers all types of schools including SSK, MSK, and alternate school excluding private schools. Thus there are enough schemes and incentives to realize the goal of universal elementary education in India. SSA is providing infrastructure, recruiting teachers, establishing schools, introducing innovative school curriculum, providing on job training of teachers, striving for quality education and sustaining the movement with all-out effort. Mid-day meal is supplementing the SSA effort through serving nutritious and tasty food to children for physical as well as cognitive growth. These are all supply side intervention but the demand side factor must work positively. Demand side factor generates from children's household. Households must be economically strengthened so that they not depend on child's earnings. Parents need to feel that return to child's education must be positive.

Education is a driver of human capital formation. The district of Murshidabad is by and large poverty-stricken. The penury of the people as revealed in the official statistics formulated on the basis of consumption expenditure survey needs no further elaboration. Poverty flourished in the predicament of illiteracy. Poverty illiteracy nexus is conspicuously present in the district. Children of today are adults of tomorrow. A child would grow into adult ordinarily but becoming an adult does not necessarily mean worthy adult. A country to grow in a harmonious way needs skilled, educated, trained, motivated, intelligent, healthy adults. The citizens are human resources; they are capital quite distinct from physical capital. Capital enhances productive capacity. As the country needs improved physical capital, technology, innovation, research and development so she also needs better workforce, trained and motivated manpower, skilled technicians, professionals, artisans and educated farmers. Physical capital and human capital reinforces each other. One cannot be separated from others to accomplish economic prosperity of a nation. The history of economic development of prosperous nations is testimony to the perpetual interdependence between human and physical capital. Universal primary education had preceded removal of mass poverty in major South-East Asian nations whose industrial achievement and spectacular prosperity has become 'mythical'. They are now referred as East Asian Tigers. They removed illiteracy well ahead of the elimination of poverty through industrialization, technology and trade. They had built human capital base that was prepared for industrial enterprise, absorption of new skill, and attitude for moving forward, a zeal for drive and dynamism, an outward looking orientation and attitude of learning emerging technical knowhow. Promotion of human capital does not end in formation of skill but also a shift in change in outlook in favour of growth, in favour of taking up the challenge to face the world. But the building of human capital is not easy and automatic. Government has to generate resources for spending on building of human capital. Poor countries cannot allocate enough resources on this expenditure head. The low rate of investment on public education is caused by economic hardships, low level of income and savings, inability to generate revenue in a distressed economy. The question of survival overtakes the need for public education. But history does not always stand to support the poverty argument as a main hurdle in the way of providing basic education.

Japan and Korea, even the tiny country of Sri Lanka could achieve universal literacy when they were poor, measured by per capita income. There are poorer nations whose per capita income stands similar to what those countries had years ago.

But these countries are steeped in massive illiteracy despite substantial flow of international aid to support education programmes. Dictatorial and anarchist regime in many African countries have misused the donor fund. They have failed to generate own resources for investment in education. They lack the political will and commitment. The system is not in place. Institutions are defunct. Corruption is rampant. There is no accountability. Thus public investment in mass education requires commitment, dogged determination, vision, governance, accountability to the people, and solid institutions. The expenditure on education, building schools, recruiting teachers, formulation of curriculum and imparting of skill in basic numeracy and literacy are investment that has positive return. A country cannot overlook this vital task. The priority should be to invest in human capital formation process. The government must establish schools for children so that they can easily access them. School must offer joyful learning environment. The education must be meaningful and beneficial.

FEATURES OF SCHOOLING : CHILDREN OF THE STUDY VILLAGES

Physical Accesses

The Kothari commission, constituted by the Government of India after independence made a host of recommendations for modernizing education system in India. The commission prescribed for a uniform education structure for the entire country. It envisioned a prosperous India built on the edifice of modern education, science and technology. It dreamed of an inclusive education system in India, particularly of basic education. The commission had cherished an egalitarian system of delivery of quality basic education in India abandoning elitist approach that marked almost the period preceding our independence. The commission strongly recommended a system of neighbourhood school for children. All habitations in India must have at least one primary school. The government must ensure physical access for schooling in the formative years of life of her budding citizens. The future of India lies in the hands of her today's tiny tots. The commission did foresee that if schools do not come up in every villages or hamlets, children of lesser gods, poor and distraught would not be able to access school. The ultimate aim of this costly recommendation to the government is to move forwarded for universal primary education as articulated in our constitution. Poor parents cannot afford private transport to attend school outside their habitations. Villages do not have motorable roads for transportation of children. Children would take a long walk to reach the nearest school. But the journey could be too exhaustive for them. Poverty and the resultant malnutrition could deepen the exhaustion. This could be the reason for discontinuation and end of schooling in the mid-way. In villages children undertakes different types of household work. They also help parents in farm work particularly during hectic crop season. Thus distance always increases the chance of dropout when the distance cannot be bridged by any other means. Unfortunately, the commission's recommendation of *'neighbourhood'* school remained in paper for a long period until Sarva Shiksh Abhiyan came in 2001. It was realized after many years and the folly is now acknowledged that millions of children cannot access schools in India not because they are unwilling to do so. They do not find school in the vicinity. Remote areas are worst sufferers. Hilly areas, forest areas, desert areas and many other inaccessible areas are mostly cut-off from mainstream schooling.

TABLE 10.1
Children's Residences to Primary Schools (Distance in Kilometre)

Distance Category	*Frequency*	*Percentage*
Up to 1 K.M.	2189	82.30
1 to 2 K.M.	330	12.40
2 to 3 K.M.	141	5.30
Total	2660	100

Source : Household Survey in Murshidabad in 2008.

This is evidently an improved picture of school accessibility of children. Without going into the quality of school, they can attend, a large magnitude of children, 82.30 percent of all children in our survey villages can attend schools that are housed within one kilometre of their residences in the village. A small minority of children, 5.30 per cent of all, have to walk a distance over 2 kilometres to attend school. We have included SSKs in considering the distance because SSKs are prototypes of formal primary schools that were established in school-less habitations after the introduction of SSA all over the state of West Bengal. Although a small minority of children would have to take a long walk, despite the SSA initiative to bring school close to the children the picture is less than perfect. This calls for a closer scrutiny of the arrangement and a renewed effort.

TABLE 10.2
Children's Residences to High Schools
(Distance in Kilometre)

Distance Category	*Frequency*	*Percentage*
Up to 1 K.M.	877	32.97
1 to 2 K.M.	114	41.88
2 to 4 K.M.	669	25.15
Total	2660	100

Source : Household Survey in Murshidabad in 2008.

To gauge the distance of High Schools we also considered MSK as they are parallel institutions imparting elementary education. We considered either of the two that stands nearest to the residences of the children. We find a different scenario with regard to physical accessibility. While primary schools or SSKs comes up within the habitations of the vast majority of children, elementary schools are not easily accessible for children of post primary school stage. Only 34 per cent of children find their elementary school within one kilometre of their residences. A significant number of children almost one-forth of them would need to walk more than 2 kilometres to reach. We have recorded the distance for all households although many children are not actually attending school.

SCHOOL ATTENDANCE

Children must attend school regularly. Teaching and learning process take place in classrooms. Thus evading school even for a single day is damaging for children, particularly for those who do not receive supplementary tuition at home. Private tuition is too costly to afford for many parents. Thus school absenteeism retards the learning process. The loss is less acute if the absence is infrequent or once in a full noon. But it may be disastrous if the absence is regular and for a longer period at a stretch. Children skip school for a variety of reasons. During peak agricultural season, children help their

TABLE 10.3
Number of Days of Attendance in School and Gender of the Children

No. of days of attendance in school last two weeks	*Gender*		*Total*
	Female	*Male*	
0	0	1	1
3	1	0	1
4	1	3	4
5	10	7	17
6	33	29	62
7	70	76	146
8	308	249	557
9	341	304	645
10	302	376	678
11	48	53	101
12	1	5	6
1115	1103	2218	—

Source : Household Survey in Murshidabad in 2008.

parents in agricultural work where hiring of outside labour goes beyond reach for small farmers. Children thus substitute the hired work in hectic crop seasons. In many instances, school going children join wage work in agriculture occupation to supplement family income. Agricultural work is few and far between in our study area. Children are born to the world of tobacco. They grow in the atmosphere of *beedi* rolling in which they pick up the skill from the infancy. They join the family work in tobacco with their nimble fingers.

School going children skip schools and the most possible reason might be their engagement in tobacco work. When a family is committed to the company agent to supply a fixed amount within a stipulated period, children are drawn to work to meet the commitment. They help in running the family's only source of livelihood. Table 10.3 presents gender-wise attendance in school during last 12 school days preceding the date of survey. We carried out our survey on 2218 children over the selected 6 villages marked by household occupations on Beedi rolling. Out of 2218 children, 1103 are males and the rest 1115 are female. If we reflect on attendance record from the perspective of gender, boys are ahead of girls in respect of attendance for more than ten days during the last 12 days. We come across only one boy out of 2218 school going children who did not turn up even for a single day. Almost 91 per cent of children did attend school from 7 days to 10 day during reference period of 12 school days. Gross absenteeism is not detected in this study and there is also an absence of acute gender divide in the pattern of attendance excepting a lower attendance of girls compared to boys in 10 days and above school days.

We now try to relate school attendance of children with membership to BPL categories. The purpose of this exercise is to see whether BPL membership of the children's households has something to do with or interfere with school attendance.

A quick glance of the table evokes interest as to the connection between the two variables: Poverty, as measured by the BPL membership of the households, causes absenteeism in the absence of any other casual factors like disease, disinterest, etc. Out of our student population of 2218, a total of 940, that is 42.39 per cent belong to BPL households. There is an

TABLE 10.4
School Attendance and BPL Status

No. of days of attendance in school last two weeks	*BPL family or not*		*Total*
	Non-BPL	*BPL*	
0	0	1	1
3	1	0	1
4	3	1	4
5	11	6	17
6	34	28	62
7	80	66	146
8	275	282	557
9	363	282	645
10	437	241	678
11	68	33	101
12	6	0	6
Total	1278	940	2218

Source : Household Survey in Murshidabad in 2008.

obvious linkage between poverty and truancy. We do not find a single child in BPL family attending all the 12 school days. All the children attending all days of schooling belong to non-BPL families. We find that 101 children have attended 11 days out of 12 days. Non-BPL children comprise of 67.32 per cent of them while the rest, 32.68 belong to BPL families. The trend holds good for 10 days of school attendance where we find 678 children could attend. The share of non-BPL children is 64.55 among this group and that for BPL is far less at 35.55 per cent.

This is second attempt to explore the connection between economic standing of the households and the school attendance of the children. The BPL listing, done by the local authority, is beleaguered by controversy and contestation. There is large scale allegation that the listing is beset with error. We have formulated our own measure of poverty that captures comprehensive dimensions of poverty. Instead of relying only on binary classification of BPL and APL of the

TABLE 10.5
Attendance in School and Standard of Living Index

Days of attendance	*Standard of Living Index*					*Total*
	Destitute	*Very Poor*	*Poor*	*Middle*	*Rich*	
0	0	0	1	0	0	1
3	0	0	0	1	0	1
4	1	2	1	0	0	4
5	3	6	7	1	0	17
6	12	20	22	8	0	62
7	28	53	45	20	0	146
8	71	208	157	105	16	557
9	54	215	189	155	32	645
10	30	165	215	201	67	678
11	3	21	13	52	12	101
12	0	0	1	2	3	6
202	690	651	545	130	2218	

Source : Household Survey in Murshidabad in 2008.

households under the study, we made 5 classifications according to standard of living score. The lowest in the poverty rung is destitute. The highest category is rural rich, very poor, poor and middle in between the two extreme categories. Relating the family's economic rank with school attendance of their children reveals almost similar trend we observed in case of BPL connection. Children of the rural rich had never missed school for seven days out of 12 days. We find that 130 school going children belong to rich families and all of them had attended school for eight days onwards to 12 days, the complete school days available during the last two weeks. The percentage share of children who attended all 12 days is 50 per cent whereas the share of the rich student in total population of students in our study villages is only 5.87 per cent, the proportion of 'Middle' group children who attended all 12 days class was 33.34 and the same is 16.67 per cent for poor category. We did not find a single student in both 'destitute and very poor' category who could attend all 12 days school days. Similar is the attendance trend for 11 days, 10 days, 9 days and so on that establishes that relatively prosperous and economically secured families would tend to send their children to school for all days of the week. If we consider the number of children attended for 11 days during the last 12 days of schooling, only 1.48 per cent of destitute children could do so whereas 9.54 per cent and 9.24 per cent from middle and rich children could do that. The trend is also evident in case of children attend 10 days of schooling, we find that 51.54 per cent of rich children could do so, 36.89 of middle children, 33 per cent of 'poor' children, 23.92 per cent of 'very poor' children and finally 14.86 per cent of destitute children could do so.

Government must ensure physical accessibility to school for all children. This is the first initiative to accomplish universal education. But establishing school in the neighbourhood is not the guarantee that all children of the neighbourhood will automatically get themselves enrolled. Even when all children are enrolled, there is no system at place to ensure regularity of attendance. Poor parents cannot afford any alternate private arrangement to make good the losses incurred for missing class room transactions. Thus absence from school is an irreparable damage to academic achievement for majority of households in the study area. More is the absence; more is the damage in learning processes. Poverty comes in the way of school attendance. The results of our exercise corroborate this negative impact. BPL category children are less likely to attend classes regularly. Our classification of households in five categories on the basis of level of living bears the similar result. Comparatively well-off families in our study area, identified in this study as 'rich' and 'middle' send their children to school in larger number than their counterparts in 'poor', 'very poor' and 'destitute' categories. Mid-day meal programme is now universal. Retention has jumped up manifold after the launch of the scheme. Thus starvation as dominant cases of absenteeism for many children in our study is not logically tenable. Children's work in home-based tobacco processing, which they undertake intermittently is the obvious reason of such absence.

Parental schooling background has been found to have positive influence on children's schooling participation. We have explored the connection between parental educational attainments measured in years of schooling with days of attendance of children in school. We tried with fathers' years of schooling in the first go.

TABLE 10.6

Education of Father's and No. of Days of Attendance

Correlations

		Education of father in years of schooling	*No. of days of attendance in school last two weeks*
Education of father in years of schooling	Pearson Correlation	1	.227**
	Sig. (2-tailed)		.000
	N	2521	2117
No. of days of attendance in school last two weeks	Pearson Correlation	.227**	1
	Sig. (2-tailed)	.000	
	N	2117	2218

**. Correlation is significant at the 0.01 level (2-tailed).

Source : Household Survey in Murshidabad in 2008.

The correlation between father's education in years and days of attendance of their children is positive and statistically significant. The correlation between mother's education and days of school attendance is positive and also statistically significant. Mother's education as an influencing education of offspring is well documented in various research studies on determinates of children's education. Mother's educational exposure positively affects girls compared to boys.

Where both parents are literate and had exposure to schooling in their past, children generally do not miss school

TABLE 10.7
Education of Mothers and No. of Days of Attendance

Correlations

		Education of mother in years of schooling	*No. of days of attendance in school last two weeks*
Education of mother in years of schooling	Pearson Correlation	1	.213**
	Sig. (2-tailed)		.000
	N	2645	2215
No. of days of attendance in school last two weeks	Pearson Correlation	.213**	1
	Sig. (2-tailed)	.000	
	N	2215	2218

**. Correlation is significant at the 0.01 level (2-tailed).
Source : Household Survey in Murshidabad in 2008.

accepting under unavoidable circumstance. Educated parents can understand the usefulness of attending classes. They can teach the value of classroom transaction which uneducated parents generally do not do.

ACADEMIC COMPETENCY

The study has focused on 2660 children inhabiting the six tobacco villages. The primary purpose is to reveal the nature of child labour that prevails overwhelmingly over there. Education can be deterrent to child labour if other contributing factors that generate and perpetuate this inhuman practice can be kept at bay. Not all children in these areas attend school. School participation rate is 83.39 per cent among children from 6 to 14 years of age. School enrolment is a statistical figure used by government to drumbeat its achievement. Even the data on retention and school continuation which has remarkably gone up in recent years may be soothing to ear. There may be a euphoria and celebration of impending universal elementary education. But that may be more hype than reality.

Primary school completion rate in the post DPEP period is satisfactorily high, a big leap forward compared to what prevailed before 1994 when DPEP come in to effect. Dropout rate is on the wane now in primary stage. The scenario at the upper primary level is far improved now, thanks to SSA. There is significant accomplishment in quantitative expansion in elementary education. But the quantitative improvement achieved in recent years under the auspices of SSA is moving too fast leaving far behind quality learning and academic competency. Educationists are raising the issue of quality learning which is blatantly overlooked in the zeal for quantitative expansion. An organization based in Mumbai, named, *PRATHAM*, has been looking tirelessly into the issue. They conduct competency test on primary school going children in reading skill, writing skill and rudimentary arithmetic standardized for the entire country. Their findings are shocking. Many children cannot correctly read a few lines. They can not write two to three sentences correctly in their own vernaculars. Many of them are horribly bad in arithmetic and unable to perform simple two digit summation or subtraction. PRATHAM is doing wonderful work in the domain of primary education in India. It publishes ASER (Annual Survey of Education Report) every year to bring to light state of primary education in our country. Their annual report, widely circulated and read, contains the quality aspect. This revelation has triggered debate on the efficacy of primary schooling system currently underway. There is widespread regret that public money is going down the drain because of dysfunctional delivery system. Millions of children in India are learning almost nothing of three Rs, comprising of reading, writing and arithmetic after a full course of four years in primary education.

Our study of the six tobacco villages also looked into this aspect of quality attainment of all school-going children but in a different methodological frame. We could not use same kind of methodology adopted by PRATHAM. Our primary purpose is to look into child labour use in these tobacco villages and related to this occupation is educational participation. But we did depend on results of school examinations written by the children during the last occasion. For primary school-going children, we collected the Marks/Grade Slip of their grade performance during last evaluation examinations. For them who could not furnish the Marks/Grade Slip for the last exam, we had asked for the one before the last school examination

Primary schools including SSKs now provide grades instead of only marks as a measure of competency for each student. Grades are allotted for each subject separately and composite grade incorporating all subjects. Grades in descending order are A, B, C, D, E. In primary stage, full marks in each subject are 50. A student will obtain A if her total marks fall between 50-41. B grade is conferred to examines, if the total marks fall between 40-30. Likewise C relates to marks between 32-26 and D to 25-18. Lastly E rates to less than 18, A, B, C, D, E, respectively stands for very good, good, satisfactorily average and unsatisfactory. Interestingly we did not come across any student in primary stage to have obtained 'E' grade. We have based our assessment of achievement through obtaining of grades. Therefore, the grades are limited to four in this analysis. In upper primary grades, seven grades are allotted: AA, A+, A, B+, B, C, D. We brought down those into four grades, A, B, C, D, for simplicity and parity with primary school grades. Full

TABLE 10.8

Score in the Last Exam and Standard of Living Index

Score	*Standard of Living Index*					*Total*
	Destitute	*Very Poor*	*Poor*	*Middle*	*Rich*	
A	0	9	25	64	32	130
B	99	382	335	318	76	1210
C	81	241	232	145	21	720
D	21	58	58	20	1	158
Total	201	690	650	547	130	2218

Source : Household Survey in Murshidabad in 2008.

marks in each subject are 100 in upper primary grades. Thus A stands for 60 and above, B stands for 45 to 60, C for 25 to 35 and D is less than 25

The table presents that only 5.87 per cent of students could achieve A grade. B grade is rather more populated, 54.56 per cent of them could achieve B grade, followed by C grade obtained by 32.47 per cent and D grade by 7.13 students. This table shows the result of cross-tabulation between standard of living categories and grades of students obtained in the school examination. The purpose is to see how poverty can influence grade achievement of the students. There are 201 school-going children in the 'destitute' category. No one has obtained 'A' grade. But 49.26 per cent of them has obtained B grade, 40.30 per cent has got C grade the rest 10.45 per cent has got D grade. When the level of living slightly improves, the grades of children improve correspondingly. In the 'very poor' category, the next higher rung to destitute, we find that 1.31 per cent of them has obtained 'A' grade compared to nil in destitute category. Similarly, B grade is obtained by 55.37 per cent, slightly higher than percentage score of destitute children. Likewise, promotion to 'poor' strata also results in higher share of A grades. 'A' graders comprises of 3.85 per cent in 'poor' category. The share of 'A' graders goes up to 11.71 per cent in 'middle' category the next higher strata above poor category. The 'rich' category is at the top in having A graders in it's fold. A staggeringly high percentage of these children, 24.62 per cent have achieved this highest grade. What has occurred in case of A graders holds good for B graders but not robust as the earlier case is. Here we find that B graders constitute 49.26 per cent in destitute group, 55.37 per cent in very poor group, 51.54 per cent in 'poor' group, 58.14 per cent in 'middle' group and 58.47 per cent, the highest achievement in the rich group. The relationship between school achievement of the children and their corresponding membership with stratified 'living standard' groups indicates that poverty sometimes turn out to be inhibiting factor. Children of poor families in these 'tobacco villages' divert much time in family occupation to assist their families with whatever means they have under this command. Here they can give only labour time and as much time is extracted from them for child labour, little time is left for study at home. Engagement in work also interferes with school attendance. This inescapable engagement of poor children for seeking livelihood and survival cause lower attainments in competency as assessed by the school.

EDUCATION OF PARENTS : DOES IT AFFECT CHILDREN'S ACADEMIC PERFORMANCE?

Fathers' educational background expected to bear on children's school performances. The possible scenario is that educated fathers can assist their children in preparing of lessons at home. When class rooms are overcrowded and

TABLE 10.9
Education of Father's Score of Children

Education of father in years of schooling	*Score in the last exam*				*Total*
	A	*B*	*C*	*D*	
0	20	548	398	86	1052
1	1	29	21	1	52
2	3	29	16	10	58
3	1	31	18	8	58
4	6	104	39	9	158
5	6	68	32	6	112
6	8	65	30	6	109
7	1	30	14	2	47
8	17	111	40	10	178
9	16	50	22	2	90
10	25	62	27	4	118
11	0	7	2	0	9
12	8	16	6	0	30
14	12	20	6	0	38
15	1	2	0	0	3
17	3	2	0	0	5
Total	128	1174	671	144	2117

Source : Household Survey in Murshidabad in 2008.

teachers at school cannot pay attention to the needs of individual students, paternal help at home can compensate. We have measured father's education by years of schooling they have completed. Almost half of the fathers, we have visited, are unlettered. The highest schooling is for 17 years by fathers of 5 children among 2117 children in our study area. They are privileged few who have completed Madhyamik examination, the variant of secondary examination in our state. They went up to Higher Secondary and even to under graduate level.

Children of fathers having 17 years of schooling exposure are all A and B graders. The same is also true for father having

TABLE 10.10
Education of Mothers and Scores of Children

Education of mother in years of schooling	*Score in the last exam*				*Total*
	A	B	C	*D*	
0	20	548	398	86	1052
0	49	889	599	141	1678
1	0	3	0	0	3
2	1	23	5	0	29
3	1	24	17	2	44
4	6	63	27	6	102
5	5	40	17	5	67
6	14	65	20	1	100
7	6	19	6	0	31
8	13	50	19	2	84
9	21	13	9	1	44
10	6	9	0	0	15
11	1	0	0	0	1
12	6	7	0	0	13
14	1	3	0	0	4
Total	130	1208	719	158	2215

Source : Household Survey in Murshidabad in 2008.

15 years of schooling experiences. We find that fathers having schooling experience of 11 years onwards do not find any child obtaining D grade. Unlettered fathers can see 1.91 per cent of their children achieve A grade. A graders constitute of 3.80 per cent for fathers who have completed primary schooling.

Fathers with background of full upper primary education of eight years can see that A graders constitute as high as 9.56 per cent of their children. This exercise thus establishes that paternal education positively affects children's accomplishment in school examinations.

Maternal illiteracy is quite high in our study villages. We find that 75.76 per cent of school going children are born to illiterate mothers having no schooling experiences. Children whose mothers have four years of primary level of learning comprises of 4.61 per cent of all. Less than one percent (0.68) percent of mothers have completed 10 years of schooling. Proportion of mothers who have gone beyond secondary level is 0.82 per cent. All the mothers from 10 years of education onwards find this children in A and B grade, not even a single one below B grade. The frequency of D graders the worst performs gradually comes down with improvement in mother's schooling years. The worst achievers, D graders are highest in magnitude at 8.41 per cent for unlettered mother's. This occurrence has come down to 5.89 per cent in case of mothers having had primary level of schooling. School performance is improving and incidence of worst performance is slowing down with further improvement in mothers educational back ground. Mother's having full course of elementary education of eight years see only 2.39 per cent of their children obtaining D grades. No D graders are found for mothers having 10 years of schooling. Mother's education is thus a factor to reckon with in determining grade achievement at school.

PRIVATE TUITION

Private tuition has come to stay in the educational scenario as an occupation for unemployed youth and as other source of extra income for employed teachers. Private tutoring as occupations as well as a practice of seeking supplementary coaching at home is a long-standing activity. For hundreds of years, a privileged few among the students could receive private tuition as the cost of such private provisioning was beyond means for majority of parents. In recent times, it has become widespread. Parents take it for granted that they have to cough up money for providing tuition for their children. Schools, as they understand, are not well-equipped to provide quality education to the children. Parents clamour for it. There has been a latent demand for good education for children by the parents. Private tuition has thus turned out to be an

TABLE 10.11

Private Range and Score in the Last Examination

Expense on private tuition per head (in Rs.)	*Score in the last exam* A	B	C	D	*Total*
0	33	495	260	63	851
20- 45	5	259	121	23	408
46-70	31	257	194	55	537
71-95	9	61	49	9	128
96-120	11	81	67	5	164
121-145	2	8	1	0	11
146-170	9	24	14	2	49
171-195	1	1	0	0	2
196-220	10	9	12	1	32
221-245	0	0	1	0	1
246-270	5	5	0	0	10
296-320	8	6	1	0	15
346 and above	3	1	0	0	4
Total	127	1207	720	158	2212

Source : Household Survey in Murshidabad in 2008.

unavoidable option.

We have also explored this aspect of private spending on education even though government has committed for provision of free and compulsory education for children. The 'free' education is narrowly defined; therefore, it excludes many other private costs in which private tuition has dominant share. We are interested to know whether children who receive private tuition achieve better than those who cannot afford to do. The basic presumption is that children who get the benefit of higher amount of spending on supplementary tuition must score high grades. The table shows that A graders and B graders respectively constitute 3.88 per cent and 58.17 per cent of children who are unfortunates to receive any supplementary tuition. Where families spend between Rs. 146 to Rs. 170 or Rs. 158 on average per month per child, the share of A graders goes up by 18.37 per cent and the share of B graders also stands at 49 per cent. At higher levels of spending, the proportionate share of A graders and B graders improves. When spending goes above Rs. 246, almost all students get A and B with major share in A grade.

Table 10.12
Private Tuition Fees and Standard of Living

Correlations

		Private tution fees per month	*Standard of Living Index*
Private tution fees per month	Pearson Correlation	1	.392**
	Sig. (2-tailed)		.000
	N	2218	2218
Standard of Living Index	Pearson Correlation	.392**	1
	Sig. (2-tailed)	.000	
	N	2218	2660

**. Correlation is significant at the 0.01 level (2-tailed).
Source : Household Survey in Murshidabad in 2008.

The spending capacity of parents is obviously dependent on earning capability that goes into our measure of living standard. The positive correlation between the amounts of private spending on tuition and the level of living expressed as living index score is obvious. Poor parents, bereft of the capacity to spend cannot provide for quality education of their unfortunate off springs. While public provisioning for education of children is inadequate and incapable for imparting quality education, private market seizes the opportunity. Poor are thus kept out of the market for lack of purchasing power that is valid in the similar vein for all commodities and services that are bought and sold in the market. Exclusion of poor from the educational process that builds human capital through imparting quality and meaningful learning is the negation of basic human right of children to education. It stifles the growth potentiality of our nation by fostering unskilled, untrained, uniformed and unmotivated human persons who could otherwise be human resources. The nation is deprived of their monumental contribution to growth for which they are not responsible.

OBSERVATIONS

We can not say, for sure that education delivery system under public domain is in disarray. School level statistics did not come by. But schools are not evidently well-equipped to cater to the individual needs and provide for personal attention. Schools are overcrowded everywhere in the state that is out of line with desired pupil teaching ration of 40:1. We have looked in to daily attendance of school going children in those study villages. Education is universally recognized as a dominant driver of human capital formation. Children have to attend school regularly to take part in teaching and learning process that takes place in class rooms. Recurrent absenteeism is a symptom of sporadic discontinuation and ultimate drop-out. This study finds that children of BPL families miss classes in larger proportion than the children of APL families. BPL classification is an official exercise beset with methodological inaccuracy and allegation of subjective judgment. We have carried out our own measure to see whether any particular family is placed in one of the five categories formed on the basis of standard of living score.

We find the same trend here also. Poor households do not seem to insist on school attendance while the affluent households, relatively speaking, send their children to school in larger proportion. Children of poor families assist the family work in *beedi* processing, the dominant means of living in the study villages. Thus they miss the school in larger number. Education of parents also makes a difference. Educated parents send their children to school more or less regularly while the urge is less intense in case of unlettered parents. Score obtained in the last school examination is our gross yardstick of academic competency. Richer children have done comparatively better than their counterparts in the poorer categories. Supplementary private tuition has a bearing on school score. Private tuition is widespread in villages also and has become an inescapable option for parents. Poor children are thus left out of the private market for education, thereby signally an unwelcome development in future. A large number of children are thus deprived of their basic rights to quality and meaningful education.

11

Determinants of Child Labour : An Exploration with Household Survey Data

Data were collected through canvassing and recording in the survey schedule specially designed for the research study. The household schedule was pretested before it was put to use for final data collection. Each schedule was meant for one household. Our unit of enquiry is individual child of the reference household. Thus we have details about 2660 children and they belong to 1224 children households spread over 6 villages of Murshidabad district. Our primary purpose of carrying out logistic regression is to locate the factors, generated at the household level that causes child labour. We have considered only those households having children within 6 to 14 years age bracket. Therefore, dependent variables are children. We consider 5 child status categories and every sample child belongs to one of these categories. There are K child attributes and each sample child has a K-vector of observed values of these attributes.

We postulate that the probability of the ith child belonging to such categories depends on a set of explanatory variables. An appropriate functional form between the dependent variable and the explanatory variables must satisfy two requirements. One requirement is that it translates the values of the explanatory variables to a probability that ranges in value from 0 to 1. Another requirement is to maintain the property that increase in any of these variables is associated with increase in the probability in question. These requirements are satisfied by a cumulative probability function. The resulting probability distribution is represented as:

$$P_i = P\ (Y_i = 1) = F\ (\beta_o + \beta_1 \times i_1 + \ldots\ldots + \beta_k \times i_k)$$

where F is the cumulative probability function. A special form of F is the cumulative logistic probability function.

The logit model is based on this probability function and is specified as :

$$P_i = p\ (Y_i=1) = F\ (\beta_o + \beta_1 \times i_1 + \ldots\ldots + \beta_k \times i_k)$$

$$= \frac{1}{1+e^{-(\beta o+\beta 1\times i1+\ldots\ldots+\beta k\times ik)}}$$

where F is a cumulative logistic function and e represents the base of natural logarithm. The specification leads to the following form

$$\text{Log}\ \frac{p_i}{(1-P_i)} = (\beta_o + \beta_1 \times i_1 + \ldots\ldots + \beta_k \times i_k)$$

One feature of the logit model is that it transforms the problem of predicting probabilities within (0.1) interval to the odds of an event occurring.

DATA AND VARIABLES

We estimate a multinomial logistic regression with the maximum likelihood estimation procedure by using the data set generated through our intensive household survey of

TABLE 11.1
List of Variable

Variable Name	*Dependents*
Child 1	1 If the child is full time student, 0 otherwise
Child 2	1 If combining school and work, 0 otherwise
Child 3	1 Full time work, 0 otherwise
Child 4	1 No work and no school, 0 otherwise
Child 5	1 Part time work and idleness, 0 otherwise
Explanatory Variables	
Chilage	Age of child in completed years
Gender	1 Male 0 Female
Mother's Characteristics	
Mothage	Age of mothers in years
Mothedu	Education of mothers in years
Moccu	Occupation of mothers
Moread	Whether mother can read and write, 1-yes, 0-no
Father's Characteristics	
Fathage	Age of Fathers in years
Fathedu	Education of Fathers in years of schooling
Faoccu	Father's occupation
Faread	Whether father can read and write, yes-1, no-0
Family Characteristics	
Famistru	Structure of the family, 1- single parent, 2-Nuclear, 3-Joint family
Famihead	Head of the family 1-father headed, 2- Mother headed
BPL	0-Non BPL, 1- BPL
MPCE	Monthly Per Capita Consumption Expenditure
Members	Total family members of the household
Children	Total no. of children (6-14 years)
Sliscore	Standard of living score
Jobless	Days of unemployment during last year by the head of the family
Engel	Engel's ratio

TABLE 11.2
Children's Status and Age in Years

Age in completed years	*Only Study*		*Study and work*		*Fullt ime work*		*No work no school*		*Work and idleness*	
(1)	*(2)*	*(3)*	*(4)*	*(5)*	*(6)*	*(7)*	*(8)*	*(9)*	*(10)*	*(11)*
6	149	164	2	11	0	1	56	38	0	0
7	146	113	5	20	2	5	14	13	0	0
8	137	133	11	51	1	3	12	4	0	1
9	108	111	15	56	2	5	6	0	0	0
10	171	163	31	101	13	10	9	1	0	0
11	87	110	23	80	7	11	4	0	0	1
12	130	132	37	120	27	21	6	1	1	1
13	82	98	39	82	19	34	3	2	0	1
14	92	92	33	85	56	50	2	0	1	0
Total	1102	1116	196	606	127	140	112	59	2	4

children households. In this survey a total of 2660 children of 1224 families spread over 6 tobacco villages were taken up for recording information. Explanatory factors that affect children's time use are broadly grouped in three categories and are presented in Table. These three categories are: child characteristics, parental characteristics and family characteristics. Child characteristics include children's age and sex. While child age is continuous variable but child sex is dummy variable. These two characteristics are important in their own way. Child labour, particularly full time employment of children is prevalent, comparatively in higher intensity, among grown up children. The younger children undertake part time work on irregular basis. The younger children are found in larger proportion, in school rather than in work places. The mean age of the children in the study area is 9.78 years.

TABLE 11.3
Descriptive Statistics

Name	*Number*	*Minimum*	*Maximum*	*Mean*	*S.D.*
Chilage	2660	6	14	9.78	2.655
Gender	2660	0	1	.50	.500
Mothage	2645	19	70	35.98	7.013
Mothedu	2645	0	14	1.29	2.69
Engel	2660	41.46	93.10	79.09	7.477
MPCE	2660	161.54	2150.00	446.62	194.27
Members	2660	2	20	6.90	2.459
Children	2660	1	9	2.74	1.217
Jobless	2660	0	210	73.15	54.24
Standard of living index	2660	1	5	2.76	1.084
Age of father	2522	24	64	41.58	8.708
Fathedu	2522	0	17	3.04	3.929
Occupation of Father	2522	0	10	4.21	2.07

The next category of explanatory variables is parental characteristics. Mother's age is a significant variable that affects children's time use, specifically of girl children. Older mothers are obviously less capable of undertaking household chores as well as income earning activities. Children, particularly girl children are more prone to be drawn in to mothers' role as house makers as mothers turn older and feeble. The mean age of the mothers in our study area is 35.98 years with a standard deviation of 7.013. Mother's education is measured by years of schooling. The minimum year of schooling is 0 which indicates that these mothers have no schooling back ground. The maximum years of schooling are 14 years. The standard deviation of schooling in years is 2.69. The mean years of schooling of mothers are 1.29. The minimum age of father is 24 years and the maximum of 64 years with mean and standard deviation of 41.58 years 8.708 respectively. The maximum years of father's education is 17 years. The third set of explanatory variables comprise of family characteristics. Fertility and household poverty are frequently invoked in the discourse on child labour. Our survey has recorded number of children in each household. The minimum is 1 and the maximum is 9 with the mean and standard deviation of 2.74 and 1.217 respectively.

Household size is equally important factor in determining children's participation in labour activities. With limited employment opportunities and low family income, larger families fall back on children for income support. The household size is minimum at 2 and maximum at 20 with mean and standard deviation of 6.90 and 2.459 respectively. The average family size is bigger in the study villages that evoke the issue of child labour and fertility nexus. Joblessness of the head of the household results in economic adversities that compel the younger children of the household to look for income opportunities. We have recorded the number of days of unemployment by the head of the household during the reference year. The maximum days of unemployment are 210 days with mean and standard deviation of 73.15 and 54.24 respectively. We have recorded and calculated monthly per capita consumption expenditure (MPCE) for each family as a measure of economic well-being. The MPCE is lowest at

Rs. 161.54 and Rs. 2150.00 at maximum with a mean and standard deviation of 446.62 and 194.24 respectively. The Engel's ratio is minimum at 41.46 and maximum at 93.10 having a mean value of 79.10 and standard deviation of 7.417 respectively.

ESTIMATES OF MULTINOMIAL LOGIT MODEL

We find that probability of the child of remaining in school decreases as child grows. The younger children are more likely to remain in school while the older ones are more likely to stay outside school. A parameter or logit co-efficient gives the change in log-odds ratio associated with one unit change in the independent variable when all other variables are controlled. The sign of an estimated co-efficient gives the direction of the effect of a change in the explanatory variable on the probability of success.

The negative parameter for child indicates that a unit increase in age will bring down the probability of child going to school. On the other hand, probability of child joining labour force increases with the increase in age. These findings in our survey villages are in consistent similar revelation by Ray (2001). The probability of a child remaining idle (child 4) also increases with age. The probability of belonging to child 2 and child 3 categories also goes up with age of the child. Aged mothers are less likely to send their children to school. This scenario is quite common in the rural area where aged mothers relinquish domestic duties to their children particularly to grown up daughters. Therefore, increase in mother's age lowers down the probability of children attending school and increases the probability of children combining work and school (child 2). It also increases the likelihood of a child joining labour force. Aging of mothers decreases the possibility of their remaining idle. This is quite obvious and children would replace their aged mothers in domestic chores as well as in income earning activities. Children can remain idle (child 4) when their mothers are aging and incapacitated.

Mother's characteristics play an important role in household decision about children's time use. We find that educated mothers are more likely to send their children to

TABLE 11.4
Multinomial Logistic Estimate
Dependent Variables : Child Status

Variables	*Child 1*	*Child 2*	*Child 3*	*Child 4*	*Child 5*
Chilage	- .136**	.360**	.627**	0.52	.406*
	(.022)	(.021)	(.042)	(.048)	(.199)
$Chilage^2$	.065	0.024	0.035	0.76	0.058
	(.089)	(.043)	(.067).	(.056)	(.098)
Gender	0.005	0.004	0.022	0.013	0.0116
	(.009)	(.008)	(.013)	(.014)	(.081)
Mothage	-0.005	0.004	0.022	-0.013	0.116
	(.009)	(.008)	(.013)	(.014)	(.081)
Mothedu	.025*	-0.118	-065**	-0.011	-.125**
	(.080)	(.055)	(.110)	(.128)	(.617)
Engel	-.48*	0.014	.043**	0.057	.009*
	(.011)	(.009)	(.015)	(.018)	(.094)
MPCE	.003**	-.001*	-.004*	-.002**	-0.007
	(.001)	0.000	(.001)	(.001)	(.007)
Members	.097*	0.058	0.165	-0.023	-0.034
	(.043)	(.034)	(.059)	(.065)	(.294)
Children	0.204	0.052	0.214	0.15	0.316
	(.059)	(.028)	(.080)	(.080)	(.413)
Jobless	-.003***	0.001	0.002	0.004	0.009
	(.001)	0.000	(.002)	(.002)	(.010)
Gender	-.263*	1.808	-.043**	-0.693	0.68
Ref. male	(.111)	(.106)	(.149)	(.177)	(.887)
Moread	.815*	-.498**	-0.99	-0.83	-0.638
Ref. illiterate	(.473)	(.326)	(.659)	(.725)	(.601)
Single parent	-0.277	0.044	1.018	-0.408	0.562
Ref. joint	(.135)	(.437)	(.789)	(.207)	(.275)
Family					
Male headed	0.37	-0.264	-0.159	-0.74	0.318
Ref. female head	(.226)	(.222)	(.789)	(.360)	(.001)
Non-BPL	.086**	.064***	-0.229	-.088*	-.467*
Ref. category BPL	(.123)	(.111)	(.163)	(.163)	(.962)

Notes : (1) The bold numbers indicate logit co-efficients.
(2) The numbers within bracket indicates standard error.
(3) *** indicates significant at 10% level, ** and * indicate. significant at 5% and 1% level respectively.

school. A unit increase in mothers' education measured by years of schooling enhances the probability of children to remain in school (child 1). Mother's education also decreases the probability of child joining labour force (child 3) and decreases the likelihood of remaining idle (child 4). It also decreases the probability of child combining work and school (child 2) as well as the probability of child combining work and idleness (child 5). This finding on the efficacy of mothers' education is supported by similar findings by Burki and Shahnaz (2001) that reveals mothers with primary and secondary education are less likely to allow their wards to become child labourers. Similar impact of mother's education on school participation of children also came out in a study by Ray (2001). Literate mothers are more likely to send their children to school than the illiterate mothers are more likely to send their children to school than the illiterate mothers. Literate mothers are less likely to allow their children combining work and school (child 2). Literate mothers are also less likely to allow their children to become child labourers (child 3) and idle (child 4). Mothers' literacy is also important for the choice between education and work of children in general and girl children in particular. It is commonly believed that education of mothers affects the girls in the household (Grootaert, 1998). The probability of child going to school is lower for a unit increase in the Engel's ratio. Engel's ratio is a measure of relative affluence of the family. Rise in the ratio is an indication of relative poverty and lower standard of living. The decrease in Engel's ratio is, on the other hand, is an indication of lessening of poverty and higher standard of living. Rise the Engel's ratio is associated with rise in incidence of child labour. The probability of child joining labour force is higher for unit increase in Engel's ratio. Children are more likely to become idle (child 4) with increase in Engel's ratio. Children are equally likely to combine work and school (child 2) and combining part time work with idleness (child 5) with increase in Engel's ratio.

Monthly per capita consumption expenditure (MPCE) is another measure of economic well-being of a family. Higher is, therefore and indication of economic affluence while lower MPCE is just the opposite. The probability of a child going to school (child 1) is higher for a unit increase in MPCE. In the similar vein, the probability of child undertaking income earning activities (child 3) is lower for a unit increase in MPCE. The probability of becoming 'no where' (child 4) as well as combining school and work (child 2) is lower for a unit increase in MPCE. The same is also true for child 5.

Household size has a role to play in influencing children's time use in a family. A large family having a good numbers of members can be of immense benefit for the children. There is also a possibility that larger household can not help children in enhancing their development process. The influence of family size on the children's time use is mediated by the level of family income and relative affluence. Large families beset with poverty would tend to see children as earning hands; on the other hand economically well-off large families would send their children to school. This study finds that a unit increase in the size of the family enhances the probability of children going to school (child 1) and lessening the probability of joining labour force (child 3) and also reduces the probability of remaining idle (child 4). But it raises the probability of combining work with school (child 2). Number of children in the households is also a factor in distributing family resources among children and their time use. Families with large number of children are less likely to send their children to school (child 1) and more likely to allow their children to combine work with school (child 2). A unit increase in number of children in the family also increases the probability of joining labour force by the children (child 3). The likelihood of children becoming idle (child 4) also increases with unit increase in the number of children. Unemployment of the head of the household decreases the probability of attending school (child 1) and increase the probability of becoming child labourers (child 3) and probability of remaining idle (child 4). Unemployment of the head of the household raises the probability of combining school and work (child 2) as well as combining part time work and idleness (child 5). Male headed families are more likely to send their children to school (child 1) than female headed families. Male headed families are less likely to allow their children to combine work with school (child 2), allow their children to become child labourers (child 3) and allow these children to remain idle. Non-BPL families are more likely to send these children to school (child 1) than BPL families. Non-BPL families are also less likely to allow their children to become child labourers (child 3) and idle (child 4). Children of the nuclear families are less likely to attend school (child 1) compared to children of the joint family. They are more likely to combine work and school (child 2) and more likely to become child labourers (child 3) and idle children (child 4). Girl children are less likely to attend school (child 1) and less likely to become child labourers. They are more likely to combine work with school (child 2) and remaining idle (child 4) girls are more likely, compared to boys, to combine part time work with idleness.

DISCUSSION

Older among the children are more likely to be in labour force and less likely to be in school. Girls are less likely to remain in school and also in labour force but they are prone to become idle. Poverty and lack of alternative gainful employment in the study area are primary causes of prevalence of child labour. We have measured household's economic standing in four different ways to capture the influence of poverty on the generation and perpetuation of poverty. These measures are: Engel's ratio, monthly per capita consumption expenditure, days of unemployment of household heads and membership of BPL listed categories among the survey households. The reason for adopting so many measures of poverty or relative opulence is to rule out the possibility conceptual incomprehensive of any singular measure. We have taken up Engel's ratio as one measure of relative economic affluence. A lower ratio indicates higher standard of living, therefore less economic adversity. A higher ratio is thus an indicator of poverty and economic distress. Families having lower Engel's ratio tend to send their children to school instead of sending them to work. Thus poverty, as an over-whelming reason of child labour, is established through this measure. Similarly, lower MPCE is also associated with poverty and low income. We find that households with lower MPCE are sending their children to work rather than sending them to school. Extent of unemployment by the head of the household, particularly in a situation where they lack productive resources is an obverse of household poverty. Here also, we find the development distress of the children. Children of unemployed adults are more likely to join labour force and abandon schools. BPL households, the identified poor families as listed by the local Governments, are also more likely to send their children to labour force instead of sending them to school. This study, revealing household poverty as dominant factor behind child labour and schooling deprivation is in tune with similar studies by Bequele and Boyden (1988), CACL (1993), Jain (1994), Grootaert and Kanbur (1995). Analyses of household survey also present a negative effect of low household income on schooling (Levy, 1985, Buragohani, 1997, Singh and Santiago, 1997). Surveys of child workers report that poverty is almost the first reason given by households (CPSS, 1985, APARD, 2000.) The next important characteristic is thought to be adult illiteracy which leads to lack of demand for education (Weiner, 1991, Bhalla, 1995, Burra, 1995, GOI, 1998). The strong effect is found in nearly all studies based on statistical inferences (Rosenzweig and Evenson, 1977, Kanbargi and Kulkani, 1991). In particular, it is widely recognized that female literacy contributes to the enhancement of child welfare particularly education. Our findings come across similar result of maternal education on child schooling and child labour.

12

Concluding Remarks

Child labour, as a retarding block, in the human capital formation process is still posing formidable challenge, particularly in the developing world. The developed world had confronted it in the past but still to go a little far for a turn of complete elimination. The Declaration of the Rights of the Child (DRC) was adopted in 1924. Since then, the world community began to promote and disseminate the idea that children are no longer *physical possessions* of their procreators. They are individual human beings having inner selves, wishes and autonomy. They are rights holders. The central focus of these new thinking of the global leaders is to initiate the bestowal of decent childhood to all children on this planet. They are to be protected from all odds that come in the way. The persistence of child labour is thus an obvious indication that multitude of children in this world are not protected from inhuman economic exploitation of them by the adults. Children are, in many corners of the world, are compelled to undertake income earning activities unsuitable for their levels of maturity, both physical and psychological. Many of the works, they perform are intolerable, exploitive and hazardous. This is most shocking to learn that, presently we are living in a world that still shelters around 246 million child labourers. They work in agriculture, in manufacturing, in mining and in construction and quarrying. Many of them live and work on the street of metropolis. Many underage girls are placed in sex trade for the sake of the profits of their recruiters. Tourism sector is rapidly expanding in many locations of the world. But it comes with its abominable derivative: sex tourism. Underprivileged girls are sourced from vulnerable areas to keep the booming industry on track.

The League of Nations ceased to exist after the Second World War. The United Nations was born with renewed hope and vigour to build the world ravaged by the ghastly war that immensely harmed humanity at large. The new global body was formed on the principles of peace, stability, development and human liberty. Articulation and promotion of human rights were her priority agenda. The Universal Declaration of Human Rights came in 1948 under the auspices of this newborn body. But the year of 1989 was something special for the children on this planet. The United Nations Conventions of the Rights of the Child was adopted in that year. Article 32 of the Convention stipulates that State parties recognize the right of the child to be protected from economic exploitation and from performing any work that is likely to be hazardous or to interfere with the child's education or to be harmful to the child's health or physical, mental, spiritual, moral or social development.

The International labour Organization (ILO) was born as constituent of the League of Nations to take care of workers' rights everywhere. It lays down minimum standard at work places, stipulates working hours, pleads for decent minimum wages and promotes workers' rights. It binds the member-nations through passing and adopting Conventions with a view to persuade the member-states to enact in their respective legislative domain. Child labour would naturally come under its purview of actions. ILO was much concerned about 250 million child labourers during nineties. This figure was based on the ILO definition of work that obviously excludes non-economic activities mostly carried out at homes. The figure would have touched plus 300 million in the event of inclusion of the vast army of non-economic child workers. The magnitude appeared alarming for ILO. Later on, ILO was advised from different corners to relook at the 'overwhelming figure', re-examine the methodology of counting and to reconsider the definition of child labour. ILO, since 2004, has been segregating three different categories: worst form of child labour, unacceptable child labour and acceptable child work in particular context. It now asks for immediate abolition of the first category. The second has to be eradicated through long-term policy and actions and it now condones the third if it does not come in the way of normal development of the child. This is pleasing to note that the worst form of child labour has come down from 171 million during 2000 to 126 million during 2004. But the decline is not proportionately distributed across nations. This has swelled in some locations of the world and had come down significantly somewhere.

The world is now far more integrated than at any period in the past. Trade and exchange among countries are far more unhindered now. This economic globalization can affect child labour positively as well as negatively. This new coin has harmful side as well as beneficial side. Proponents of globalization claim that child labour would be a thing of past under neoliberal global order if properly pursued. The opponents, on the other hand, warn that globalization is *child labour-enhancing*. There is other strand of argument that reconciles these two opposite stances. It says that globalization may harm as well as can shower benefits to the underdogs of the society. But which one would accrue depends on the quality of governance, level of human development, government action, social protection and public policy. The state should provide protective shield for the vulnerable population and make the best use of global opportunity for free trade and exchange. The flow of technology, knowledge and investment would eradicate many social ills including child labour that had remained as a consequence of longstanding poverty and underdevelopment.

But the stimulating debate in the discourse of child labour relates to the diagnoses of the causes that generate and perpetuates it. Is the poverty only reason? If that is accepted then what specific poverty is invoked? Household level poverty, cluster level poverty, regional level or even poverty at the national level? Is it possible that a poor child residing in a relatively rich neighbourhood is prone to be child labourers?

Or conversely, a question can be put whether a rich child residing in a poor neighbourhood is less likely to fall back on child labour. These contrasting possibilities thus raise the issue of supply side as well as demand side factors that make the whole of explanatory causes. Household poverty works as push factor but the availability of work opportunities at lower wage or worse income prospect in the immediate surroundings of disadvantaged children must be there as pull factors. Both push and pull must be present simultaneously to make child labour happen. Poverty, as measured and manifest at any level of household; cluster, region or nation can not singularly cause child labour. Take the example of Kerala in India to buttress the imprecise connection. Kerala is poorer than Andhra Pradesh measured by per capita State Domestic Product (SDP). But child labour is alarmingly high in Andhra Pradesh and pleasurably very low at less than one per cent in Kerala. The reason is not far to seek. Children are drawn to labour market when the latter is segmented. Adult unemployment is high in Andhra Pradesh still child labour persists in a massive way.

The persistence of disagreement on the causal factors is largely due to definitional incongruity among scholars and activists. The perception as to what constitute child labour widely varies. The 'Broader' definition of child labour entails all children out of school. They like to segregate the 'out of school children' into two categories: active child labour and potential child labour or child labourers in waiting. They put them in a singular box. On the other hand, the 'narrow' definition differentiates between child work and child labour. The former is enabling while the latter is disabling. But there is no disagreement on the issue of its elimination because the perpetuation of the menace is growth retarding as well as violating the basic human rights of children. However, the elimination of child labour is a daunting task. We need to formulate effective plan of action. Before that we need to know how grave the danger is. What is the enormity of the problem? Is it on the wane globally? Or it is on the rise? Is it declining in India? We need to know the real magnitude before we engage ourselves for eradication. Child labour is widespread in developing countries led by Asia having 61 per cent of world's working children. Asia is followed by Africa in sheltering 32 per cent and the share of Latin America is 7 per cent. The remaining is scattered over in different other world regions. It is comforting to learn that during last forty years, from 1950 to 2000, child labour participation rate, on global scale, has come down from 27.6 per cent to 11.30 per cent. Back home in India, the child labour estimate, as provided by the government, is rather upsetting. During the inter-census period, from 1991 to 2001, the number of working children has gone up from 11.28 million to 12.67 million. This estimate is obviously based on restrictive definition which is unacceptable to many scholars and activists on the ground that this is underestimation. As many as 87.12 million children are out of school in 2001. Taking out 12.67 million working children from that category, we are left with 74.25 million children who are neither in work nor in school. The National Sample Survey that also counts child labourers in India, from time to time, however has estimated 7.23 million child labourers in India in 2004-05.

The fundamental object of the present study is to examine the circumstances that generates and perpetuates child labour in *beedi* rolling or processing in a particular region in the state of West Bengal in India. Demand side factors behind child labour are overwhelmingly present in the district of Murshidabad. The latter is marked by poverty and is discredited with very low score in human development index, constructed by the state government for each district within it. We have purposively selected this district to undertake the study on children, born and raised in families dependent on tobacco processing as primary source of sustenance. *Beedi* rolling, as a family-based occupation and undertaken in the family setting, draws little children to this perilous work. We are curious to know whether the prevalence of this most hazardous variety of child labour in this region is purely poverty-driven. Our study reveals that poverty is just manifestation of long drawn neglect of this underdeveloped region during colonial as well as in post-colonial period. One obverse of the backwardness is the ostensible lack of alternative employment opportunities for the working population here. There is deplorable dearth of non-agricultural manufacturing, agro-processing and rural service sector activities. The inter-generational transfer of low skill in the tobacco processing is other feature of the persistent economic adversity. There is perpetual cycle of low skill transfer, poverty, ill-health, illiteracy, immobility, inward looking orientation and governmental neglect. The cycle needs to be broken in no time. We have looked in to variation in the presence of child level factors, parental level factors and family level factors that collectively work on supply side to cause child labour here. The production chain in the tobacco enterprises evokes interest. There are large number of *beedi* companies who source the raw materials from Bihar, Jharkhand and its adjoining districts of West Bengal. *Munshis* are middlemen who work as conduits between family workers and the companies.

The district of Murshidabad in which our study villages are located is itself mired in developmental distress. Underemployment and backwardness mark in every nook and corner. There are varieties of manifestations of this economic ill-health. Socio-economic indicators that reflect the development outcomes come in handy to support this pessimistic disclosure. The pace of urbanization is shockingly low. Population density that speaks for itself population size as well as land-man ratio is alarmingly high at 1102 per square kilometre. This is far above the state average of 904 per square kilometre for West Bengal which is, in turn, the most populated state in India. The population density for the whole of India is 325 per square kilo metre. Poverty as measured by per capita monthly consumption expenditure (MPCE) is Rs. 428 for the district and state average for the same is Rs. 562. These estimates were published by NSS on the basis of their consumption expenditure survey carried out in 2004-05. It was revealed in course of the 61st round of NSS survey that 56 per cent of the rural population is poor. Murshidabad thus turned to be the poorest district in West Bengal. The annual growth rate of population is 2.37 per cent here while the growth rate for India as a whole is 1.93 per cent during 1991-2001. The literacy rate for the state of West Bengal is 68. 6 per cent while for the district of Murshidabad the same is 54 per cent. The female literacy is alarmingly low at 47 per cent.

Muslimabad's traditional industries in handicrafts, silk and brassware are on the verge of disappearance. Handicrafts that had flourished during the reign of Nawabs were forced to perish under colonial rule. De-industrialization during the period had almost decimated them. It did not receive needed boost for revival even in the post-independence era. Agriculture in its pre-modern structure and hazardous occupation in *beedi*-rolling have come to stay as principal provider of bread and butter in these areas. Poverty and low level of human capital seem to persist for quite some time from now. The Human Development Index score is 0.46 for the district compared to 0.61 for the entire state of West Bengal. At least 0.3 million (three lakh) people are officially registered as *Beedi* workers. More than the quoted magnitude of labour force is working as family labourers in the same occupation without official registration. The last category is most vulnerable as they have no access to whatever provisions are there for the registered workers.

We have studied the family structure of these 1224 children's families to examine the influence of family structure on the well-being of the children. One revelation is that children of single-parent families are least food secure. But the incidence of child labour is higher in nuclear families. However, structure of family has nothing to do with both school participation and school attendance. School performance as measured by the score obtained by the children at school examination is worst for pupils from nuclear families. But caste factor, that generally affect children well-being elsewhere in India does not seem to play here. This is because the majority of children belong to Muslim families and they are bereft of any caste facility despite their ostensible poverty. Children of the mother-headed families have been found to be more likely to be child labourers. The paternal literacy at 47 per cent in the study villages is below the district average and far below the state average of 64 per cent. Maternal illiteracy in our study villages is quite high at 78 per cent. Literate mothers have been found to send their children in greater magnitude than the illiterate mothers. Unemployment of fathers increases the likelihood of their children joining full time labour. In contrast, children of salaried fathers attend school and do not join full time work. Fathers are engaged in wide varieties of occupations here. But three occupations are dominant: *beedi* work, non-agricultural labour and petty trade. However, neither school participation nor labour participation is linked to specific pattern of job in a systematic way. But what matter is the quality of jobs and income accrual from them.

The average MPCE in our study areas is Rs. 446 which is almost close the district average. The National Commission on Enterprises in the Unorganized Sector headed by Prof. Arjun Sengupta had revealed in 2004 that 77 per cent of India's population were poor if the narrow concept of nutritional poverty is replaced by the holistic concept of economic vulnerability. The commission came with an estimate that all people below the MPCE of Rs. 600 are vulnerable. We have estimated, by the same measure, that 86 per cent of the population in our survey locations are vulnerable if not officially poor.

Still in this ambience of poverty and economic distress, variation in the economic standing of the households largely matter in the affairs of their children. Childhood is not same for all children in these locations. Relatively better-off families are sending their children to school instead of engaging them for income earning job. Many of surveyed families are food insecure. This was observed in course of our household visits which aimed at gaining access to all facts and information of their daily living. Food insecurity was manifest in their expressed fear of food shortage in the immediate future. A significant section of households have reported their bitter experiences of running out of food on several occasions. They had adjusted themselves in the habit of taking thin meals instead of full ones, one square meal a day instead of two square meals. The food insecurity however is not universal. There are households who had never experienced such odds in the past. Relatively well-off household, even in this poverty stricken areas are food secure. Food insecurity and poverty seem to move together in the same direction. Childhood adversities are more intense in food insecure households. They send their children to work places, in larger number than the food secures households.

Even the diehard critic of the government would not allege that education delivery system in the public domain is in doldrums here. A few school buildings came to our view in course of traversing the survey villages. The ramshackle school buildings with frail walls and porous roof are now giving way to new construction and added class rooms. Thanks to DPEP and SSM for their benevolence and priority for school infrastructure. But class rooms are still over-crowded. Inadequacy of teachers adversely affects learning attainments of pupils. Well-off families can make good the loss at class rooms by engaging private tutors. The poor families to which a significant majority of our children belong cannot afford such 'luxury'. Thus for poorer children, one time losses at the class rooms turn out to be life long missing. Still whatever benefit that accrues to the pupil in the class room process is of immense gain to them. Therefore, school bunking on several occasions, by these children takes away that little bit precious gain in learning. This study finds that school absenteeism of children has something to do with economic standing of the families they hail from. Children of the families below poverty line are irregular in school attendance in higher proportion than the children above poverty line. Recurrent absenteeism is a symptom of sporadic discontinuation that ultimately results in drop-out for ever. This is a major malady that afflicts the education delivery system in vulnerable areas bereft of any surveillance and monitoring by the appropriate authority. This issue has to be addressed seriously. There is, on the whole, an easy access to primary schools located in the vicinity for the children but accessing high schools for attending upper primary grades is little problematic. High schools are located far away from children's residences and many of them have to take a long walk of more than three kilometres to reach the school. Our study also finds that daily attendance of children at schools is related to family's economic standing as well as parental educational background. Educated parents have been found to send their children in higher proportion than the unlettered ones. In the same vein, pupils of relatively well-off families hardly bunks schools. We find that children of richer households have fared better in school examinations than their counterparts in the poorer families. One obvious reason of this differential learning outcome is the role of private tuition which richer families can afford.

Older among the children are more likely to be in labour force and less likely to be in school. Girls are less likely to remain in school and also in labour force but they are prone to become idle. Poverty and lack of alternative gainful employment in the study area are primary causes of prevalence of child labour. We have measured household's economic standing in four different ways to capture the influence of poverty on the generation and perpetuation of poverty. These measures are: Engel's ratio, monthly per capita consumption expenditure, days of unemployment of household heads and membership of BPL listed categories among the survey households. The reason for adopting so many measures of poverty or relative opulence is to rule out the possibility conceptual incomprehensive of any singular measure. We have taken up Engel's ratio as one measure of relative economic affluence. Families having lower Engel's ratio tend to send their children to school instead of sending them to work. Thus poverty, as an overwhelming reason of child labour, is established through this measure. Similarly lower MPCE is also associated with poverty and low income. We find that households with lower MPCE are sending their children to work rather than sending them to school. Extent of unemployment by the head of the household, particularly in a situation where they lack productive resources is an obverse of household poverty. Here also, we find the development distress of the children. Children of unemployed adults are more likely to join labour force and abandon schools. BPL households the identified poor families as listed by the local Governments are also more likely to send their children to labour force instead of sending them to school. This study, revealing household poverty as dominant factor behind child labour and schooling deprivation is in tune with similar studies by similar studies undertaken mostly in developing world by eminent scholars.

Poverty and 'occupational trap' are conspicuously present in the surveyed localities. Families seem to be caught in the perpetual inter-generational cycle that centres on low paid and extremely hazardous job in tobacco rolling. This vicious cycle has to be broken apart and families have to be rescued from the trap. This is only possible through the diversification of rewarding economic activities and lessening of dependence on tobacco as only source of living. Workers everywhere move from low-paid jobs to higher paid ones that hold out better prospects and greater opportunities. One possible option is the expansion and encouraging horticulture and fruit processing enterprises. The region has the distinction of producing world famous varieties of mango and litchi. Public-private partnership model can be explored to bring in private capital in this potential sector. The industries would need skilled man-power. The government must come forward with a scheme of intensive training programme for skill development for the 'entrapped' *beedi* workers. Family workers would grab the new opportunities if they come along with better prospects and higher income. Handicrafts units that once commanded reputation across length and breadth of the country can be revived through infusion of latest technology. Agro processing may be one area for creating employment opportunities provided this sector gets attention, priority and investment. There may be many more, still unexplored, areas of economic activities pregnant with immense job prospects. The onus of exploring and creating such opportunities rests with the government which can seek private capital if situation demands to meet the ends.

However, those obviously very few, who want to stay back on their own volition must be protected from exploitation. Firstly, all workers need to be registered as *beedi* workers by the government agency preceded by household visits. There must be a separate list of families employing children in this family occupation. The names of child workers obtained through the survey should be cross-checked with the attendance register of the schools where they have reported to be currently enrolled. The daily attendance register of the schools can be checked with the help of the V.E.C (Village Education Committee) to have a look at their attendance and duration of stay at school. Each panchayat constituency at village level must maintain a child register that must be updated regularly to keep record and monitor activities of all children within its jurisdiction. Each adult worker must be provided with free medical check up at regular intervals by their employers in collaboration with local elected body. The companies or their agents must be compelled by the government to provide each worker with protective gear and musk to rule out any possibility of lung infection. The wage should be fixed in the presence of labour inspcctor where all terms and condition relating to contracts between the company and the workers can come under scrutiny. Workers must be protected from exploitation, maltreatment and abuse.

Thus we need supply side intervention as well as demand side actions to bring an end to this hazardous occupation of children. Child labour families have to be economically strengthened through anti-poverty programmes. The suffering families and the distraught children cannot wait for GDP growth to take care of them. The remarkable economic growth, our nation has accomplished in recent years, does not seem to percolate down to this area. These villages have been breeding child labour of most dangerous variety for last many years. Therefore, the growth has obviously bypassed these places and has shunned these underprivileged people. Let the economic growth take its own course and let the people enjoy the fruits of it. But the child labour in tobacco rolling should be eliminated in no time. The National Rural Employment Guarantee Scheme (NREGS) is great opportunity to empower the families through providing wage employment for adults. Adult women can form Self-Help Groups with support from banks and local governments to undertake income earning activities. The labour department must monitor the family units on regular basis to make sure that no child is engaged in home-based tobacco units. Panchayats must be proactive to sensitize the families regarding the ill-effects of tobacco on children. The schools must be well equipped to provide joyful and meaningful education to all children. There must a balanced mix of persuasion and compulsion in the pursuit for elimination.

Bibliography

Ashagrie, Kebebew (1998), *"Statistics on Working Children and Hazardous Labour in Brief"*, www.ilo.org/stats.htm

Antony, Piush (2002), *"Child Work in Bihar: A Leeway for Household Food Insecurity"* in Ramchandran, Nira and Lionel Massun edited (2002), "Coming to grips with Rural Child Work, A Food Security Approach", Institute For Human Development, New Delhi.

Basu, Kaushik (1999), *"Child Labour: Cause, Consequences and Cure, With Remarks on International Labour Standards"*, *Journal of Economic Literature*, Vol. 37.

Becker, G.S. (1962): Investment in Human Capital: A Theoretical Analysis, *Journal of Political Economy*, Vol. LXX, Part 2.

Bequele, A. and Boyden, J. (1988): *Combating Child Labour*, Geneva, ILO.

Bhalla, A.S. (1995) : *"Uneven Development in the Third World : A Study of China and India"* : London, St. Martins Press.

Bhatty, K. (1998) : "Educational Deprivation in India : A survey of Field Investigation", *Economic and Political Weekly*. No. 27 July.

Bonnet, Michel (1993) : "Child labour in Africa", *International Labour Review*, Vol. 132, No. 3.

Boyden, J. (1993) : The Relationship between Education and Child Work (Innocenti Occasional Papers No. 9), Florence, Italy, *International Child Development Centre*.

Burki, Abid and Lubna Shahnaz (2001): *The Implication of Household Level Factors For Children's Time Use In Pakistan,* Paper presented at IDPAD International Conference on Child Labour in South Asia, New Delhi, CSRD, JNU.

Burra, N. (1995): *"Born to Work: Child Labour in India"*. Delhi, Oxford University Press.

CACL (1997): *Child Labour in India: A Dossier*, UNICEF, Maharashtra State Office.

Buragohain, T. (1997) *"Differentials in Literacy Rate by Social Group,* Margin, Vol. 29, No. 3.

Chaudhuri, D.P (1996): *A Dynamic Profile of Child Labour in India 1951-91*, New Delhi, ILO.

Chakraborty, Sudip (2004), *"Child Labour and Child Rights in India"*, paper presented at International Interdisciplinary Course on Child Rights, Child Rights Centre, Ghent University, BELGIUM.

Chakraborty, Sudip (2006), *"Child Health"*, Amsterdam Masters in Medical Anthropology (Amma), University of Amsterdam, Netherlands.

Chakraborty, Sudip and Lieten, G.K. (2004), *"What do child labourers do?"* Working Children Around the World, Irewoc, University of Amsterdam, Netherlands

Chakraborty, Sudip (2006), *"Child Labour In Rural Context: Concern, Causes and Cure"*, Mittal Publications, New Delhi.

Chakraborty, Sudip (2003), "Child labour in Rural India: Concern, Concepts and Causes—Panchayat as a Change Agent", *Asian Economic Review*, Hyderabad.

Chakraborty, Sudip (2003), "Child work, child labour and Educational Deprivation: The Study of Socio-economic context and factors in a Bengal Village". *Indian Journal of Social Development*, New Delhi.

Chakraborty, Sudip (2004) "School Participation and Child labour: A recent Survey of Rural Households in North Bengal", *Journal of Social and Economic Development*, Bangalore, Vol. 6, No. 1, June 2004.

Chakraborty, Sudip (2006), "Demand Side Factors of Children's School Participation: An exploration with household survey data for Rural North Bengal", *Journal of Educational Planning and Administration*, National Institute of Educational Planning and Administration, New Delhi, Volume XX, No. 2, April 2006.

Chakraborty, Sudip (2006), *Children's Rights to Development: Issues, Extent and Nature of Violation of Child Rights to Education in India,* Seminar Paper series, Save the Children, Sweden and Child Rights Centre, Jamia Milia University, New Delhi.

Chakraborty, Sudip (2008), "Universal Child Rights in the Discourse on Child Labour: Settling the debate over needs vs. Rights", *Social Action,* Volume 58, No. 4.

Chakraborty, Sudip (2008) "Household Vulnerability, Child Labour and Schooling Deprivation: A recent survey of poor households in the Sub-Himalayan West Bengal", Sent to Social Change, New Delhi for Publication.

Chakraborty, Sudip (2008) *"Situating Child Labour in the Context of Neo Liberal Global Order",* unpublished paper, Department of Economics, A.C. College, North Bengal University.

Colclough, C. (1973) : *"Human Development : Towards a more Integrated Framework for Planning in the 1990,* Institute of Development Studies, Paper 323.

Daily, G., D. Bhattacharyya and B.P. Dash (2002), *"Food Security and Child Work in Rural India" in* Ramchandran, Nira and Lionel Massun edited (2002), "Coming to grips with Rural Child Work, A Food Security Approach, Institute For Human Development, New Delhi.

Dreze, J. and Kingdom, G.G. (1999) : *School Participation in Rural India,* Delhi School of Economics.

Dube, Leea (1981: *The economic role of children in India: Methodological Issues,* In Gerry Rodgers and Guy Standing (1981), The Economic Roles of Children in Low Income Countries, Geneva, ILO, 179-214.

Edmonds, Reic V. (2007), *"Child Labour",* NBER Working Paper 12926, Cambridge, MA., USA.

Enney, J. (Ed.) (1995) : Learning or Labouring—A Compilation of key texts on Child Work and Basic Education (Innocenti Readings in Children Rights), Florence, Italy, *International Child Development Centre.*

Ennew, J. (1993) : *"Learning or Labouring",* Innocenti Research paper, International Child Development Centre, Italy.

Fyfe Alec (2001) *Child Labour, Policy Option,* Akshant, Amsterdam.

Government of India, Department of Education, MHRD, New Delhi (1998).

Government of India, Department of Education, MHRD, New Delhi (1992-93).

Government of India, Ministry of Labour Annual Report (1996-97).

Grootaert, C. and Kanbur, R. (1995) : "*Child Labour: An Economic Perspective*", *International Labourer Review*. Vol. 134, No. 2.

Grote, U., Basu, A., Child Labour and the International Policy Debates, Weinhold, D. (1998). *Centre for Development Research*, Bonn.

Himanshu (2007), "*Recent Trends in Poverty and Inequality: Some Preliminary Results*", *Economic and Political Weekly*, Vol. 62, No. 6.

Hirway, Indira, J. Cottyn and Pushkar Pandya (1991), (Ed.) *Towards Eradication of Child Labour*, Oxford & IBH Publishing Co. Pvt. Ltd., New Delhi.

Hirway, Indira (1991), "*Child Labour in the Developing Economies Today*", In Hirway *et. al.* (Ed).

ILO (1992): *Towards action against child labour in Zimbabwe*, Geneva, ILO.

Jain, Mahaveer (1994), *Child labour in India: a Select Bibliography*, New Delhi National Labour Institute.

Jafarey, S. and Lahiri, S. (1999): "*Will Trade Sanction Reduce Child Labour*", University of Essex.

Jayraj, D. and Subramaniam (1997), "*Child labour in Tamil Nadu*", Preliminary Accounts of its Nature, Extent and Distribution, Madras Institute of Development Studies, Chennai.

Kambhampati, U. and R. Rajan (2005), "*Economic Growth: A Panacea For Child Labour*", World Development, Vol. 34.

Kanbargi, R. and Kulkani, P.M. (1991), "*Child Work, Schooling and Fertility in Rural Karnataka, India* in Kanbargi R. (ed.) 'Child Labour in the Indian Subcontinent, Dimension and Implications', New Delhi, Sage.

Kashyap, S.P. (1991), *"Earning Profile and Prospects for Child Labour in Diamond Processing Units: A Case Study of Surat"*, In Hirway *et. al.* (Ed).

Lieten, G.K. (2000) : Children, Work and Education", *Economic and Political Weekly*, 25, 2037-43.

Levison, D. (1993): *"Child Work and Schooling in Brazil's cities , lesson from survey data"*, unpublished manuscripts.

Lloyd, C.B. (1993) : *'Fertility, Family size, Consequence for Family and Child"*, New York, Population Council.

Maharatna Arup (1997) : Children's Work Activities, Surplus Labour and Fertility, *Economic and Political Weekly*, February 15, 1997.

Mahendra Dev, S. and C. Ravi (2002) *"Food Security and Child Work in South India: Determinants and Policies"* in Ramchandran, Nira and Lionel Massun edited (2002), "Coming to grips with Rural Child Work, A Food Security Approach, *Institute for Human Development*, New Delhi.

Mehra Kerpelmau, K. (1996) : Children at work—How many and where, *World of Work*, Vol. 15, No. 8.

Mehta, S.S. (1991), *"Why Child Labour? The Indian Case"*, In Hirway *et. al.* (Ed).

Mehta Niti, *"Child Labour in India: Extent and Some Dimensions"*, Paper presented at National Workshop on Socio-Economic Issues in Child Labour, 16-17 March, 2007, organised by *Mahatma Gandhi Labour Institute*, Ahmedabad. http://ssrn.com/abstract=996574

McEwan P.J. (1999): "Private cost and the Rate of Return to Primary Education, *Applied Economics letters*, Vol. 6, No. 11.

Mincer, J. (1958) : "Investment in Human Capital and Personal Income Distribution", *Journal of Political Economy*, Vol. No. 4, pp. 281-302.

Nangia (1987) : *Child Labour : Cause and Effect Syndrome*, Janak Publishers, New Delhi.

Nieuwenhuys, O. (1994): *Children's Life Worlds, Welfare and Labour in the Developing World*, London, Rutledge Press.

Psacharopoulos, G. and Woodhall, M. (1985), *"Education for Development: An Analysis of Investment Choices*, Oxford University Press.

Psacharopaulos, G. (1997) : "Child Labour versus Educational Attainments: Some evidence from Latin America", *Journal of Population Economics,* Vol. 10, Part 4.

Rao Surda, V. (1985) : *Education and Rural Development,* New Delhi, Sage.

Ramchandran, Nira and Lionel Massun edited (2002) : "Coming to Grips with Rural Child Work, A Food Security Approach, *Institute For Human Development,* New Delhi.

Ramchandran, Nira and Anup Kr. Karan (2002) : *"Hunger, Illiteracy and Child Deprivation in a Tribal Region: A Study of Jharkhand"* in Ramchandran, Nira and Lionel Massun edited (2002), "Coming to grips with Rural Child Work, A Food Security Approach, *Institute for Human Development,* New Delhi.

Ray, R. (2000): "Analysis of Child Labour in Peru and Pakistan: A comparative Study", *Journal of Population Economics,* 13(1), 3-19.

Rosenzweig, M.R. and Evenson, R. (1977), "Fertility, Schooling and the Economic Contribution of Children in Rural India: An Econometric Analysis", *Econometrica,* Vol. 45, No. 5.

Glasinovich, W.A. (1996) : Better schools—Less child work, Child work and education in Brazil, Columbia, Ecuador, Guatemala and Peru (Innocenti Essays No. 7), Florence, Italy, *International Child Development Centre.*

Singh, R.D. and Santiago, M. (1997) : "Farm earnings, Educational attainments and Role of Public policy, some evidence from Mexico, *World Development,* Vol 29, No. 3.

Sinha Shantha (1996) : Child Labour and Education Policy in India, *The Administrator,* Vol. XLI, July-September.

Schultz, T.W. (1960) : "Capital formation by Education" *Journal of Political Economy,* Vol. LXVIII, No. 6.

Sharif, Mahammad (1994) : Child Participation, Nature of Work and fertility demand : A Theoretical Analysis, *The Indian Economic Journal,* Vol. 40, No. 4.

Swaminathan, Madura (1998) : "Economic Growth and the Persistence of Child Labour: Evidence from an Indian City", *World Development*, Vol. 26.

Tilak, J.B.G. (1987) : *The Economics of Inequality of Education in India*, Sage Publication, New Delhi.

Todaro, M.T. (1997) : *Economic Development,* Longman, Lond Meier, G.M. and Ranch, J.E. (2000), Leading Issues, Oxford University Press.

Weiner, M. (1991) : *"The Child and the State in India: Child Labour and Education Policy in Comparative Perspective,* Princeton University Press.

Index